Using PFS®:
First Publisher™

Katherine Murray

Foreword by

Jill Groginsky
Software Publishing Corporation

CORPORATION

LEADING COMPUTER KNOWLEDGE

Using PFS®:
First Publisher™

Copyright © 1989 by Que® Corporation.

Library of Congress Catalog No.: 88-63764
ISBN 0-88022-401-0

92 91 90 89   8 7 6 5 4 3

Interpretation of the printing code: the rightmost double-digit number is the year of the book's printing; the rightmost single-digit number, the number of the book's printing. For example, a printing code of 89-1 shows that the first printing of the book occurred in 1989.

Using PFS: First Publisher is based on Versions 2.01 the earlier Versions 2.0 and 1.0, and Version 2.01—DeskMate.

D E D I C A T I O N ▼

To my kids—Kelly, Christopher,
Mashawn, and Mike—who put
up with the late hours and
weekends lost to this book, and

To Bob, our resident technical
genius. I couldn't have done this
without you.

–km

Publishing Manager

Lloyd J. Short

Production Editor

Gregory Robertson

Editors

Sandra Blackthorn
Kelly Currie
Kelly D. Dobbs
Jeannine Freudenberger
Alice Martina Smith
Richard Turner

Technical Editor

Dennis O. Gehris, Ed.D.

Indexed by

Sherry Massey

Book Design and Production

Dan Armstrong
Cheryl English   Joe Ramon
Lori A. Lyons   Dennis Sheehan
Jennifer Matthews   Louise Shinault
Cindy Phipps   Carolyn A. Spitler

Composed in Times Roman and Excellent No. 47
by Que Corporation

Screen reproductions in this book were created by
means of the InSet program from INSET Systems Inc.,
Danbury, CT.

ABOUT THE AUTHOR

Katherine Murray

Katherine Murray is the president of reVisions Plus, a writing, editing, and desktop publishing company that deals primarily with the development and production of microcomputer-related materials. Author of the *IBM PC, XT, and DOS Workbook* and the *IBM PC, XT, and DOS Instructor's Guide*, as well as a contributing author to *Using HyperCard: From Home to HyperTalk*, Katherine has also published many family-related articles in national general interest publications.

C ONTENTS AT A G LANCE

TABLE OF CONTENTS ▽

I   An Introduction to First Publisher ▽

8   Printing the Publication **275**

III Advanced Techniques

Foreword

Creating documents in today's business world no longer has to be a confusing process of writing, cutting, and pasting. The scratching of pens and the snipping of scissors is rapidly giving way to the tapping of keys and the clicking of mouse buttons. Advancing computer technology raises questions for first-time users, but it also brings an exciting array of newly discovered possibilities.

A personal computer, a decent printer, and good, easy-to-use desktop publishing software make it possible for the ordinary business person to produce high-quality newsletters, memos, fliers, and brochures. You no longer need to be a graphic designer to give a professional shine to that company newsletter or that announcement about your latest store "special." And you don't have to sit through hours of classes, spend hundreds of dollars on expensive software, or have the newest pricey hardware, either.

PFS: First Publisher provides an inexpensive solution to the problem of producing professional-looking documents. First introduced in 1985, PFS: First Publisher has rapidly become a national best-seller, the standard in the entry-level desktop publishing market. Its low price, ease of use, and capability of quickly producing polished, visually appealing documents on a wide variety of computer systems and printers have made PFS: First Publisher the favorite of many thousands of people who had never before even heard of *fonts* or *leading*.

It is important to stress that PFS: First Publisher is an entry-level desktop publishing package, designed for people whose days are filled with a lot more than producing desktop publications. Software Publishing Corporation is not attempting to replicate the capabilities of a professional typesetter. What we hear from entry-level desktop publishers across the country and from all types of business people is that they need to produce the highest-quality output possible from the relatively inexpensive hardware already available to them. We designed PFS: First Publisher to meet this need by offering the ordinary business person all the tools needed to produce professional-looking documents quickly and easily.

By no means, however, is PFS: First Publisher a flimsy tool made just for beginners. It offers more than enough functionality and sophistication to challenge the most experienced user. Many First Publisher users have produced great-looking publications for years without even touching some of the more sophisticated features. Software Publishing Corporation has continually added to PFS: First Publisher as First Publisher users have indicated the need for new capabilities. Our continuing challenge is to make the software easy to use, even as we offer more sophistication. Our goal is to make desktop publishing accessible to everyone by keeping PFS: First Publisher the easiest and most intuitive desktop publishing software on the market today.

To that end, I welcome and highly recommend Que Corporation's *Using PFS: First Publisher*. Katherine Murray's well-written and insightful text provides a natural supplement to First Publisher's own documentation, which is designed more as a reference book. *Using PFS: First Publisher* will take you through a series of new and useful tips compiled from the suggestions we have received from First Publisher users across the country. Ms. Murray suggests approaches that we hope will speed your learning of First Publisher and enhance your enjoyment of our product.

Que's book has the same goal as Software Publishing Corporation: to take the frustration out of learning and doing desktop publishing and to make desktop publishing accessible and satisfying to you. If you are new to desktop publishing and need to produce professional-quality documents quickly and easily, you can do no better than to use PFS: First Publisher. And if you use PFS: First Publisher, *Using PFS: First Publisher* can be your best source for new and more creative ideas for your next publication.

Jill Groginsky
Product Manager, PFS: First Publisher
Software Publishing Corporation

▼ ACKNOWLEDGMENTS

Writing a book can be a lonely and trying experience. Thanks to the contributions of many friends and First Publisher fans, this one was neither. I would like to personally thank the following people:

Jill Groginsky, of Software Publishing Corporation, for the time and effort she invested in this project, adding many tips and suggestions that will prove tremendously helpful to readers and that have helped make this a better book,

Sherry Duerre and Jennie Tan, of Software Publishing Corporation, for their enthusiasm and their invaluable—and friendly—insight,

Lynne Ranieri, John Dimsdale, and Tom Jenkins, for providing me with important tips and traps they found during the development and production of their First Publisher projects,

Douglas Kerns, manager of The Printing Center, for walking me through the publication of more than one project, and for being a great resource person,

Ann Campbell Holcombe, for the use of her terrific illustration,

Greg Robertson, the production editor of this book, whose warm sense of humor and natural editing ability made being edited a fun, non-threatening experience,

Jeannine Freudenberger, for teaching me a lot about editing computer texts almost half a decade ago, and for not beating me over the head when I turned in the illustrations late, and

Lloyd Short, publishing manager, who believed in this project when few others did, and who continually helped me keep things in perspective with his M R DUKS personality. Thanks.

TRADEMARK ACKNOWLEDGMENTS

Que Corporation has made every effort to supply trademark information about company names, products, and services mentioned in this book. Trademarks indicated below were derived from various sources, Que Corporation cannot attest to the accuracy of this information.

1-2-3 is a registered trademark of Lotus Development Corporation.

Apple, Macintosh, and LaserWriter are registered trademarks of Apple Computer, Inc.

AutoCAD is a registered trademark of Autodesk, Inc.

CompuServe is a registered trademark of H&R Block, Inc.

DeskMate and Tandy are registered trademarks of Tandy Corporation.

Epson FX-286e is a trademark of EPSON America, Inc.

Hercules Graphics Card is a trademark of Hercules Computer Technology.

IBM and QuietWriter are registered trademarks and ProPrinter is a trademark of International Business Machines.

Linotronic is a trademark of Allied Corporation.

Mouse Systems is a trademark of Mouse Systems Corporation.

MS-DOS, Microsoft Mouse, Microsoft Word, and Microsoft Windows Paint are registered trademarks of Microsoft Corporation.

MultiMate and dBASE III Plus are registered trademarks of Ashton-Tate Corporation.

OKIDATA and Microline are registered trademarks of Oki America, Inc.

PageMaker is a registered trademark of Aldus Corporation.

PC Paintbrush is a registered trademark and Publisher's Paintbrush and ZSoft are trademarks of ZSoft Corporation.

PFS is a registered trademark and First Publisher, First Choice, Professional Write, and Harvard Graphics are trademarks of Software Publishing Corporation.

ThinkJet is a registered trademark and LaserJet is a trademark of Hewlett-Packard Company.

Ventura Publisher is a registered trademark of Ventura Software, Inc.

Wang is a registered trademark of Wang Laboratories, Inc.

WordPerfect is a registered trademark of WordPerfect Corporation.

WordStar is a registered trademark of MicroPro International Corporation.

CONVENTIONS USED IN THIS BOOK

The conventions used in this book have been established to help you quickly and easily learn to use PFS: First Publisher. As much as possible, the conventions correspond with those used in the PFS: First Publisher documentation.

1. Information that you are to type (usually found in examples with numbered steps) is indicated by italic type (for example, ''At the prompt, type *cd \pub*'') or is indented and set on a line by itself.

2. Names of menus (such as File, Page, and Text) are shown with the initial letter capitalized. Options on those menus appear in boldface type (for example, **Get art** and **Save art**).

3. Messages and prompts that appear on-screen are represented here in a special typeface (Printer number).

4. Special tips and questions often asked by First Publisher users are highlighted by a special design box.

5. Text-related information of interest to First Publisher users is boxed and has a title.

In addition to these conventions, figures, graphics, and diagrams are used liberally throughout the book to illustrate the publication examples in various stages of completion.

Throughout the book, information for users of the DeskMate version is indicated by a special design element to help you find these items easily.

Introduction

Welcome to desktop publishing.

If that sounds intimidating, it doesn't need to. Like everything else in computerdom, desktop publishing is just a means to an end: a way to get your booklets, brochures, newsletters, and other documents produced with the least possible amount of trouble and expense.

If you are the person responsible for producing the company newsletter, annual reports, or press releases, you will discover that PFS®: First Publisher™ allows you to produce professional-looking documents with a minimum of effort. Whether you publish company materials, community newsletters, or advertising fliers for your own business, First Publisher offers you everything you need to merge text and graphics, enabling you to create effective, quality publications.

If you will be using First Publisher as part of your day-to-day routine, you will find that the program is easy to learn and use—even if you have had no previous computer experience. If you plan to use First Publisher only occasionally—when you redesign a flier, for example—you will see that once you have used First Publisher, it is easy to go back to: Everything you need is available in the pull-down menus or in the tools row, so you have no complicated commands to remember and no sophisticated procedures to recall.

In this book, you will learn how to use the PFS: First Publisher desktop publishing program to produce materials that might normally go through conventional publishing methods. You can use First Publisher for a variety of projects, such as the following:

❏ Newsletters

❏ Brochures

❏ Business reports/Proposals

❏ Announcements

❏ Fliers

❏ Resumes

❏ Business stationery

❏ Letterheads

❏ Disk labels

❏ Business cards

❏ Greeting cards

Whatever you want to publish, First Publisher will help you design, lay out, illustrate, and print your project.

Whether you already have invested in First Publisher or are simply exploring the possibility of purchase, *Using PFS: First Publisher* will help you evaluate the "dos and don'ts" of the program, learn the process of creating First Publisher publications, avoid trouble spots, and explore the basics of production stages from design to printing.

What Is First Publisher?

First Publisher is a desktop publishing program that allows you to create short publications such as newsletters, brochures, and fliers. Unlike some other desktop publishing programs, First Publisher comes with everything you need to write, design, illustrate, and print your projects.

If you, like thousands of other businesspeople, are pinching pennies, you will find First Publisher's price attractive. If you are just exploring desktop publishing and feel insecure about spending hundreds of dollars on a program you may never use, you will have trouble justifying a $795 expense for a sophisticated desktop publishing program like PageMaker® or Ventura Publisher®. Additionally, unlike competing desktop publishing programs, First Publisher does not require the use of a high-end computer system that possesses features such as a hard disk and more random-access memory (RAM), which can add another $500 to your investment.

Why should you invest in a sophisticated program and a feature-laden system in order to produce a simple newsletter when First Publisher gives you all the tools you need? At the low price of $129 (retail), First Publisher is a "can't lose" choice for first-time desktop publishers.

Advantages of First Publisher

First Publisher is a page-composition program that gives you everything you need to merge text and graphics, create exciting layouts, and print professional-looking documents. As you begin to explore the program, the following benefits become apparent:

❑ First Publisher is so easy to use you can produce a document the first day you work with the package. In Chapter 3 of this book is a First Publisher "QuickStart," which shows how to use various features in the program and produce a publication—at one sitting.

❑ First Publisher is a "complete" package in itself. Unlike other programs, First Publisher comes with clip art that you can use in your own publications. Additionally, you can use First Publisher's free-hand art capabilities to produce custom graphics. You can enter text using First Publisher or import it from other programs. These options allow you to create a complete document entirely within First Publisher if you prefer, without switching back and forth between word processing and graphics programs.

❑ First Publisher offers flexibility that other programs cannot. You can make text or graphics changes easily, flow text around graphics, and move various elements on-screen with a minimum of trouble.

Why a Book on First Publisher?

When you are learning something new, whether you're learning to speak French or learning to drive a 5-speed, your point of reference means everything. If you try to learn French by reading the French translation of Shakespeare's *Macbeth*, or attempt to learn to drive a stick shift by starting on the German autobahn, chances are you will be defeated (or flattened) before you start.

Learning about desktop publishing is not nearly as complicated as either of those two tasks, especially if you have previous computer experience and some idea of what you want a desktop publishing program to do. Although First Publisher is phenomenally easy when compared to more powerful (and expensive) programs like PageMaker and Ventura, don't be fooled: a learning curve is still involved.

In general, people expect low-priced software to be easy. For some reason, price and ease of use seem to go hand-in-hand. Perhaps it's the connection between price and the features available in most programs. For example, Software Publishing Corporation's PFS: Professional Write™ is substantially less expensive than dBASE III Plus™—but Professional Write also is less powerful. People apply that same logic when they approach desktop publishing software. First Publisher may surprise them. Although the more powerful desktop publishing programs possess features that are helpful when working with long, complex projects, First Publisher packs all the punch necessary for short publications such as newsletters, business reports, fliers, and press releases.

Although First Publisher is far from being the most complicated program on the market, it does have some tricks and traps. This book answers questions often asked by First Publisher users. Some additional techniques are included to help you hurdle trouble spots and shorten design and layout time.

You also will find that this book does some "hand-holding," something not often found in computer books, because a friendly, helpful attitude is in keeping with the overall tone of the software. The First Publisher program provides a pleasant, nonthreatening introduction to desktop publishing and this book does the same. For example, Appendix A explains how you can turn your First Publisher document into a finished publication; this appendix includes tips for choosing paper weight, inks, and other items related to production. Appendix B provides design tips from professionals, tips you can use to make your projects outstanding.

Who Should Read This Book?

First Publisher still is an emerging product. Already, hundreds of thousands of users are using the program to produce newsletters, business reports, resumes, fliers, and a myriad of other publications. Specifically, *Using PFS: First Publisher* addresses the following users:

❏ People in small- or medium-sized businesses who are responsible for the publication of materials related to their companies

❏ Owners of small businesses who need to produce advertising materials, newsletters, reports, and miscellaneous materials related to their businesses

❏ Home users who want to publish community or organizational newsletters

❏ Potential desktop publishers who are investigating the possibility of publishing materials for clients

Whether you use First Publisher to produce press releases at work, invitations at home, or newsletters at school, you will find the examples in *Using PFS: First Publisher* informative and helpful. Additional material, such as expert design tips, has been included to help you produce the most appealing publications possible.

Conventions Used in This Book

Using PFS: First Publisher uses several conventions of which you should be aware. They are listed here for your reference.

❏ Information that you are to type (usually found in examples with numbered steps) is indicated by italic type. For example, ''At the prompt, type *cd \pub*.''

❏ Names of menus (such as File, Page, and Text) are shown with the initial letter capitalized. Options on those menus appear in boldface type (for example, **Get art** and **Save art**).

❏ Messages and prompts that appear on-screen are represented here in a special typeface (Printer number).

❏ Special tips and questions asked often by First Publisher users are highlighted by a special design box.

❏ Text-related information of interest to First Publisher users is boxed and has a title.

In addition to these conventions, figures, graphics, and diagrams are used liberally throughout this book to illustrate the publication examples in various stages of completion.

What Is in This Book?

This section explains the various parts and chapters—the overall game plan—of *Using PFS: First Publisher*.

Part I

Part I, "An Introduction to First Publisher," starts at the beginning of the beginning and, using a First Publisher QuickStart, takes you through the production of a sample document.

Chapter 1, "Desktop Publishing: A Primer," covers desktop publishing concepts and terms, the evolution of desktop publishing, the position of First Publisher in that evolution, and what First Publisher can—and cannot—do.

Chapter 2, "Installing First Publisher," shows you how to install First Publisher on your system if you haven't already done so. In addition, this chapter describes the required hardware and shows you how to add a mouse and a printer to your system. This chapter also covers the basic procedures for setting up directories and organizing your First Publisher files.

Chapter 3, "Getting Started with First Publisher," provides a tour of the basic elements involved in First Publisher: layers, text, art, tools, menus, baselines, and fonts. This chapter also explains how to use the on-line help system and introduces you to the templates available with First Publisher. Chapter 3 concludes with a First Publisher QuickStart that uses the program's NEWS.PUB template to illustrate how you can "borrow" a design and use it as the basis of your own publications.

Part II

Part II, "The Basics: Creating a Publication," is a hands-on, step-by-step tutorial for creating your First Publisher document.

Chapter 4, "Beginning the Publication," takes you through the basics of planning and starting the publication. Design considerations for various project types are included in this chapter. Additionally, this chapter relates the procedures for opening publications, defining pages, checking the status of the system, and saving and deleting files.

Chapter 5, "Entering and Editing Text," includes topics and procedures for creating text in First Publisher or importing it from popular word processing programs. Included are instructions for editing text; deleting text; selecting fonts; using the clipboard; moving, inserting, and erasing text; saving text; and copying and pasting text.

Chapter 6, "Creating and Using Graphics," explains the tools used to produce and modify graphics in First Publisher. Topics include importing graphics files, using text as graphics, rotating text images (new with Version 2.0 of the program), importing images (including special information about using scanned images), changing art, saving graphics as art, erasing art, creating personalized art, and making attention-getting mastheads.

Chapter 7, "Finishing the Layout," teaches you to put text and graphics together. Topics include reviewing the definition of the page, setting baselines, aligning text, setting and changing margins, controlling text flow, adding rules and boxes, inserting a page, and viewing the whole page.

Chapter 8, "Printing the Publication," shows you how to print what you have created. Information about printing with dot-matrix and laser printers is included in this chapter. Also included are tips for using the Hewlett-Packard DeskJet and LaserJet™ printers, and the new scaled and unscaled printing options available with First Publisher Version 2.01.

Part III

Part III, "Advanced Techniques," takes you through the second stage of preparing documents. Once you have designed and printed the first drafts, you may want to design your own templates for documents used repeatedly. You also may want to work with some of the special features in First Publisher, such as FONTMOVE and SNAPSHOT.

Chapter 9, "Creating Your Own Templates," gives you information about setting up your own templates so that you can use them instead of redesigning the same documents over and over again. this chapter shows you how to set up templates for various publications.

Chapter 10, "Using First Publisher's Special Features," is a "catch-all" chapter covering aspects of the program that don't fit within typical chapters. FONTMOVE (the utility that moves fonts in and out of First Publisher) is discussed, as is SNAPSHOT, the program's screen-capture utility.

Appendixes and Glossary

This book concludes with two appendixes and a glossary. Appendix A takes you through the process of turning your First Publisher document into a finished product. Appendix B provides design tips gleaned from graphic designers. Appendix C includes important information for users of the First Publisher DeskMate version. Finally, the Glossary provides definitions of various terms used throughout the book.

Now that you know the basic course of the book, it's time to get started.

Part I

An Introduction to First Publisher

Includes

Desktop Publishing:
A Primer

Installing First Publisher

Getting Started with
First Publisher

Desktop Publishing:
A Primer

Whether you are new to personal computers or you have been using a computer for years, when you enter the desktop publishing arena for the first time, you wind up either learning a new set of skills or building on the skills you already have. If you envision yourself as a budding publisher, having a healthy interest in writing, editing, layout, or graphic design will help you produce professional-looking documents, but even that interest is not mandatory. First Publisher is a learn-as-you-go type of program that allows you to combine text and graphics to produce a quality document with a minimal amount of effort and expertise.

In this chapter, you will learn what the term *desktop publishing* means, how the publishing industry has evolved, and where First Publisher fits into that evolution.

What Is Desktop Publishing?

Desktop publishing gives you the flexibility to combine text and graphics in one document. Whether your desktop publishing tasks include creating the company newsletter, designing advertising brochures, or pounding out attention-getting press releases, First Publisher is a low-priced yet powerful program that allows you to design, create, and produce your publications with a minimum of effort and investment.

Benefits of Desktop Publishing

As you become proficient with First Publisher—or any other desktop publishing system—you will discover dozens of benefits. If you are currently producing fliers by writing them out by hand or by using a word processor and then literally cutting and pasting the text, you will find that the documents you produce with First Publisher require less effort and look substantially more professional. Along the same lines, training handouts that are typed on a typewriter and then photocopied are not nearly as visually appealing as a handout that combines text and graphics in an effective layout.

The three major benefits, the benefits you will recognize right away, also are the primary reasons most people get into desktop publishing. With a desktop publishing system, and with First Publisher in particular, you can save time, save money, retain quality control of your projects, and produce better-looking documents.

Saving Time

As you will see later in this chapter, desktop publishing drastically reduces the time spent on complex procedures related to typing, typesetting, designing, and pasting up documents. A project that takes days to accomplish with conventional methods may be reduced to hours with a desktop publishing system. Additionally, with desktop publishing, you retain the ability to make last-minute changes—right up to the minute you print the publication. Then, if modifications are needed on the printed document, you can make the changes quickly and print the document again. With a conventional method, you would need to travel back and forth to the printer in order to make corrections, and you would lose valuable time in waiting to see the results.

When you use a typesetting system or a more complicated desktop publishing program such as Ventura Publisher or PageMaker, you go through a steep learning curve because of the variety of procedures and commands you must learn. Not so with First Publisher. First Publisher saves you even more time because its user-friendly interface, easy-to-understand menus, and numerous help screens take the confusion out of desktop publishing. With First Publisher, you can create your first document the same afternoon you pop the shrink-wrap on the package.

Saving Money

Typesetting systems are *expensive*. Not too many people go out and purchase a typesetting system—which could cost up to several hundred thousand dollars—in order to produce a series of newsletters or advertising fliers. If you are currently producing those publications by taking them to a printer and having them typeset, you are paying for some of the cost of that typesetting system. On the average, typesetting charges run $18 to $20 per page.

By comparison, desktop publishing offers many less-expensive alternatives. If you start with the bare essentials, you need a computer, a mouse, and desktop publishing software. You also must own a printer or have access to one that outputs the quality you want. Even better, if you already own a personal computer, First Publisher probably will run on your system as-is. With other competing products such as PageMaker or Ventura, you may need to upgrade your system by increasing the system's memory or by adding a hard disk, which can require a significant investment.

Depending on the power and capacity of the computer you choose (First Publisher will work on a system that has two disk drives and no hard disk), your cost may be as low as $2,000. If you plan to invest in a laser printer, however, add at least another $2,000. (The laser printer cost given is an estimate; costs for laser printers range from $1,500 to more than $8,000.)

Retaining Control and Convenience

Another important benefit of desktop publishing is the amount of control you retain over your projects. Suppose that you currently create the company newsletter by gathering articles, entering them into your word processing program, printing on a high-resolution dot-matrix printer, and pasting on a few graphics. Perhaps you have someone else proofread the newsletter quickly, and then you take the newsletter to the printer or to a good photocopier.

With First Publisher, you never need to pull the paste out of your desk drawer. After you type the articles into your word processor, you can import the text into First Publisher, use the program's clip art to illustrate the newsletter, and use the program's graphics tools to further enhance the design.

In a more elaborate publishing cycle, you might take the quarterly sales report to be typeset, and then you would have to trace the publication through a series of steps: to the typesetter, back for page proofs, back to the typesetter for corrections, and then to the printer—you could have a wait time of several weeks involved, depending on the workloads of the printer and the typesetter.

With First Publisher, you can create new text or bring in existing text, create and use graphics, lay out the publication, and print it yourself. You can be the writer, editor, typesetter, designer, proofreader, and layout artist for the project, which gives you ultimate control over the quality, timeliness, and cost of your publication.

Producing Better-Looking Documents

One of the additional benefits of desktop publishing is the difference you can make in the publications you produce. If you have previously been typing press releases on the company letterhead and sending the release out to prospective buyers, you will find that the choice of fonts in First Publisher, the capability of importing scanned images, and the graphics features of the program will greatly enhance the material you create. For example, you can use First Publisher to spruce up your press releases by doing the following:

❑ Using one font for headlines and a second font for the body text

❑ Scanning a photo of the product and incorporating the scanned image in the publication. (You also can edit the scanned image by using the options available on the Art menu.)

❑ Adding rules to highlight the product information

❑ Adding a quick-look box that provides technical specifications of the product

Similarly, suppose that you are responsible for creating a quarterly sales report that will be distributed to all sales managers in your district. In the past, you simply typed the text into your word processor (in a one-column format), left blank space for spreadsheets and graphs (which you created in 1-2-3® and printed), and printed the text on a Hewlett-Packard laser printer. You then had to paste the printed spreadsheet and graphs in place and have the publication copied. With First Publisher, you can cut down on the amount of work and time involved and produce more professional-looking output by using these features:

❑ Select the margin and column formats before entering text

❑ Import text directly from the word processor with fonts already specified (by using First Publisher's *FONT* commands)

❏ Use SNAPSHOT (First Publisher's screen-capture utility) to take a picture of the 1-2-3 spreadsheets and graphs and import those items as graphics into your publication

❏ Use the program's graphics tools to add rules and highlight boxes to your publication

❏ Use the Hewlett-Packard soft fonts to produce professional-quality text

Desktop Publishing and First Publisher

In this section, you will get an overview of what you can do with desktop publishing. Desktop publishing gives you the power to combine text and graphics into a pleasing layout to produce a professional-looking publication. Figure 1.1 shows the basic elements involved in the desktop publishing process. Each of these elements is described in the following pages.

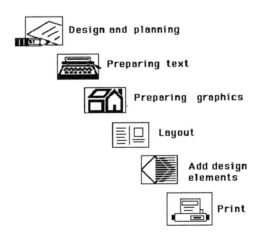

Fig. 1.1. Elements in the desktop publishing process.

Designing and Planning

Anyone with parents has heard the admonition "before you do anything, *think*." Although parents seem to use the phrase to point out something obvious (like, "Next time you back the car out of the garage, open the door first"), it really *is* a good rule. Planning the layout and design of your publications is no exception to that rule (see fig. 1.2).

Before you begin typing text, creating graphics, or pondering attention-getting headlines, you should think about the design of your publication. You can plan on-screen, in-head, or on-paper. Ask these kinds of questions: What type of document am I producing? Do I want three columns? One? Will I use photos? Who will read this publication? What will they expect?

In Chapter 4, you will learn to plan various aspects of your publication before you put finger to keyboard (or hand to mouse). This stage in desktop publishing is comparable to the design stage in traditional typesetting: in both processes, someone has to *think* about the design. In desktop publishing, that someone is you.

Preparing Text

With the advent of word processing, typewriters are fast becoming obsolete. Word processing allows typists to enter data at lightning speed, while simultaneously fixing errors, formatting paragraphs, and performing a multitude of other tasks such as tabbing, spacing, hyphenation, spelling, and adding headers and footers—things either impossible or extremely time-consuming with a typewriter.

The typist can save the finished document in a file that can be printed as-is or used as text in a desktop publishing program such as First Publisher. Literally hundreds of word processing programs are on the market. The most popular of these programs are supported by First Publisher, meaning that text generated with them can be used in First Publisher. First Publisher can use text that you have generated using one of the following programs:

❏ PFS: First Choice

❏ PFS: Write

❏ PFS: Professional Write (Version 1.0 or 2.0)

❏ Microsoft® Word (Version 3.0)

❑ MultiMate®

❑ Wang® PC

❑ WordPerfect® (Version 3, 4.1, or 4.2)

❑ WordStar®

Fig. 1.2. *Planning the page layout on paper.*

If you use a word processing format other than the ones listed, you may be able to output your file in ASCII format; First Publisher can read such a file. (For more information, see Chapter 5, "Entering and Editing Text.")

You also can type text using First Publisher, whether you want to enter new sentences or paragraphs or edit what's already there. First Publisher also gives you the option of treating text as graphics—a valuable feature when you want to create eye-catching mastheads or ornate paragraph openings. Figure 1.3, for example, shows a newsletter with its name printed vertically along the left side of the page. To achieve this vertical positioning, the text was treated as a graphic and rotated to fit on the side of the page.

Preparing Graphics

Without some form of graphics, your publications would be nothing more than pages full of type. Graphics add a degree of professionalism to your projects that simple typed documents cannot offer. Most people using desktop publishing want to integrate text and graphics to produce a document that is visually inviting, informative, and professional.

Before desktop publishing, the creation of graphics required the expertise of a trained artist. The artist would combine creativity, tools, and talent to produce an image that—it was hoped—fulfilled the client's vision. Before the finished image could be used in a publication, it was "shot down" to size (meaning that it was captured on film and sized to the meet the requirements of the publication).

If your projects didn't warrant the use of an artist, you probably had to type the text in a word processor, print the text, leaving blank space so that you could cut and paste in the graphics, and then draw in rules or special design elements by hand.

With First Publisher, you can draw rules and boxes; use text as graphics; place, edit, and resize images created with paint (graphics) programs; and use clip art (predrawn elements) with only a few simple procedures. First Publisher even accepts scanned images, which means you can use photos —or actually art created from photos—in your publication. (And because First Publisher allows you to edit scanned images, you can produce an image taken from a photo that actually looks better than the original photo.) First Publisher doesn't take the mystique—or the need for talent—out of creating dynamite graphic elements; it just makes the process easier for those persons who will never paint a Mona Lisa. Figure 1.4 shows an example of First Publisher's graphics capabilities.

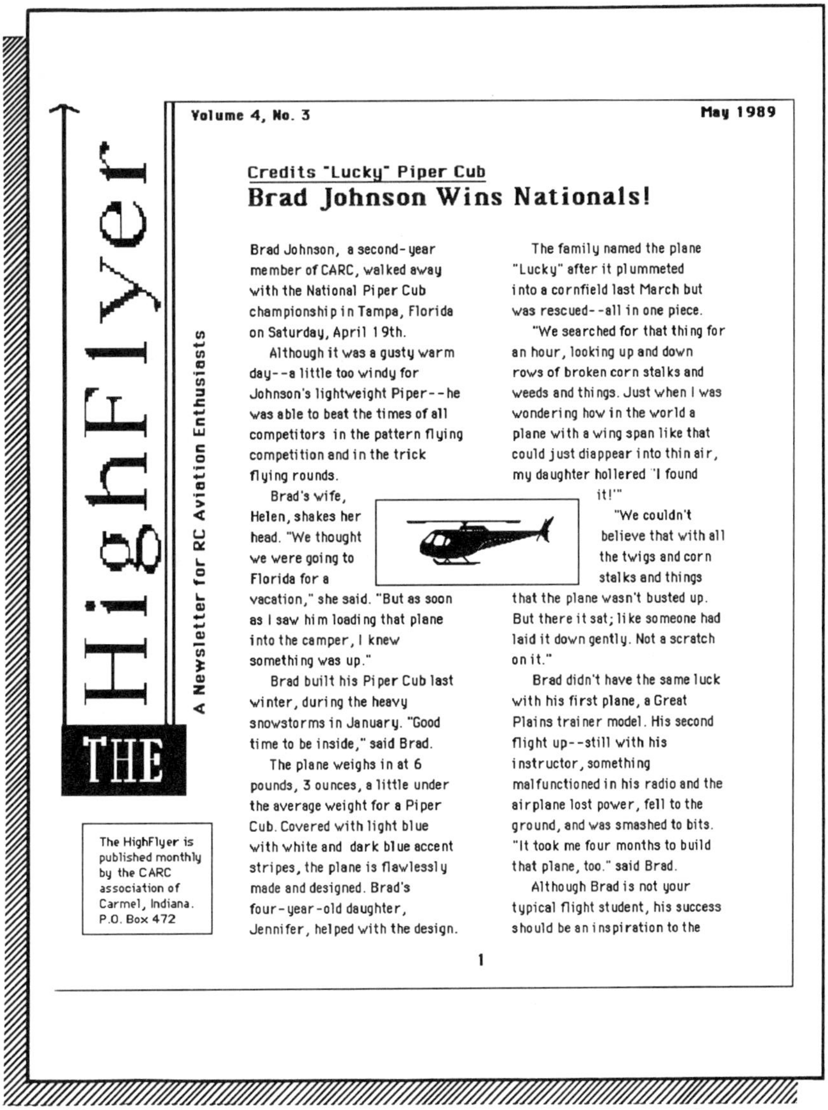

THE HighFlyer

A Newsletter for RC Aviation Enthusiasts

Volume 4, No. 3 May 1989

Credits "Lucky" Piper Cub

Brad Johnson Wins Nationals!

Brad Johnson, a second-year member of CARC, walked away with the National Piper Cub championship in Tampa, Florida on Saturday, April 19th.

Although it was a gusty warm day--a little too windy for Johnson's lightweight Piper--he was able to beat the times of all competitors in the pattern flying competition and in the trick flying rounds.

Brad's wife, Helen, shakes her head. "We thought we were going to Florida for a vacation," she said. "But as soon as I saw him loading that plane into the camper, I knew something was up."

Brad built his Piper Cub last winter, during the heavy snowstorms in January. "Good time to be inside," said Brad.

The plane weighs in at 6 pounds, 3 ounces, a little under the average weight for a Piper Cub. Covered with light blue with white and dark blue accent stripes, the plane is flawlessly made and designed. Brad's four-year-old daughter, Jennifer, helped with the design.

The family named the plane "Lucky" after it plummeted into a cornfield last March but was rescued--all in one piece.

"We searched for that thing for an hour, looking up and down rows of broken corn stalks and weeds and things. Just when I was wondering how in the world a plane with a wing span like that could just diappear into thin air, my daughter hollered 'I found it!'"

"We couldn't believe that with all the twigs and corn stalks and things that the plane wasn't busted up. But there it sat; like someone had laid it down gently. Not a scratch on it."

Brad didn't have the same luck with his first plane, a Great Plains trainer model. His second flight up--still with his instructor, something malfunctioned in his radio and the airplane lost power, fell to the ground, and was smashed to bits. "It took me four months to build that plane, too." said Brad.

Although Brad is not your typical flight student, his success should be an inspiration to the

The HighFlyer is published monthly by the CARC association of Carmel, Indiana. P.O. Box 472

1

Fig. 1.3. The name of this newsletter treated as a graphic and rotated.

Fig. 1.4. An example of First Publisher's graphics capabilities.

The following paint programs produce files that can be used with First Publisher:

❑ PC Paintbrush®

❑ PC PaintPlus®

❑ Microsoft® Windows Paint

❑ Publisher's Paintbrush™

❑ LOGIPAINT

Many graphics programs have a conversion utility that you can use to convert the graphics files to a format that can be recognized by First Publisher (PCX files). To see whether your graphics program can be used with First Publisher, check your program's documentation or ask your dealer.

Laying Out the Publication

With conventional publishing methods, "laying out the publication" means just that. After assembling the finished art and the typeset and printed article (referred to as the *galleys*), you use a special knife, a T-square, glue or hot wax, and a burnisher to manually paste everything onto boards (cardboard pages on which the text and graphics are waxed or glued). First text, then art, then rules and other graphic elements, and then headers, footers, and page numbers are carefully pasted into place. A great deal of work is involved for one page (see fig. 1.5).

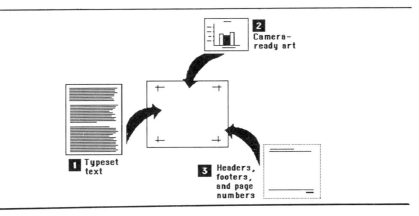

Fig. 1.5. The paste-up process used with conventional publishing.

With First Publisher, you can pull text from one program and art from another, or create all the elements within the program, producing a publication on-screen in a few short steps. When you print the publication, the text, art, and graphic elements are all together—straight from your printer. No hot wax, no slips of the knife, no separate pieces of artwork to keep track of. The document is completed on-screen and printed as a completed publication.

Printing the Publication

The last phase in the desktop publishing cycle—the actual printing—is not much different from conventional methods. At this stage in the conventional process, someone boxes up the boards (the pasted-up manuscript) and ships them to an offset printer. (An offset printer uses a printing press to produce the best print quality possible.) Or, depending on your method of publishing, perhaps you take the pasted-up document to the photocopier.

If the project is a newsletter, the newsletter goes to the printer to be printed and folded (or stapled, if necessary). Perhaps several weeks later, after the proofing stage, the publication is returned to you in its finished state.

In recent years, photocopying has evolved to the point where many people produce their materials by copying them on a high-quality copier. Some people still prefer to use an offset printer. Because of the time, cost, and patience involved, few people publish 150 copies of a monthly newsletter on their laser printers—but it can be done. Let your own standards be the guide for handling the final printing of the document. Appendix A gives you additional tips for dealing with a printer about the choices regarding your publication.

The future promises improved printer technologies, fax boards, networking of desktop publishing systems, and color photocopiers and color laser printers (which are currently available but costly).

Conventional Versus Desktop Publishing: Summing Up

Desktop publishing combines the power of a personal computer, the flexibility of a page-composition system, and the basic procedures of conventional publishing to constitute an easy-to-use, cost-effective, and timely alternative to the complicated publishing process.

You can spend hundreds of thousands of dollars on a typesetting system that produces beautiful type, is difficult to learn, expensive to run, and difficult to maintain. Desktop publishing is a low-cost, low-maintenance solution that allows you to produce professional newsletters, brochures, manuals, books, and fliers. Table 1.1 compares conventional and desktop publishing and shows why even large companies with the capacity to do in-house typesetting are exploring the possibility of desktop publishing.

Table 1.1
Benefits of Desktop Publishing

Conventional Publishing	Desktop Publishing
Expensive hardware	Inexpensive hardware
Extensive coding	Minimum coding (none with First Publisher)
Complicated process	Flexible process
Costly materials	Less costly materials
Involves many people	Requires only one person
Requires tight scheduling	Minimizes time investment
Hard to control project	Easier to control project
	Minimum effort expended
High-quality output	Professional-quality output

An Overview of First Publisher

First Publisher occupies a unique position in the desktop publishing market. Instead of costing hundreds of dollars, First Publisher retails for $129 and includes templates and clip art files you can use to create your own publications.

As a result, First Publisher rapidly has acquired devoted users. These people are ''taking a chance'' on desktop publishing. If your company publishes a three-page newsletter once a month for day-care moms, do you need a desktop publishing package that costs $795 and will take you months to learn to use effectively? If your radio-control airplane club has voted you the editor-in-chief of the *HighFlyer*, do you want to tap the club's reserves (or your patience) by investing in an expensive, complicated program? Figure 1.6 shows three examples of the kinds of publications you can produce with First Publisher.

Fig. 1.6. Examples of publications produced with First Publisher.

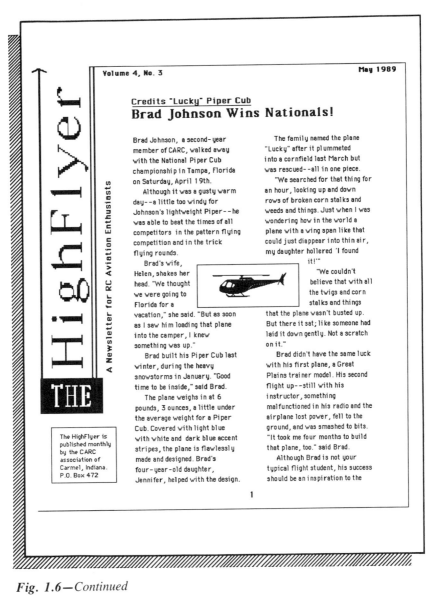

Volume 4, No. 3   **May 1989**

THE HighFlyer
A Newsletter for RC Aviation Enthusiasts

The HighFlyer is published monthly by the CARC association of Carmel, Indiana. P.O. Box 472

Credits "Lucky" Piper Cub
Brad Johnson Wins Nationals!

Brad Johnson, a second-year member of CARC, walked away with the National Piper Cub championship in Tampa, Florida on Saturday, April 19th.

Although it was a gusty warm day--a little too windy for Johnson's lightweight Piper--he was able to beat the times of all competitors in the pattern flying competition and in the trick flying rounds.

Brad's wife, Helen, shakes her head. "We thought we were going to Florida for a vacation," she said. "But as soon as I saw him loading that plane into the camper, I knew something was up."

Brad built his Piper Cub last winter, during the heavy snowstorms in January. "Good time to be inside," said Brad.

The plane weighs in at 6 pounds, 3 ounces, a little under the average weight for a Piper Cub. Covered with light blue with white and dark blue accent stripes, the plane is flawlessly made and designed. Brad's four-year-old daughter, Jennifer, helped with the design.

The family named the plane "Lucky" after it plummeted into a cornfield last March but was rescued--all in one piece.

"We searched for that thing for an hour, looking up and down rows of broken corn stalks and weeds and things. Just when I was wondering how in the world a plane with a wing span like that could just disappear into thin air, my daughter hollered 'I found it!'"

"We couldn't believe that with all the twigs and corn stalks and things that the plane wasn't busted up. But there it sat; like someone had laid it down gently. Not a scratch on it."

Brad didn't have the same luck with his first plane, a Great Plains trainer model. His second flight up--still with his instructor, something malfunctioned in his radio and the airplane lost power, fell to the ground, and was smashed to bits. "It took me four months to build that plane, too." said Brad.

Although Brad is not your typical flight student, his success should be an inspiration to the

1

Fig. 1.6—Continued

Fig. 1.6—Continued

First Publisher is used by people all over the country (and internationally) as a low-cost, easy-to-use solution to the problem of personal publishing. Newsletters, training materials, fliers, proposals, reports, manuals, magazines, brochures, invitations—all kinds of professional-looking documents are being produced by First Publisher users.

Where Does First Publisher Fit in Desktop Publishing History?

First Publisher truly is a unique product. It combines powerful features, an easy-to-use design, and extra elements such as clip art files, a screen-capture utility, 20 different dot-matrix fonts, and support for leading laser printers—all wrapped up in the *least expensive* desktop publishing program available.

When the term *desktop publishing* first became a buzzword at cocktail parties, people used it synonymously with PageMaker. In those early days, desktop publishing *was* PageMaker—there really was no competition.

PageMaker was a phenomenal advancement for the new desktop publishing industry. Like its chief competitor, Ventura Publisher, PageMaker is expensive, difficult to use, and complicated.

Since computers first became tools that real people could use—no longer confined to people with degrees in engineering and computer science—they have become easy-to-use, user-friendly machines. This user-friendliness is evidenced in the evolution of the Apple Macintosh® and the IBM® PC.

In general, software has followed that same evolution. Early spreadsheet programs that were difficult to decipher now can carry out complex operations with one keystroke. Word processors that required a series of commands to move a paragraph now allow you to identify and move a block of text with minimum trouble. More and more often, software companies provide help screens and better documentation with their products, hoping to improve the user-friendliness of the software.

First Publisher is the "easy-to-use, user-friendly" contribution to the desktop publishing market. Not only does it bring you up to speed on desktop publishing techniques, it makes the whole process as easy to understand as possible. In addition, by offering you a variety of templates and designs, First Publisher helps you learn to create your own publications; you provide the text and graphics, and First Publisher provides the layout. When you are ready to create your own designs, First Publisher provides help screens to assist you in trouble spots and clip art to spark interest in your publications.

What First Publisher Can— and Cannot—Do

Although the cost of First Publisher is only a fraction of that of its more complicated competitors, First Publisher isn't "missing" anything. In fact, First Publisher has some features that the high-end desktop publishing programs do not have, such as graphics editing, clip art files, and so forth. To produce virtually any short publication, you will find everything you need to design, write, edit, lay out, and publish your project.

Among its many features, First Publisher offers the following:

❏ Layout of up to four columns. You can easily specify up to four columns by using the **Define page** option in the File menu. Additionally, First Publisher comes with a library of templates that provide a variety of column formats.

❏ Text entry and editing. With First Publisher, you can choose to enter text directly into the document by typing it, or you can import text from most popular word processors. First Publisher also offers text editing features and allows you to control the amount of space between lines; to control the fonts used in body text, headlines, and banners; and to customize the way in which the text flows on the publication.

❏ Placement of text around graphics. First Publisher offers an automatic **Picturewrap** feature that automatically flows text around a graphic. You also can tailor the way in which the text is positioned by shortening or lengthening each text line to fit a particular format.

❏ Library of clip art. Unlike any other desktop publishing program on the market, First Publisher is packaged with five different clip art files. Each file offers many individual pieces of clip art that you can use in your own documents. Additionally, many other clip art files are available separately from Software Publishing Corporation.

❏ Capability to resize graphics. In First Publisher, you can select and resize graphics—something other desktop publishing programs cannot claim. Resizing capability allows you to tailor an image to fit a particular location in the text or to reduce an image so that it appears more clearly (this is particularly useful for hand-drawn or scanned images).

❑ Capability to rotate graphics. Other desktop publishing programs have extremely limited—if any—graphics editing features. First Publisher gives you many options for working with graphics, and one of the most useful is the ability to rotate graphics. This capability allows you to create side banners and special effects that other programs cannot create.

❑ Speed keys. First Publisher offers what the manufacturer refers to as ''speed keys,'' which lessen the keystrokes necessary to perform certain operations that you use frequently. Instead of going through a menu selection sequence each time you want to save a file, for example, you can press Alt-S.

❑ Capability to preview full pages. With the **Show page** option on the File menu, First Publisher displays the entire page of the document so that you can see how the text and graphics are organized on the page.

❑ Capability to import scanned images. You can use scanned images in your First Publisher documents, and because the program offers graphics editing techniques, you can ''clean up'' scanned images by using **Magnify** from the Art menu, for example, to straighten lines or remove unwanted shadows.

❑ Support of laser printers and soft fonts. First Publisher supports the Hewlett-Packard LaserJet series and the Apple LaserWriter® printer. Additionally, the program works with the DeskJet printer, which is not technically a laser printer but produces output that is near-laser quality. You also can use soft fonts and several Hewlett-Packard cartridges to give you an almost limitless choice of fonts to use.

Currently, the following features are *not* offered by First Publisher:

❑ Creation of master pages. Master pages are pages that record the design of the publication—no text or graphics are placed on master pages. In longer documents, master pages are useful so that certain design elements need not be repeated from page to page. For most First Publisher documents, this feature is not necessary. For those documents that require the same or a similar design (such as a monthly newsletter), you can create a template file on which you build each newsletter so that you don't have to re-create the design each time you use it.

❑ Production of indexes, tables of contents, headers or footers

❑ Automatic page numbering

❑ Shading of graphics (although images from paint programs that do include shading can be imported)

❑ Multiple page sizes

❑ Landscape printing

❑ 300 dpi (dots per inch) graphics

What's in the Future?

Speculating on what the future will bring to First Publisher and to desktop publishing in general is difficult. By examining where the industry has been, perhaps deductions can be made about where it's going. In general, expect to see these improvements in the desktop publishing industry:

❑ More typefaces

❑ More powerful graphics packages

❑ Faster processing and reforming on-screen

❑ More context-sensitive help screens

❑ Decrease in cost of desktop publishing peripherals

❑ More powerful laser printers

❑ Multiple page sizes

❑ Landscape printing

❑ 300 dpi graphics

First Publisher itself also will continue to evolve. Although the desktop publishing industry has been progressing at a furious pace in the last few years, it still only has begun to fulfill its development potential. If people know how much money, time, and effort desktop publishing saves them and are aware that they can better control the quality of their publications, produce more professional-looking documents, and automate tasks they now do by hand, why hasn't desktop publishing become the explosion it has the potential to be? Simple. Because many people who are in a position to learn desktop publishing skills are intimidated by the language and concepts they don't understand. As the first truly user-friendly desktop publishing program, First Publisher takes the intimidation out of desktop publishing and helps users produce appealing, professional publications in the manner most comfortable for them.

Chapter Summary

In this chapter you learned about the concept of desktop publishing and some of the benefits it provides the user. In addition, you learned which word processors and paint programs work with First Publisher. An overview of First Publisher was included in the chapter in order to highlight First Publisher's features and to show how versatile the program is. Finally, the chapter looked at the future development of desktop publishing programs. The next chapter tells you what hardware you need and how to install First Publisher for your system.

Installing First Publisher

Before you can start producing knockout publications with First Publisher, you must find out what hardware and software you need, install First Publisher for your particular system, and set up the mouse and the printer you will be using. This chapter introduces you to all those things and shows you how to start the program.

In the first half of this chapter, the discussion deals with the various hardware setups possible with First Publisher. Explanations for backing up First Publisher disks and installing the program on your particular system are provided. Because several different systems are discussed, you may want to skip the sections that don't apply to your system: much of the information is the same and only details relating to the hardware have been changed. You can use the icons to help you locate quickly the procedures for your system.

What Comes with First Publisher?

First things first. When you open the First Publisher box for the first time, you should find the First Publisher *User's Guide* and five disks:

❑ Program Disks 1 and 2

❑ The Fonts Disk (Disk 3)

❑ The Sampler Disk (Disk 4)

❑ The Laser Support Disk (Disk 5)

If you are using a system that has 3 1/2-inch drives, such as the PS/2 Models 30, 50, or 60, you will find the *User's Guide* and three disks:

❑ The Program and Fonts Disk (Disk 1)

❑ The Program Disk (Disk 2)

❑ The Laser Support and Sampler Disk (Disk 3)

If you are missing any of these items, contact the dealer who sold you the program.

Be sure to send in the registration card that is packaged with the First Publisher program. Doing so puts you on a list to receive upgrade notices and offers of additional clip art and sample disks.

If you are using the DeskMate version, you also have a DeskMate Runtime disk. Consult your software manual for a list of the disks with your program.

What Do You Need?

Although First Publisher isn't as demanding on your computer's RAM capacity (or your pocketbook) as some other leading desktop publishing programs, your system does have to meet some essential requirements. Most likely, First Publisher will work on your IBM or 100 percent IBM-compatible computer just as you have it set up. You do need either a Color Graphics Adapter (CGA), Enhanced Graphics Adapter (EGA), or Hercules® Graphics Card that is installed inside your computer, however. If you do not have one of these graphics cards, your local computer dealer can help you with this choice and installation. Before you can use First Publisher, you need the following items:

❑ An IBM PC, XT, or PC AT; a Personal System/2 30, 50, or 60; or an IBM-compatible computer. (The computer must have two floppy disk drives or one floppy disk drive and a hard disk.)

❑ DOS (Version 2.0 or higher)

❑ A monitor (monochrome or color)

❑ A graphics card (CGA, EGA, or Hercules)

❑ A mouse (optional)

❑ A printer

The sections that follow explore each hardware necessity in more detail. If you already have the hardware and software you need to run First Publisher and are eager to get started, you can skip the next section and go on to "Installing First Publisher."

In the following section, three tables show you the basic, enhanced, and top-of-the-line setups for a First Publisher desktop publishing system. Remember that if you already own a personal computer, chances are that the program will work on your system as-is.

Table 2.1 lists the essentials for a system that will run First Publisher. Table 2.2 shows you the type of system many First Publisher users own; and Table 2.3 shows you the top-of-the-line (and most expensive) system used for First Publisher.

Table 2.1
Minimum Hardware and Software Setup for First Publisher

Component	System Has
System unit	8088 microprocessor
Disk drives	Two 5 1/4-inch disk drives
Memory	512K of memory (RAM)
Monitor	Monochrome
Display adapter	CGA card
Printer	Dot-matrix printer
Operating system	MS-DOS or PC DOS (2.0 or higher)

Table 2.2
Enhanced Hardware and Software Setup for First Publisher

Component	System Has
System unit	8088 or 80286 microprocessor
Disk drives	One 5 1/4-inch disk drive, 20M hard disk[1]
Memory	640K of memory (RAM)
Monitor	Monochrome or color
Display adapter	EGA card
Printer	Dot-matrix, inkjet, or laser printer
Operating system	MS-DOS or PC DOS (2.0 or higher)
Mouse	Microsoft, LOGITECH, or Mouse Systems mouse[1]
Text editor	PFS: First Choice

[1] The hard disk and the mouse are optional components. First Publisher will work without them, but their use is recommended.

Table 2.3
"Top-of-the-Line" Hardware and Software Setup for First Publisher

Component	System Has
System unit	80286 microprocessor
Disk drives	One 3 1/2-inch or 5 1/4-inch disk drive, 40M hard disk
Memory	640K of memory (RAM)
Monitor	EGA
Display adapter	EGA card
Printer	Laser printer (HP or Apple)
Operating system	MS-DOS or PC DOS (2.0 or higher)
Mouse	Microsoft, LOGITECH, or Mouse Systems mouse
Scanner	Hewlett-Packard
Text editor	PFS: First Choice
Graphics editor	Publisher's Paintbrush

The Computer System

You have several options for the type of computer you use to run First Publisher. You can go from a simple two-drive IBM PC or IBM-compatible system to a feature-laden IBM Personal System/2 (see fig. 2.1). The number of applications you run, the speed you desire from your machine, and the quality of screen display and printer output you need all figure greatly in your computer hardware decision.

The type of documents you produce also helps determine the type of computer you purchase. For example, if you are creating multipage newsletters that combine many graphic elements, a considerable amount of text, and several different typefaces, you may want to consider purchasing a hard disk. More complex documents take up more storage space; therefore, if you are creating long or complicated projects, an investment in a hard disk drive will pay off. Additionally, if your projects require frequent use of graphics, purchasing a mouse can save you a large amount of time that otherwise would be spent capturing and positioning graphics by using the keyboard.

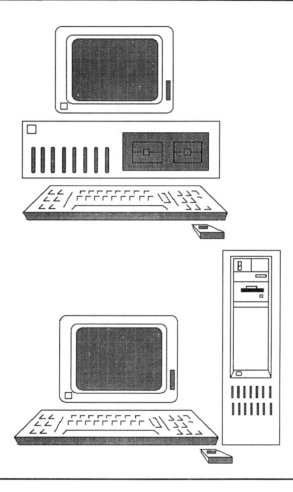

Fig. 2.1. *An IBM PC and a PS/2 Model 60.*

Monitor

For many people, the choice of monitor is one of the most important hardware decisions they make. After all, without the monitor, you wouldn't be able to see what you're doing. (It is possible to use a computer without a monitor, as people did when output was produced on punch cards or magnetic tape.)

With First Publisher, you have the choice of selecting a monochrome or color monitor. You can also choose the quality of the display you want by selecting a CGA, EGA, or Hercules® Graphics Card.

On all monitors, the display is composed of hundreds of small dots of light, called *pixels*. Each character is a pattern of pixels displayed on the screen. The higher the number of pixels used to display a character, the better the quality of the display. Monitors that can display a high number of pixels are known as high-resolution monitors; monitors capable of displaying a lower number of pixels are low-resolution monitors.

A CGA adapter is capable of displaying characters within a grid of 8 by 8 pixels. By comparison, an EGA adapter displays 8 by 14 pixels for one character, and the Hercules graphics card provides a display of 9 by 14. A few extra pixels per character can greatly increase the readability and clarity of on-screen text and graphics. If you plan on doing a great deal of work with First Publisher, it would be worth your investment to get a monitor with better resolution than is possible with the CGA.

As a First Publisher user, the question of high versus low resolution really depends on what you want from your system. If cost is a major consideration, a low-cost option is to use a CGA card and monitor, although that combination also gives you the lowest screen resolution. A better solution is to use an EGA card and monitor or a Hercules card with a monochrome monitor for higher resolution.

SNAPSHOT and the Hercules Card

Here's an important note if you are still shopping for a monitor and a graphics card. As you may know, First Publisher comes with a screen-capture utility called SNAPSHOT that allows you to take a ''picture'' of any screen displayed on your monitor (whether that screen is a WordStar document, Harvard™ Graphics chart, Auto-CAD® image, or from some other program). You can then ''develop'' the picture and use the image as a graphic in your First Publisher documents. If you plan to use SNAPSHOT on a system that is equipped with a Hercules card, however, you should be aware that the text on the screen will not be captured. If you are capturing only graphics, or if you do not plan to use screen shots in your publication, this consideration is minimal; but if the screens contain text, SNAPSHOT will not recognize the text when the screen shot is captured.

Just remember that the higher the resolution of your display, the more accurately your First Publisher screen will reflect the printed publication. Although First Publisher is a ''what you see is what you get'' program, meaning that what you see on-screen is what you get as a printed product, the resolution of the screen does affect the accuracy of the display. If you have a CGA, for example, when you print the publication, you may find that although it appears basically the way you created it, the size and location of some elements may be different from what you anticipated.

Also, if you are using a CGA card, First Publisher displays only one-quarter of a publication page at one time, and the letters and graphics are a little ''stretched out.'' If you are using a Hercules card or an EGA, half a page is displayed at one time, and the letters and graphics are formed the way you see them in print. (*Note:* With any of these graphics adapters, you can use the **Show page** command to display the entire page. Remember that this ''whole page'' display gives you only a thumbnail picture of the entire page, however; you will not be able to read individual characters in the text. Later chapters explain more about this command.)

First Publisher and Color

As you know if you have a color monitor, First Publisher does not display in color, at least at the present time. When the opening screen is displayed, it is black text (or gray tones) on a white screen.

If you use another graphics program that does display in color, such as PC Paintbrush or LOGITECH's Paintshow, you need to change that image to a black-and-white image before you import it into First Publisher. If you try to import a color graphic into First Publisher, a message is displayed telling you that First Publisher cannot retrieve that file. Check your paint program's documentation for information on how to save the art as a black-and-white image.

Printer

Like the monitor, your choice of printer dramatically affects the quality of your finished documents. Dot-matrix printers are given ample support by the First Publisher program; a wide variety of fonts is available for dot-matrix printers. Laser printers provide professional-quality output that is not achievable with dot-matrix printers, but they also represent a substantial investment. The Hewlett-Packard DeskJet printer produces output that rivals laser printers, but at a fraction of the cost. When you are considering which printer to purchase, ask yourself the following questions:

Does the type of publication I'm producing require near-typeset-quality print? Consider what type of documents you will be producing with First Publisher. If you plan to create documents for business purposes—to woo clients or to communicate information outside your company—a laser printer may be in order. For internal documents, reports, or announcements, a dot-matrix printer may be as much as you need.

Who will be reading the document? What type of quality will your audience expect? If you are producing a newsletter for your gardening club, chances are that the members will be impressed with the print quality you can produce on a dot-matrix printer. Many newsletters, fliers, and announcements don't demand laser-quality output. If that's your niche, you could use a dot-matrix printer. If you are producing a quarterly report that will be circulated at the regional sales meeting, however, your publication needs a more polished look. For this use, printing with a laser printer will give your document the professional quality it needs.

Will I be selling the publication? If you hope to make money using desktop-published materials, examine the publications of your major competitors. Whether they are producing house publications for various nonprofit organizations or catering to the needs of school PTOs across the district, look at the quality of their publications. Do they use typeset material? Is the newsletter simply typed on someone's typewriter and then duplicated 200 times? Consider the needs of your clients, and then take steps to go a little beyond their expectations. Keep in mind, however, that as the industry evolves and the price of laser printers comes down, more and more people will expect laser-quality output.

As table 2.4 shows, you have a wide variety of printers from which you can choose. From basic dot-matrix to letter-quality to laser printers, you are sure to be able to find a printer that gives you the quality you want at affordable cost.

Table 2.4
Printers Compatible with First Publisher

Manufacturer	Models
Apple	LaserWriter, LaserWriter® Plus, LaserWriter II
EPSON	EX, FX, JX, LX, MX, RX, LQ
Hewlett-Packard	LaserJet, LaserJet +, LaserJet Series II[1], QuietJet, QuietJet Plus, ThinkJet®, DeskJet[2]
IBM	Graphics, QuietWriter® II, ProPrinter™, ProPrinter™ XL, ProPrinter II, ProPrinter XL24, ProPrinter X24
NEC	P5, P5XL, P6, CP6, P7, CP7, P9
OKIDATA®	Microline® models 92, 93, 182, 183, 192, 193, 292, 293, 294
Panasonic	1080, 1090, 1091, 1092, 1093, 1592, 1595
Star Micronics	Gemini 10X/15X, NR-10/15, NX-10/15, NB24-10/15, NB-15
Tandy®	DMP-130, 430, 2110, 2200
Texas Instruments	855
Toshiba	P321, P341, P351, P351C, P1340, P1350, P1351

[1] First Publisher supports all Hewlett-Packard soft fonts and font cartridges B and F.

[2] First Publisher supports cartridges A, D, E, F, G, H, J, P, and Q.

Figure 2.2 shows you the differences between a First Publisher document printed on an EPSON FX-286e and a Hewlett-Packard LaserJet.

Users of the DeskMate version have the option of setting color specifications for First Publisher. For more about setting color with First Publisher —DeskMate, see Appendix C.

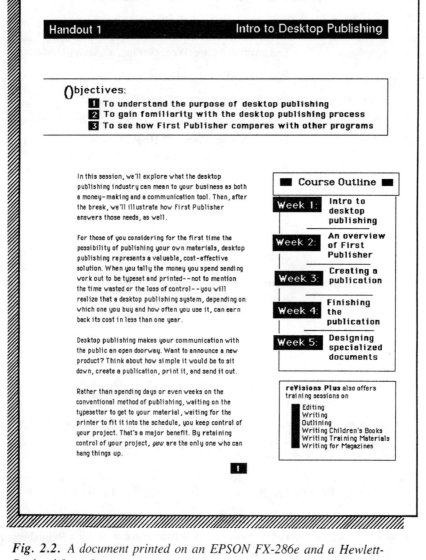

Fig. 2.2. *A document printed on an EPSON FX-286e and a Hewlett-Packard LaserJet.*

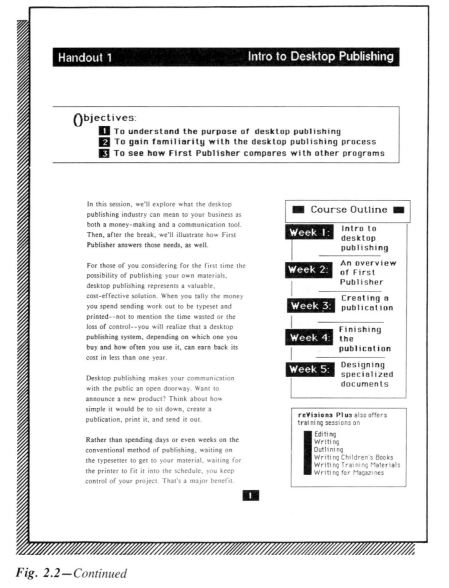

Fig. 2.2—Continued

> ### Dot-Matrix Printers: 9-Pin or 24-Pin?
>
> Dot-matrix printers come in two varieties: 9-pin and 24-pin. As explained more thoroughly in Chapter 8, a dot-matrix printer prints text and graphics by pressing a matrix of pins into a ribbon, which in turn prints the characters on the page. Some users and hardware manufacturers believe that 24-pin printers produce better quality print than the 9-pin varieties. Generally, the 24-pin dot-matrix printers produce only their built-in Courier fonts with any noticeable difference in quality; they actually do poorly when compared with the 9-pin printer's ability to produce fancier fonts and graphics.

As you see in table 2.4, First Publisher supports two types of laser printers: the Apple LaserWriter series and the Hewlett-Packard LaserJet series. (The DeskMate version also supports Tandy printers.) Additionally, First Publisher supports the Hewlett-Packard DeskJet as a laser printer, but it actually is a printer that can produce near-laser quality documents and costs significantly less than a laser printer. First Publisher is capable of supporting the HP soft fonts for LaserJet and LaserJet Series II only and several of the cartridges, as well. Soft font support gives you the ability to access a wide variety of other typefaces, styles, and sizes available for laser printers. Chapter 8 explains the specifics of using these features with First Publisher.

The Mouse

You don't need to have a mouse to use First Publisher—but without one, you will be spending quite a bit of time pressing keys and waiting for the cursor to move. Also, if you often work with graphics, you will find that positioning and modifying graphics is much more difficult without a mouse.

Having a mouse (the small pointing device you use to direct the cursor on the screen) gives you the freedom to capture, move, and edit graphics on the screen. Additionally, you use the mouse to move the cursor quickly and select options and commands. With a simple click of the mouse button, you can open menus, choose tools, capture art, move art, position elements on the page, resize art—and those are only a few possible uses. Doing all these tasks from the keyboard is possible—but cumbersome.

Many PC users feel uncomfortable about the idea of using a mouse; it seems like an item more of a Macintosh nature than of a PC nature. However, old standards are changing quickly, and many popular applications programs are now adopting the pull-down menu structure and mouse interface that once was exclusive to Apple computers. For new mouse users, the change from typing commands at the keyboard to physically moving your hand in order to move a cursor on-screen is quite a leap, although once you get used to it, you will find that it's much more intuitive than pressing the arrow keys. In First Publisher, the mouse is most important in the use of placing, modifying, and moving graphics, but it also provides you with a faster method of moving the cursor on the text layer, and allows you to open the pull-down menus and select options easily.

If you plan on using a mouse with First Publisher (and that is highly recommended), you need to obtain one of the following:

❏ A Microsoft® mouse

❏ A LOGITECH mouse

❏ A Mouse Systems™ mouse

Figure 2.3 shows a LOGITECH mouse.

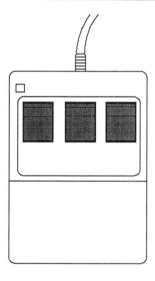

Fig. 2.3. A LOGITECH mouse.

Mouse costs range from $79 to $150, and often you will find "package deals" that offer a paint program for no extra charge with the purchase of a mouse. For example, the LOGIPAINT paint program has been pack-aged—at no additional cost—with a LOGITECH mouse. Check to see what offers are available—and before you invest, make sure that the paint pro-gram and the mouse are compatible with First Publisher.

Making Backup Copies of First Publisher

Before you install First Publisher, you need to make backup copies of the original First Publisher disks. Whether you need to copy five disks (for 5 1/4-inch disks) or three (for 3 1/2-inch disks), the copying procedure is basically the same. (Remember that First Publisher is not copy-protected, but the program is covered by the copyright laws that pertain to computer software. These laws allow you to make backup copies for your own use, but making copies for others is illegal.)

This section explains how to install First Publisher on a two disk drive sys-tem and on a computer with a hard disk. The disks you use to store the backup copy of the program must be blank, formatted disks. (If you are unsure of how to format the disks, consult *Using PC DOS,* 2nd Edition, published by Que Corporation.) In this section, you will find margin icons to help you locate your particular system.

> Remember to label the disks before you back up the program on them; use some type of identifier to indicate that they are backup copies.

If you are using the First Publisher DeskMate version, the copying and installing procedures are slightly different. Consult your software manual for details.

Making Backup Copies on a Hard Disk System with One Disk Drive

After your computer has been turned on, and the C prompt is displayed on the screen, follow these steps:

1. Type *diskcopy a: b:* and press Enter.

   (*Note:* Even though, with one disk drive, your system technically has only drive A, in this case the drive does "double duty," serving as both the source and the destination drive.)

2. Place Program Disk 1 in the drive and press Enter (for 3 1/2-inch disks, this is the Program and Fonts disk.) DOS then reads the disk and prompts you to insert the blank, formatted backup disk.

3. Remove Program Disk[1].

4. Insert the backup disk and press Enter. DOS then writes the information to the disk.

Repeat these steps until you have made backup copies of all your First Publisher disks. Remember to store the original First Publisher disks in a safe place.

Making Backup Copies on a Hard Disk System with Two Disk Drives

The backup procedure for a hard disk system with two disk drives is a little less complicated: not as much floppy-swapping is involved. When the computer is turned on and the C prompt is displayed, follow these steps:

1. Insert Program Disk 1 (or the Program and Fonts disk, for 3 1/2-inch systems) into drive A.

2. Insert the blank, formatted and labeled backup disk into drive B.

3. Type *diskcopy a: b:* and press Enter. DOS then copies the contents of the disk in drive A to the disk in drive B.

Repeat these steps until you have made backup copies of all your First Publisher disks. Remember to store the original First Publisher disks in a safe place.

Making Backup Copies on a Two Disk Drive System

If you don't have a hard disk drive, you have an additional (albeit simple) step to master. Instead of having the DOS operating system on your hard disk, you need to put the DOS disk into drive A before you turn on the computer. When the A prompt appears (perhaps after you enter the date and time), follow these steps:

1. Type *diskcopy a: b:* and press Enter.

2 Remove the DOS disk from drive A, place Program Disk 1 into the drive, and close the drive door. (This will be the Program and Fonts disk if you have 3 1/2-inch disks.)

3. Insert the formatted and labeled backup disk into drive B and close the drive door.

4. When prompted, press Enter.

The operating system then copies the contents of the disk in drive A to the disk in drive B. Repeat these steps until all your First Publisher disks have been copied. For safety's sake, use the backup copies of First Publisher for your daily use and store the original disks in a safe place.

Installing First Publisher on a Hard Disk

The next step in preparing to use First Publisher involves getting First Publisher installed on your system. On a hard disk system, the installation process actually requires three steps: (1) setting up directories for your First Publisher files, (2) copying the First Publisher files to your hard disk, and (3) configuring First Publisher to recognize your particular system.

Planning and Setting Up Directories

Some people go blazing through their hard disk, taking no time to organize files, scattering files here and there in no particular order. But let these people spend one harried afternoon searching desperately for a lost but important file, and they will realize that they're doing something wrong.

No matter how rushed you are, whether you plan to do only one project or one hundred projects, take the time to think through the organization of the directories on your hard disk.

If you think of a directory as having a "tree" structure, you will be able to visualize the storage structure of your hard disk. Figure 2.4 shows this tree structure. In the figure, you can see that the root directory (shown at the base of the tree) leads to several different directories. On the far left is the WS4 subdirectory, which stores the program WordStar. The WS4 subdirectory branches further to subdirectories for individual projects that are being done in WordStar: BOOK and MEMOS. The First Publisher directory, which is named PUB, appears in the middle of the tree, on the same level as the WS4 directory. Beyond this directory are the subdirectories of ZOO and DRAGON (two projects currently under construction in First Publisher).

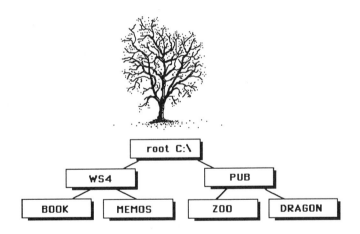

Fig. 2.4. *The tree structure of the directories on a hard disk.*

Think about the projects you will be working on and organize the directories on your hard disk accordingly.

Figure 2.5 shows the way the directory illustrated in figure 2.4 would look if the DOS command DIR were used to display the files and subdirectories in the directory.

```
[C:\PUB] dir

    Volume in drive C is COBRA
    Directory of  C:\PUB

    .             <DIR>      10-19-88    1:00p
    ..            <DIR>      10-19-88    1:00p
    ZOO           <DIR>      10-19-88    1:00p
    DRAGON        <DIR>      10-19-88    1:00p
    FP      EXE   152512     5-19-88    9:43a
    FP      HLP     7014     5-17-88    2:23p
    FP      CUT   115088     4-22-88    6:03p
    FP      WPC      892     3-18-88    4:15p
    FP      OVL   140320     5-19-88    9:43a
    FPPRINT DEF      313    10-14-88    5:09p
           10 File(s)   11030528 bytes free

[C:\PUB]
```

Fig. 2.5. *The directory and subdirectories.*

As you will learn in later chapters, First Publisher has four file types, known by their file name extensions: publications that combine text and graphics (PUB), graphics files (MAC), art files (ART), and text files (TXT). Some people opt to keep each of these file types in different sub-directories, as shown in figure 2.6. Many users, however, find it easier to keep all files (PUB, MAC, ART, and TXT) related to a particular project in one directory named for that project.

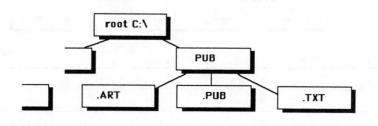

Fig. 2.6. *Alternate method of setting up directories.*

To set up your First Publisher directories, follow these steps:

1. Turn on your computer, if you haven't already done so.

2. If you have been using your computer, get to the DOS prompt and type *cd*. This command ensures that the root directory is the current directory.

3. Make a directory to store the First Publisher program by typing *md\\pub* and pressing Enter. (The *md* stands for "Make Directory," and the backslash says that the directory is off the root directory. Without the backslash, the new directory would be created under the current subdirectory. Typing *pub* assigns the name PUB to the new directory.)

4. Type *cd\\pub* and press Enter. This command tells DOS to "Change Directories" to the \\PUB directory.

If you want to go ahead and create subdirectories for your current or upcoming projects, follow these steps:

1. Get to the root directory by typing *cd* and pressing Enter.

2. Create a subdirectory of the PUB directory by typing *md\\pub* and the name of the directory you want to create (for example, MD\\PUB\\DRAGON). DOS limits the names of directories to eight characters, with an optional extension. Be sure to choose a directory name that in some way indicates what files will be stored there.

When you retrieve a file, you are asked to specify the directory in which the file is stored. You do this by entering the path to the file. For example, the path to a file stored in the subdirectory just created would be C:\\PUB\\DRAGON.

Copying First Publisher
to the Hard Disk

The installation procedure is simply a matter of copying First Publisher to your hard disk. Follow these steps:

1. At the C prompt, change to the PUB subdirectory by typing *cd\\pub* and pressing Enter.

2. Place Program Disk 1 in drive A. (If you have 3 1/2-inch drives, this is the Program and Fonts disk.)

3. Type *copy a: *.** and press Enter. Repeat this step until you have copied all files on the First Publisher disks to the PUB subdirectory.

Configuring First Publisher for Your System

First Publisher is installed on your hard disk. Now you're ready to configure the program for your particular system.

Adding a Mouse

As mentioned earlier in this chapter, First Publisher works with a LOGITECH, Microsoft, or Mouse Systems mouse. When you purchase a mouse, it comes with a program that tells the computer that a mouse is going to be used. That program is called a *mouse driver*.

Depending on which mouse you purchase, the mouse driver program may be different. Chances are, the driver program will be either MOUSE.COM or MSMOUSE.COM.

Each time you start your computer, the mouse driver program must tell the computer that the mouse will be used. You can run the mouse program by entering a specified command at the DOS prompt (the command varies, depending on which mouse you use). If you have a hard disk, copy the mouse driver to your PUB subdirectory. Then, if you wish, you can include the command to run the mouse driver program in your computer's AUTO-EXEC.BAT file so that the program runs automatically each time you start the computer.

The way in which you attach the mouse depends on the type of system and the type of mouse you have. Some systems use their serial ports (located on the back of the machine) to attach the mouse; some mice—called *bus* mice—attach directly to the card that comes with the mouse (these mice must be installed in the computer). Other systems, like the PS/2, have a dedicated mouse port, meaning that the port is used only to attach a mouse to the system.

If you have a two disk drive system, insert the disk that was packaged with the mouse into drive A; then type the command necessary to run your mouse driver program.

For more specific information about your particular type of mouse, consult the manual that is included in the package. This manual should tell you the type of mouse you have, how to connect it, what mouse driver routine is included, and how to incorporate a command in your AUTOEXEC.BAT file so that the mouse driver routine runs automatically when you start your system.

Connecting a Printer

The next step in configuring First Publisher for your system involves telling the program what type of printer you will be using.

If you have a hard disk system, follow these steps:

1. Change to the First Publisher directory by typing *cd\pub* and pressing Enter.

2. Type *printer* and press Enter. You then see a numbered list that shows several different printers (see fig. 2.7). If you don't see the printer you need, you can press Enter to display another screen of printer choices.

3. Enter the number that appears next to your printer type and press Enter.

4. Select the port you will be using by typing the number that corresponds to your printer port and pressing Enter. (If you are unsure how to determine which port you will be using, contact the dealer or service outlet from which you purchased the system.)

Unless you change printers or install First Publisher on another machine, you will not need to modify these settings.

Although the DeskMate program offers a Printer Settings screen, you must run First Publisher's Printer program (by selecting Run . . . from the File menu) for your documents to print properly.

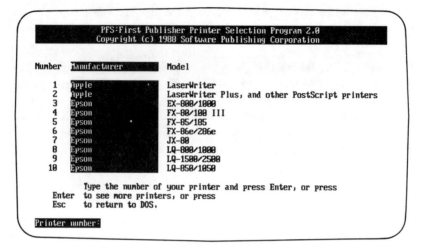

```
        PFS:First Publisher Printer Selection Program 2.0
           Copyright (c) 1988 Software Publishing Corporation

Number  Manufacturer         Model

   1    Apple            .   LaserWriter
   2    Apple                LaserWriter Plus, and other PostScript printers
   3    Epson                EX-800/1000
   4    Epson                FX-80/100 III
   5    Epson            .   FX-85/185
   6    Epson                FX-86e/286e
   7    Epson                JX-80
   8    Epson                LQ-800/1000
   9    Epson                LQ-1500/2500
  10    Epson                LQ-850/1050

        Type the number of your printer and press Enter, or press
  Enter  to see more printers, or press
  Esc    to return to DOS.

 Printer number:
```

Fig. 2.7. The printer selection screen.

If you have a two disk drive system, follow these steps:

1. Insert Program Disk 1 into drive A. (Again, that's the Program and Fonts disk if you're using 3 1/2-inch disks.)

2. When the A prompt is displayed, type *printer* and press Enter. You then see a numbered list that shows several different printers. If you don't see the printer you need, you can press Enter to display another screen of printer choices.

3. Enter the number that appears next to the type of your printer. (If you are using First Publisher Version 2.01, see the sidebar titled "Scaled Versus Unscaled Printing.")

4. Select the printer port by entering the correct number at the Printer port prompt and press Enter.

The installation procedure for laser printers is a little more complicated because it requires manipulating some of First Publisher's font files and setting up First Publisher's laser support. For details on these and other procedures related to printing, see Chapter 8.

Scaled Versus Unscaled Printing

In order to explain the scaled/unscaled concept, we need to review a little printing history. Version 1.0 of First Publisher offered unscaled printing, meaning that your printed documents closely resembled what you saw on-screen, but the proportions and sizes were a bit different. This print routine worked fairly quickly and offered good quality output. Version 2.0 of First Publisher attempted to answer users' wishes by providing a scaled print routine, meaning that everything printed appeared exactly as it was created on-screen, in the precise proportions and measurements shown in the ruler lines. Although this feature provided documents that were truer-to-form, it also introduced problems for some users. Depending on the type of printer used, some users found the newer print routine to be producing lower quality text and long print times.

To solve this problem, Software Publishing Corporation chose to give users the choice of scaled or unscaled printing. Version 2.01 allows you to decide which method works best for your projects and your printer.

If you are using First Publisher Version 2.01, after you specify the printer number you are using (in the Printer routine), a prompt may be displayed asking Scale output (Y/N)?. (Whether or not this prompt is displayed depends on the printer you use.) If you answer N, scaled output is unavailable to you. If you select Y, the system allows you to use scaled or unscaled output, depending on the needs of the publication. When you start to print the document later, the Print dialog box asks you whether you want to print the document scaled or unscaled. If you want to print unscaled, you can select No at that point, rather than disabling the feature altogether. Try both the scaled and unscaled methods and see which method gives the best results on your printer. If you change your mind about this setting later, you can simply run the Printer routine again by exiting to the DOS prompt and typing *printer*.

Starting First Publisher

To start First Publisher on a hard disk system, follow these steps:

1. Change to the PUB directory by typing *cd\pub* and pressing Enter.

2. Type *fp* and press Enter.

To start First Publisher on a two drive system, follow these steps:

1. At the A prompt, using the backup copies of your First Publisher disks, insert the copy of Program Disk 1 into drive A.

2. Insert the Fonts disk into drive B. (*Note:* If you have 3 1/2-inch disks, you can insert the Program and Fonts disk into drive A and a data disk into B.)

3. Type *fp* and press Enter.

On either type of system, after you type *fp* and press Enter, First Publisher's opening screen, shown in figure 2.8, is displayed.

Fig. 2.8. *First Publisher's opening screen.*

File Limitations on a Two Drive System

On a two drive system that uses 5 1/4-inch disks, First Publisher uses a temporary file, called PUBLISH.WRK, on the Fonts Disk to record publication changes. This fact means that you must leave the Fonts disk in drive B whenever you use First Publisher. The program must have at least 40K available on the Fonts disk, or the program will not be able to create the temporary file, and any changes you make will be lost.

To determine the amount of space available on the Fonts disk, you can use the DOS command DIR. For more information about DIR and other DOS commands that can aid you in file organization and maintenance, see *Using PC DOS,* 2nd Edition, published by Que Corporation.

To start the DeskMate version of First Publisher, run the program from the DeskMate desktop. For specific instructions, consult your programs documentation.

Chapter Summary

In this chapter, you went from an inspection of the hardware you need in order to run the program to the installation and configuration of First Publisher. At this point, you are ready to proceed to the next chapter, in which you go through a step-by-step exploration of the various elements of the program and begin hands-on learning with a First Publisher QuickStart.

3

Getting Started with First Publisher

Up to this point, you have been introduced to the basics of desktop publishing and the installation and configuration procedures for First Publisher. In this chapter, you will learn about the various elements that make up the program. First, however, the chapter briefly explains the two different ways of using First Publisher. Then, starting with a discussion of the use of layers in First Publisher documents, you are introduced to all the important features you will use as you create your own projects.

As a special feature, this chapter offers a First Publisher QuickStart tutorial that walks you through the various procedures involved in creating, editing, enhancing, and printing a First Publisher document. Because the majority of this book focuses on creating publications from ''scratch,'' the QuickStart shows you how to produce professional-quality materials by using one of the templates that are packaged with First Publisher.

Methods of Using First Publisher

Basically, First Publisher allows three methods of operation: (1) using the mouse, (2) using the keyboard, and (3) using the mouse *and* the keyboard.

The way in which you use First Publisher depends on the type of hardware you have and the methods with which you are most comfortable. Each of these methods is explained in this section.

Most people who have purchased a mouse use it for operations such as placing and modifying graphics. Accurate positioning of art elements is more difficult when you must use the keyboard.

For primarily text-manipulation tasks, the keyboard method is adequate if you use the cursor-movement keys and First Publisher's speed keys to move the cursor quickly and allow you fast access to menus and options.

Even with mouse capability, however, many users prefer to use a combination of mouse and keyboard operations in order to use First Publisher most efficiently. These users count on the mouse when they are working with graphics and rely on First Publisher's speed keys to select menus and options quickly.

Using the Mouse

If you are a dyed-in-the-wool PC fan, it may have taken you a while to try your hand at a mouse—literally. Although mouse-run programs have been common at Apple for years, it hasn't been that long since the first DOS programs with mouse capabilities were introduced.

Some people don't like using a mouse; they find that the mental shift from typing to pushing is more interruptive than helpful. If you're accustomed to working primarily with the keyboard, don't worry: First Publisher has an alternative keyboard method for every mouse action required by the program.

Although using a mouse with First Publisher is not mandatory, most people find that using a mouse allows them a significant amount of freedom when placing, moving, or modifying graphics. Additionally, on the graphics layer, using a mouse opens up the alternative of drawing free-hand. On the text layer, the mouse method requires less time to select commands and move the cursor around within the document. Throughout this book, you will see two terms related to mouse operations with which you should be familiar:

Click means to press and release the mouse button. (Depending on which mouse you use, your mouse may have up to three mouse buttons. Pressing any one of the mouse buttons produces the desired result.)

Drag means to press and hold down the mouse button and move the mouse so that the mouse cursor moves accordingly.

Using the Keyboard

Using the mouse is not mandatory with First Publisher. Although a mouse can make life easier, unless you are dealing with a lot of graphics, you can get by without one. When you use only the keyboard, moving the cursor can seem like a slow process. Luckily, other cursor-movement keys are available to you that help speed the cursor-movement operation. For a listing of these keys, see Chapter 5.

If you do not use a mouse, you can perform the mouse click and drag operation by using these methods:

Emulate a mouse click by pressing F10 twice. (Remember that the mouse click is actually two actions: pressing and releasing the mouse button. That's why two F10 keystrokes are needed.)

Drag an item by positioning the cursor on the item, pressing F10 once, and using the arrow keys to move the item in the direction you desire.

Using the Mouse and the Keyboard

As users become proficient with First Publisher and comfortable with the menu selections they use most often, most users mix using the mouse with using the keyboard. The mouse is most effective when it is used for working with graphics and for positioning the cursor; First Publisher offers *speed keys* that allow you to select menu options quickly from the keyboard. The speed keys are shown on the pull-down menus, to the right of the option name. Not all options have speed keys. Figure 3.1 shows how the speed keys appear on the File menu.

As you can see, six of the nine options on the menu have speed-key combinations. For **Get publication**, for example, you press Alt-G, meaning that you should press and hold the Alt key, and then press G. (*Note:* Although the ALT symbol on the screen is slanted, the combinations are represented here by hyphenating the key names to show that they are pressed at the same time.)

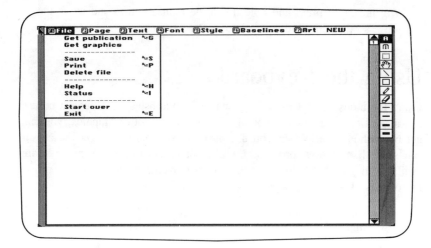

Fig. 3.1. *The File menu.*

The option **Start over** does not have a speed-key combination. To select this option without using the mouse, you use the ↓ key to move the highlight to that option and press Enter. If you are using a mouse, simply drag the mouse until the option is highlighted and click the mouse button. The next section begins the exploration of the various elements in the First Publisher program.

DeskMate users will notice that First Publisher's speed-key combinations involve the use of the Ctrl key rather than the Alt key.

Understanding the Layers in First Publisher Publications

Unlike some other desktop publishing programs, First Publisher looks at each document as a combination of two layers: text and graphics (see fig. 3.2). The text layer, as you might expect, includes the text for the document, and the graphics layer includes all clip art, rules, boxes, and text treated as graphics, such as headlines and banners. (*Note:* The First Publisher *User's Guide* refers to these layers as *overlays*.)

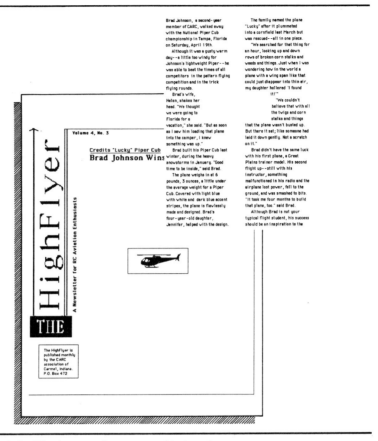

Fig. 3.2. The layers of a First Publisher document.

Working with the Text Layer

The text layer is the layer on which you work with text in your First Publisher document. Each time you start First Publisher, the program begins with the text layer—even if you are working with a new publication that, as yet, has no text. You can tell that the text layer is the current layer because the text tool (shown at the top of the row of tools on the right side of the screen) is the current tool.

Everything you do on the text layer is independent of the graphics layer. You can move, delete, reformat, place, and edit text—perform any operations you want—and not affect the graphics layer of the First Publisher document.

Figure 3.3 shows the text layer of a publication.

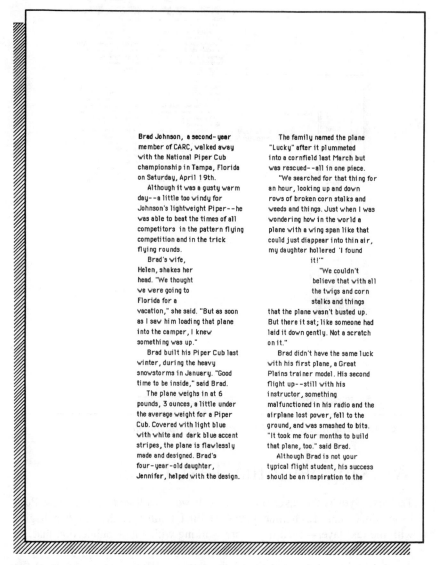

Brad Johnson, a second-year member of CARC, walked away with the National Piper Cub championship in Tampa, Florida on Saturday, April 19th.

Although it was a gusty warm day--a little too windy for Johnson's lightweight Piper--he was able to beat the times of all competitors in the pattern flying competition and in the trick flying rounds.

Brad's wife, Helen, shakes her head. "We thought we were going to Florida for a vacation," she said. "But as soon as I saw him loading that plane into the camper, I knew something was up."

Brad built his Piper Cub last winter, during the heavy snowstorms in January. "Good time to be inside," said Brad.

The plane weighs in at 6 pounds, 3 ounces, a little under the average weight for a Piper Cub. Covered with light blue with white and dark blue accent stripes, the plane is flawlessly made and designed. Brad's four-year-old daughter, Jennifer, helped with the design.

The family named the plane "Lucky" after it plummeted into a cornfield last March but was rescued--all in one piece.

"We searched for that thing for an hour, looking up and down rows of broken corn stalks and weeds and things. Just when I was wondering how in the world a plane with a wing span like that could just diappear into thin air, my daughter hollered 'I found it!'"

"We couldn't believe that with all the twigs and corn stalks and things that the plane wasn't busted up. But there it sat; like someone had laid it down gently. Not a scratch on it."

Brad didn't have the same luck with his first plane, a Great Plains trainer model. His second flight up--still with his instructor, something malfunctioned in his radio and the airplane lost power, fell to the ground, and was smashed to bits. "It took me four months to build that plane, too." said Brad.

Although Brad is not your typical flight student, his success should be an inspiration to the

Fig. 3.3. *The text layer of a publication.*

Working with the Graphics Layer

The graphics layer of a First Publisher document stores only the graphics portion of the layout, including boxes, art, lines, and any text that is used as graphics. This separate graphics layer gives you the freedom to move or resize graphics to fit the text you have imported, or vice versa. Because modifications on the graphics layer do not affect the text layer, you don't have to go through a lengthy process of reformatting text or moving columns or headings if you want to change a particular graphic element on a page. Also, when you use the eraser tool to erase something on the graphics layer, you can use the tool freely, without worrying that you might erase some of the text. Text on the text layer is unavailable on the graphics layer; *graphics text*, on the other hand, can be erased with the eraser tools. You switch the program to the graphics layer when you select any one of the options on the Art menu or one of graphics tools from the right side of the screen. When you are working on a publication and you select a graphics tool, the text appears "dimmed," but it does not disappear altogether. When you have been working on graphics and switch to the text layer, the graphics remain visible on-screen. The graphics tools available are the following:

    graphics text tool
    selection tool
    hand tool
    straight line tool
    box tool
    pencil tool
    eraser tool

Figure 3.4 shows the graphics layer of the First Publisher document shown in figure 3.3. Figure 3.5 shows both layers, as they are displayed and printed in First Publisher. (*Note:* Although these figures do show the text and graphics layers individually, this effect is for discussion purposes only. First Publisher has no capability for displaying or printing the layers separately.)

You can add text to the graphics layer by using the graphics text tool. If your publication includes a considerable amount of text, however, use graphics text only for headings and banners. Typing the entire publication in graphics text does not give you the print quality that is available from regular text. For more information on using graphics text, see Chapter 6.

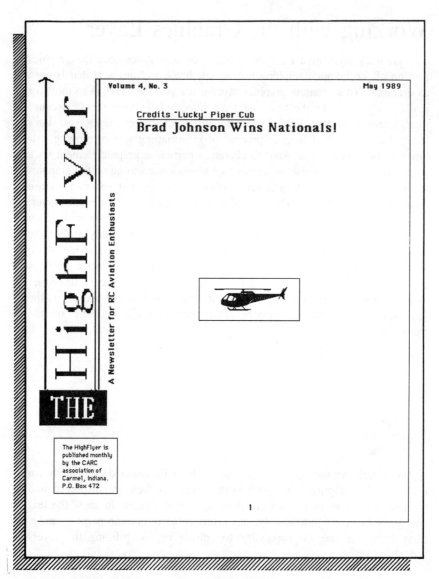

Fig. 3.4. The graphics layer of a First Publisher document.

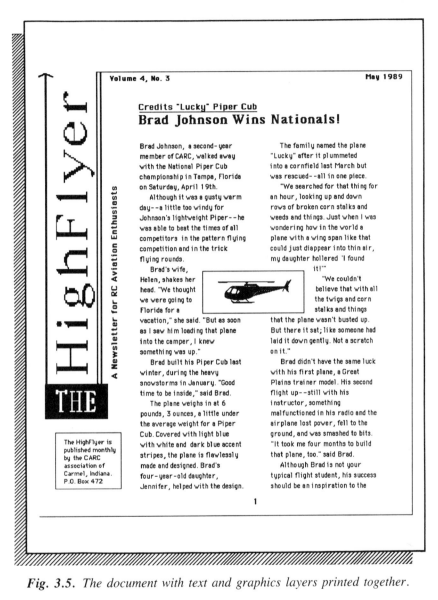

Volume 4, No. 3   **May 1989**

The HighFlyer

A Newsletter for RC Aviation Enthusiasts

THE

The HighFlyer is published monthly by the CARC association of Carmel, Indiana. P.O. Box 472

Credits "Lucky" Piper Cub
Brad Johnson Wins Nationals!

Brad Johnson, a second-year member of CARC, walked away with the National Piper Cub championship in Tampa, Florida on Saturday, April 19th.

Although it was a gusty warm day--a little too windy for Johnson's lightweight Piper--he was able to beat the times of all competitors in the pattern flying competition and in the trick flying rounds.

Brad's wife, Helen, shakes her head. "We thought we were going to Florida for a vacation," she said. "But as soon as I saw him loading that plane into the camper, I knew something was up."

Brad built his Piper Cub last winter, during the heavy snowstorms in January. "Good time to be inside," said Brad.

The plane weighs in at 6 pounds, 3 ounces, a little under the average weight for a Piper Cub. Covered with light blue with white and dark blue accent stripes, the plane is flawlessly made and designed. Brad's four-year-old daughter, Jennifer, helped with the design.

The family named the plane "Lucky" after it plummeted into a cornfield last March but was rescued--all in one piece.

"We searched for that thing for an hour, looking up and down rows of broken corn stalks and weeds and things. Just when I was wondering how in the world a plane with a wing span like that could just diappear into thin air, my daughter hollered 'I found it!'"

"We couldn't believe that with all the twigs and corn stalks and things that the plane wasn't busted up. But there it sat; like someone had laid it down gently. Not a scratch on it."

Brad didn't have the same luck with his first plane, a Great Plains trainer model. His second flight up--still with his instructor, something malfunctioned in his radio and the airplane lost power, fell to the ground, and was smashed to bits. "It took me four months to build that plane, too." said Brad.

Although Brad is not your typical flight student, his success should be an inspiration to the

1

Fig. 3.5. The document with text and graphics layers printed together.

Using First Publisher's Clipboards

First Publisher also offers you the use of clipboards; one for text, and another for graphics. You use the clipboards when you cut and paste text and graphics, when you move an item from one place to another, or when you copy text or a graphic element.

> If you have one item on the clipboard and you copy another item to the clipboard, the first item is replaced. You can, however, have one text item on the text clipboard and have another item on the graphics clipboard at the same time.

For example, suppose that you want to move the text phrase *during the heavy snowstorms in January*, as shown in figure 3.6. You highlight the phrase, thus marking it for the move operation (exactly how to highlight the phrase and move text is explained later in this chapter). You then select the appropriate commands to perform the action you want (in this case, you would select **Cut** from the Text menu, or press Del), and the text is moved to the clipboard. Because the clipboard is ''unseen,'' the text appears to have been deleted. When you move the cursor to the place you want to insert the text and select the **Paste** command (Alt-P), however, the text is copied from the clipboard and placed at the cursor position.

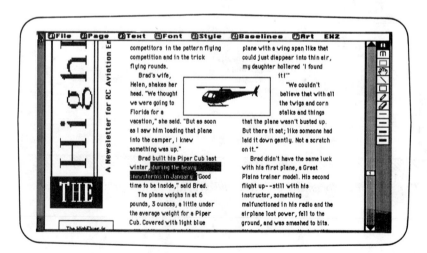

Fig. 3.6. *Marking a block of text for a move operation.*

Figure 3.7 shows the moved text. As you can see, some ''patching'' still needs to be done; for example, the *d* in *during* needs to be capitalized, the phrase about winter needs to be deleted, and the period needs to be moved.

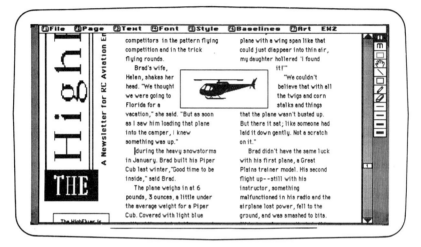

Fig. 3.7. *The inserted text is copied from the clipboard.*

Even after you place the text being moved or copied, the clipboard retains a copy of the text until you replace it by copying or cutting another text block or until you exit First Publisher.

Understanding the First Publisher Screen

This section explains the various elements on the First Publisher publication screen. You use this screen to do all of your work. Unlike other competing products, First Publisher never leaves a blank screen forcing you to guess at which keys to press. The document you are working on is displayed at all times; in some cases, windows pop up over the document to ask your input on various items.

The First Publisher screen is a combination of five major elements:

- ❏ The screen area
- ❏ The cursors
- ❏ The menu bar
- ❏ The graphics tools
- ❏ The elevator bars

Figure 3.8 shows each of these elements. In the sections that follow, each element will be explained.

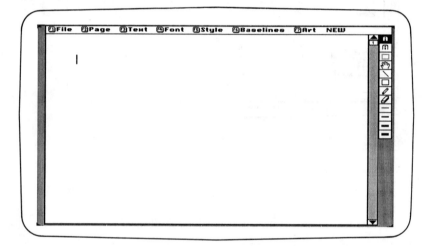

Fig. 3.8. *The elements of the First Publisher screen.*

The Screen Area

The screen area in First Publisher is the desktop on which you do your publishing. Whether you need to place, create, or edit text; draw, modify, or lay out graphics; add rules and boxes; or simply play around with design modifications, the screen area is the place where your actions are displayed.

When you call up First Publisher, the screen area is empty. When you select commands from the menu bar (discussed later in this chapter), dialog boxes may pop up over the screen area. Figure 3.9 shows the Get dialog box asking which file to open. (In this case, the user has selected **Get Publication** from the File menu.)

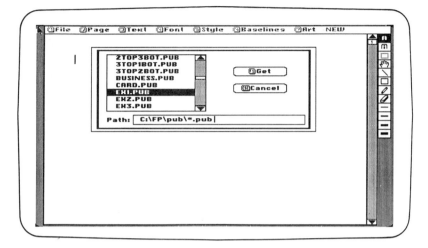

Fig. 3.9. *The Get dialog box.*

Using Cursors

First Publisher has two cursors: the bar cursor and the mouse cursor. The following sections explain each of these cursor types.

Using the Bar Cursor

When you initially bring up the First Publisher screen, the bar cursor is positioned in the upper left quadrant of the screen. You can tell that this cursor is the bar cursor because it resembles a thin vertical bar. On the text layer, this cursor marks the place that text would be inserted if you begin typing. When the graphics layer is displayed, the bar cursor is not displayed.

To move the bar cursor to another position, you must move the mouse cursor to the correct location and click the mouse button. You can also move the bar cursor by pressing the arrow keys. Figure 3.10 shows the bar cursor and the mouse cursor.

Although First Publisher's text and graphics clipboards function normally in the DeskMate version, you *cannot* use DeskMate's clipboard while you are using First Publisher.

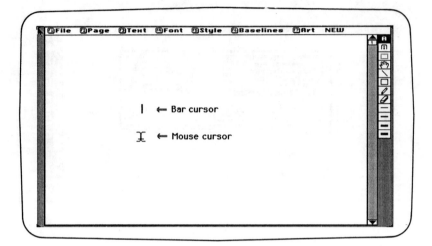

Fig. 3.10. The bar cursor and the mouse cursor.

Using the Mouse Cursor

The mouse cursor is so named because it reflects the screen position currently pointed to by the mouse. This cursor is different from the bar cursor
in appearance: the mouse cursor has curved lines across the top and bottom
of the vertical bar. When you move the mouse, this cursor moves accordingly on-screen.

When you move the mouse enough to cause the mouse cursor to move to
the menu bar, the cursor changes to the shape of an arrow. Also, when you
select one of the graphics tools on the right side of the screen, the mouse
cursor changes shape to replicate the tool selected. For example, when you
select the Hand tool, the cursor changes to a hand shape. (If you don't have
a mouse installed, the mouse cursor is not displayed on the screen. When
you choose one of the graphics tools, however, a cursor appears in the
shape of that tool, indicating the current position on the graphics layer.)

The Menu Bar

The menu bar is the line at the top edge of the screen. In this bar, you see
the names of each of the menus you will use in First Publisher. At the far-
right edge of the menu bar, the current file name is displayed. If you are

creating a new publication, the name NEW is displayed. If you are working on a file you created previously, that file's name is displayed in this space.

"Behind" the menu bar lie the various menus you use to create, modify, and print publications in First Publisher. These menus are File, Page, Text, Font, Style, Baselines, and Art. To access these menus, you have two choices: (1) use the mouse to position the arrow on the menu of your choice and press and release the mouse button, or (2) press the key shown next to the menu name (for example, for the File menu, press F1).

The Graphics Tools

The graphics tools are located along the right edge of the First Publisher screen area. Actually, "graphics" tools is the correct term for all the tools except one: The text tool, at the top of the column, is the only tool *not* used for working with graphics. When the text tool is selected, First Publisher displays the text layer. When any of the other tools are selected, the graphics layer is displayed. Table 3.1 shows you the tasks these graphics tools perform.

The last four items in the graphics tools row are not really "tools": they are line-width settings that allow you to control the width of the lines you draw with the line, box, or pencil tools.

To select any of the tools, you position the mouse cursor (which is an arrow at this point) over the correct tool and click the mouse button. If you would rather use the keyboard method, you have several options, as shown in table 3.2.

The Elevator Bars

You use the elevator bar to get around in a First Publisher document. If you are familiar with computers, you probably have seen this technique used in other programs. The elevator bar is the gray vertical bar on the right side of the screen (between the graphics tools and the screen area). At the top of this bar is a triangle pointing up; at the bottom is a triangle pointing down (see fig. 3.11).

The rectangle in the middle of the bar is called the *elevator*. The number within the elevator shows the number of the current page. The position of the elevator within the elevator bar shows where you are in the current document. For example, if the elevator is at the top of the elevator bar, the top

Table 3.1
The Graphics Tools

Tool	Name	Description
▣	Text tool	Used to switch to the text layer
ᒥ	Graphics text tool	Used to enter and edit text on the graphics layer. (*Note:* This text is treated as a graphic element and cannot be manipulated from the text layer.)
⬚	Selection tool	Used to select a graphic image for cut, copy, move, or stretch operations
✋	Hand tool	Used for placing or moving a graphic element
＼	Line tool	Used for drawing straight lines
☐	Box tool	Used for drawing boxes
✐	Pencil tool	Used for drawing items ''by hand'' and for manipulating and editing drawings pixel-by-pixel
⬛	Eraser tool	Used for erasing graphic elements

Table 3.2
Tool Selection Keys

Action	Use
To move to the text tool	Shift-F9
To highlight the next tool in the row (press this key repeatedly to cycle through the tools)	F9
To highlight a line width (press this key repeatedly to cycle through the line width settings)	Alt-F9

Fig. 3.11. *The elevator bar.*

of the document is being displayed. You can display different areas of the document by moving the elevator to the position in the elevator bar that corresponds with the area of the document you want to see. To move the elevator, you have four choices:

1. Position the arrow on the elevator; then press the mouse button and drag the elevator to the desired position.

2. Press ↑ or ↓ (if you want to move the display one line at a time) or PgUp or PgDn (if you want to move the display one screen at a time).

3. Click at the point in the elevator bar relative to the position you want to move to.

4. Click repeatedly on either of the triangles at the ends of the elevator bar. (Use this choice when you need to move the display a fraction of a screen.)

> Remember that if you use a CGA card and monitor, only a quarter of your page is displayed on the screen at one time.

Understanding First Publisher Menus

In this section, you will become familiar with First Publisher's pull-down menu system. After a brief introduction to the methods you use to pull down menus and to select options on those menus, each of the menus is discussed in detail. Each of these menus is discussed more fully at the appropriate places in the book. Look in each section for references to the specific chapter in which you can find more information.

Using First Publisher Menus

As you already know, the menu bar lists the names of the seven First Publisher pull-down menus. These menus are called *pull-down* menus because they remain hidden, giving you a maximum amount of room on-screen for your publication, until you pull the menu down to select a command.

On some early programs that used pull-down menus, the technique for pulling down a menu and selecting a command required a little extra skill. For some programs, you had to press the mouse button, pull down the menu (while holding down the button), and move the highlighting bar to the command you wanted (while still holding down the button), and then release the button to select the command. As a result, users wound up selecting a lot of commands they didn't want.

First Publisher makes the process easier by requiring only that you position the mouse cursor (which becomes an arrow when it's positioned in the menu bar) on the menu you want and click the mouse button. (Remember, *click* means to press and release the mouse button.)

When you release the button, the menu is displayed. You then can highlight the command you want and press Enter to select it, without having to worry about holding down the mouse button all the while.

If you want to select a menu by using the keyboard method, simply press the function key listed next to the name in the menu bar. The keys for selecting the various menus are listedd in table 3.3. (*Note*: These keys are different for the DeskMate version. See Appendix C.)

Table 3.3
Menu Selection Keys

Menu	Key
File	F1
Page	F2
Text	F3
Font	F4
Style	F5
Baselines	F6
Art	F7

If an item on a menu appears gray, it cannot be used in the current operation.

As mentioned earlier in this chapter, if you are using the keyboard method, you have the choice of selecting individual menu options by moving the highlight to that option and pressing Enter or by using the speed-key combination, if one is available.

To select a menu option with the mouse, you simply move the mouse cursor to the item you want (the highlight moves also), and press Enter.

When you want to close the menu, you can either press Esc or—if you're using a mouse—move the cursor off the menu.

Some menus have options that are toggled on and off. For example, figure 3.12 shows the Page menu. On that item, one toggle option is the **Show rulers** option. When the option is enabled, meaning that the **Show rulers** option is turned on, a check mark appears next to the option. To turn off, or disable, the option, you must select the option again, using one of the methods discussed previously. When the option is disabled, the check mark disappears.

A check mark next to an option indicates that the option works as a toggle. Select the option once to turn it on; select the option again to turn it off.

Fig. 3.12. *The Page menu with the **Show rulers** option enabled.*

Using the File Menu

The File menu, shown in figure 3.13, contains the options you use for manipulating files in First Publisher. Chapter 4 provides more information about the File menu. Table 3.4 provides you with an overview of each of the commands on this menu.

In the DeskMate version, the File menu has several additional options. See Appendix C for details.

Using the Page Menu

The Page menu offers some important options that you use often as you create and modify your First Publisher documents. From the initial decisions you make with the **Define page** option to **Picturewrap** and **Show page**, all the options on the Page menu help you merge text and graphics into the most appealing layout possible. Figure 3.14 shows the Page menu.

Table 3.5 lists the options on the Page menu and provides a description of each. The **Define page** option is explained in Chapter 4, and Chapter 7 provides a more complete discussion of the other options on this menu.

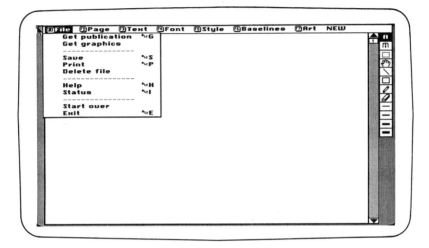

Fig. 3.13. *The File menu.*

Table 3.4
Options on the File Menu

Option	Description
Get publication (Alt-G)	Retrieves from storage a publication you have already created with First Publisher
Get graphics	Gets graphics files created in First Publisher or graphics files that are compatible with the program
Save (Alt-S)	Saves the current file (*Note:* This command saves the file and leaves the file open for further modifications.)
Print (Alt-P)	Prints the current file
Delete file	Deletes the specified file
Help (Alt-H)	Displays First Publisher's help screens (discussed later in this chapter)
Status (Alt-I)	Shows the status of the current file (*Note:* ''Status'' includes the current font, leading, printer, port, and number of characters.)
Start over	Abandons the current file and opens a new file
Exit (Alt-E)	Exits First Publisher

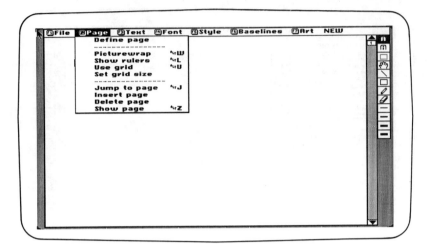

Fig. 3.14. *The Page menu.*

Table 3.5
Options on the Page Menu

Option	Description
Define page	Allows you to set margins, columns, and leading information about the page
Picturewrap (Alt-W)	Wraps text around a graphic element
Show rulers (Alt-L)	Displays rulers on the screen, enabling you to make your layout as accurate as possible
Use grid (Alt-U)	Locks the movement of the cursor into a particular ''grid'' pattern, enabling you to ensure a clean, precise look for your publication
Set grid size	Lets you modify the size of the grid so that the movement of some tools is still restricted, but within a different variance
Jump to page (Alt-J)	Moves the display to the page you specify
Insert page	Inserts page following the current page

Table 3.5—*Continued*

Option	Description
Delete page	Deletes the current page
Show page (Alt-Z)	Displays the entire page (*Note:* This command gives a ''thumbnail'' view of the entire page, so although this command allows you to see the general layout, you cannot read the text.)

Using the Text Menu

The Text menu includes only five options. These options are the ones you use when you are working with the text layer of First Publisher documents. The Text menu options allow you to move, copy, delete, rearrange, and add text to your documents. Figure 3.15 shows the Text menu, and table 3.6 provides an introduction to each of the options on that menu. Notice that on the Text menu, all items are gray except the first option, **Get text**. This ''graying'' effect means that the option is not available until a specific block of text is highlighted on-screen. Chapter 5 deals specifically with text manipulation and the options available on the Text menu.

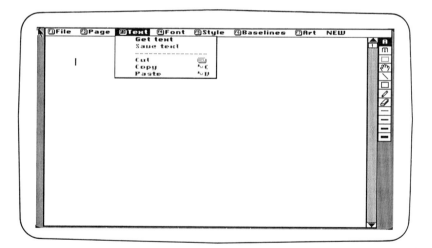

Fig. 3.15. *The Text menu.*

Table 3.6
Options on the Text Menu

Option	Description
Get text	Allows you to get and place text files
Save text	Saves a marked block of text to disk
Cut (Del)	Removes highlighted text block from publication and places the block on the text clipboard
Copy (Alt-C)	Copies a highlighted text block and places the copy on the text clipboard
Paste (Alt-V)	Inserts at the cursor position the text block currently on the text clipboard

In First Publisher, you highlight text by first positioning the cursor at the place you want the highlighting to begin. If you are using the mouse, you click the mouse button and drag the mouse to the position you want the highlighting to end. When you release the mouse button, that section remains highlighted. If you are using the keyboard method, when the cursor is positioned at the starting position of the highlight, press F10. Then use the arrow keys (or PgUp and PgDn) to move to the end of the block. When you have reached the end of the section you want to highlight, press F10 again. The highlighted section is known as a *block* or a *marked block* of text.

Using the Font Menu

The Font menu lists the names of the fonts that are available for your use. As you will learn in Chapter 10, you can change the fonts that are automatically displayed in the Font menu by using the FONTMOVE program. For now, assume that you are using the default fonts shown in figure 3.16. (If you have installed a laser printer, the fonts will be different. For more information about installing a laser printer, see Chapter 8.) The typefaces in the Font menu are toggle options, meaning that a check mark appears next to the selected typeface.

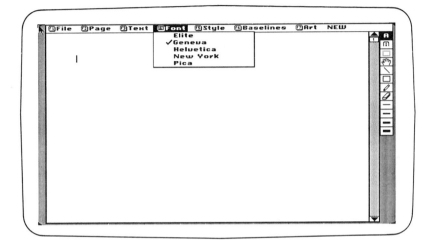

Fig. 3.16. *The Font menu.*

The Font menu lists several different typefaces that you can use to vary the type in your publication. You use this menu hand-in-hand with the Style menu, which is used to set different sizes and styles for the typeface.

> Only use one or two typefaces in your publication. Using more than two typefaces can make the page look cluttered and confusing and can detract from—rather than enhance—your design. If you choose, however, you can use as many fonts as your system memory allows.

Using the Style Menu

You use the Style menu to select the size and style for the typeface you choose in the Font menu. Figure 3.17 shows the Style menu.

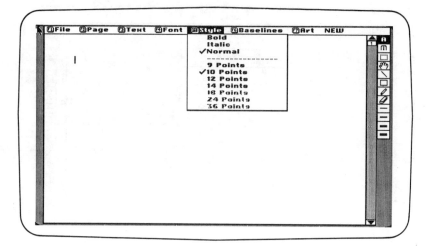

Fig. 3.17. The Style menu.

> Make sure that the body text of your publication is all the same size. Generally, 10-point is a good size for body copy, but any size from 9- to 12-point is acceptable.

The top three items on the Style menu, **Bold**, **Italic**, and **Normal**, show the options you have for the style of the text. If one of those attributes is not available for the typeface you have chosen on the Font menu, that item appears gray, meaning that the option is disabled and you cannot select it.

The remaining items on the Style menu list the various sizes available in that typeface. Again, the active size is marked by a check mark.

> Watch out for size variations among typefaces.

Using the Baselines Menu

You use the Baselines menu to adjust the layout of the text in your publications. Whether you are familiar with desktop publishing or not, the concept of baselines is probably new to you. Each line of text in First Publisher rests on a baseline that is unseen until one of the options in the Baselines menu is selected. Figure 3.18 shows how the screen looks when the **Adjust single** option in the Baselines menu is enabled.

Table 3.7 explains the options available on the Baselines menu.

Table 3.7
Options on the Baselines Menu

Option	Description
Adjust single (Alt-A)	Allows you to adjust a single baseline
Adjust column	Allows you to move the placement of a column
Adjust above	Lets you select one baseline and move every baseline on that page above and including the selected one
Adjust below	Lets you select one baseline and move every baseline on that page below and including the selected one
Center (Alt-h)	Centers a baseline (often used to center headings)
Left justify	Moves the selected baselines so that text is placed starting at the left edge of each line
Right justify	Moves the selected baselines so that the text extends evenly to the right edge of each line
Full justify	Adjusts baselines so that the text ends evenly at both ends of selected baselines
Change leading	Allows you to change the amount of space between lines
Realign text (Alt-T)	Realigns text that has been affected by the baseline modifications

In the DeskMate version of First Publisher, F1 is reserved to call up Help. The function key designations of the menus, therefore, are changed so that the File menu is F2, Page is F3, Text is F4, and so on. The DeskMate version also offers two menus that can be accessed with F9 and F10. See Appendix C for details.

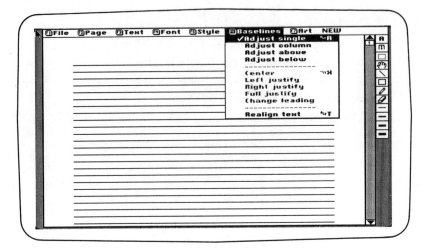

Fig. 3.18. The baselines in a First Publisher document.

The concept of baselines is often a difficult one for new First Publisher users. For now, just think of baselines as the lines on which the text "sits." Basically, you need to work with baselines only if you want to modify the way baselines are set when you choose a specific column format or when you want to move text in order to make room for a graphic element. For example, if you want to run text around an art element in the center of a page, you could shorten the individual baselines around that element so that the text flows up to—but not over—the image. In Chapter 7, you will learn how to work with the baselines in your publication.

Using the Art Menu

The Art menu gives you the options you need to work with the graphics layer of First Publisher. The options on this menu pack a lot of punch, especially when you compare First Publisher's art capabilities with the capabilities of other leading desktop publishing programs. Figure 3.19 shows the options available on the Art menu.

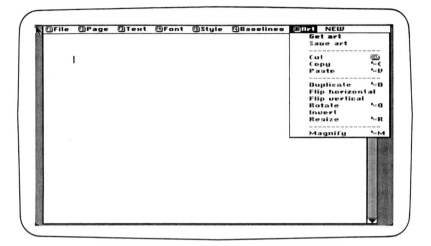

Fig. 3.19. *The Art menu.*

Table 3.8 explains each of the options available on First Publisher's Art menu. Chapter 6 explains how to use each of the options available on this menu.

Getting Help

Unlike other desktop publishing programs, First Publisher offers a help system, accessible from almost any point in the program. (The only exception to this occurs when a dialog box is displayed on the screen.) The purpose of the help system is to give you a brief overview of what to do when you get stuck—a valuable reminder to users who are returning to First Publisher after a period of time and for new users, as well.

To ask for help in First Publisher, pull down the File menu and then select **Help** or press Alt-H. First Publisher then displays a pop-up window that shows you the various subjects for which you can get help (see fig. 3.20).

If you are using the DeskMate version, you can access help by pressing F1.

Table 3.8
Options on the Art Menu

Option	Description
Get art	Retrieves art files from storage
Save art	Saves art you have created in First Publisher or art that you have selected in a graphics file
Cut (Del)	Removes selected art from the First Publisher document and places it on the graphics clipboard
Copy (Alt-C)	Copies selected art and places the copy on the graphics clipboard
Paste (Alt-V)	Places art item from the graphics clipboard to the indicated position in the document
Duplicate (Alt-D)	Creates a duplicate image
Flip horizontal	Flips selected image horizontally
Flip vertical	Flips selected image vertically
Rotate (Alt-O)	Rotates selected image 90 degrees
Invert	Turns white pixels black and black pixels white
Resize (Alt-R)	Allows you to change the size of the selected image
Magnify (Alt-M)	Magnifies selected image so that you can modify the image pixel-by-pixel

Because the program offers more help subjects than can be displayed in one pop-up window, a scroll bar is located on the right side of the window. You can click on the arrows located at the top and bottom of the scroll bar in order to show the subjects that are not displayed. When you see the subject on which you would like more help, highlight the subject by clicking it (or by using the ↑ or ↓ key to highlight it) and clicking OK (or pressing F1). A secondary screen then is displayed, offering you help on the subject you have chosen and providing a reference to which you can go for more information. A total of 14 help subjects are available, as listed in table 3.9.

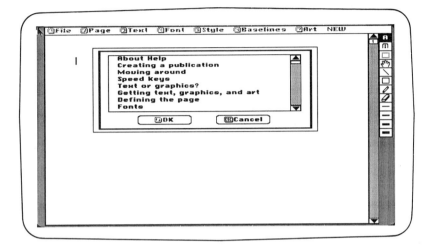

Fig. 3.20. *The Help window.*

Table 3.9
Available Help Subjects

About Help	Fonts
Creating a publication	Baselines
Moving around	Art
Speed keys	Lining up art
Text or graphics?	Deleting
Getting text, graphics, and art	Printing
Defining the page	Overflowed text

When you are ready to return to your First Publisher document, click Cancel or press Esc.

Additional First Publisher Features

First Publisher also has several built-in features that other programs cannot boast. This section introduces you to FONTMOVE, the program's utility for moving fonts in and out of First Publisher, and SNAPSHOT, First Publisher's screen-capture utility.

Adding Fonts

FONTMOVE is a program that runs outside of First Publisher; that is, you need to exit to DOS before you can run the FONTMOVE program. You use this program to move fonts in and out of the program. Why? Because many computers don't have the memory capacity for a full range of fonts, the MASTER.FNT file (the file responsible for the fonts shown on the Font menu) is configured for the smallest system, which is a two disk drive system. As you have probably already noticed, in its basic configuration, First Publisher offers only five options on its Font menu: Elite, Geneva, Helvetica, New York, and Pica. (If you have installed a laser printer, the fonts available on your Font menu will be different.) If you are working with a hard disk system that has 640K, you may be able to add more fonts to the Font menu by using FONTMOVE.

First Publisher also offers 20 different typefaces in various sizes and styles. These fonts are packaged with the program and are included in the file EXTRA.FNT (found on the Sampler Disk). In order to use these fonts in First Publisher, you need to make them accessible by adding them to the Font menu. You use FONTMOVE to add them to the menu. The procedures for using FONTMOVE are described thoroughly in Chapter 10.

With the DeskMate version, you can run the FONTMOVE program and the Printer program from within First Publisher. See Appendix C for details.

Capturing Screens

SNAPSHOT is a screen-capture utility that also runs outside of First Publisher. Like FONTMOVE, this program is started from DOS. When you are using SNAPSHOT, you can take a picture of whatever is displayed on your screen at a given time—no matter what that program is. You then use a companion program, called SNAP2ART, to turn the picture into a file (with the extension ART) usable by First Publisher. This utility is a valuable feature if you are working on a project in which you need to incorporate screen shots from another program. No matter what the program is—AutoCAD, 1-2-3®, dBASE IV—as long as the program runs under DOS, SNAPSHOT can take a picture of the screen, and you can use the screen in your First Publisher documents. SNAPSHOT is one of the main topics of Chapter 10.

First Publisher's Templates

Imitation may be the sincerest form of flattery, but it is also a great learning tool. Recognizing this fact, the makers of First Publisher supply users with a library of templates that can be used as-is or modified for individual projects. The templates packaged with First Publisher are listed in table 3.10.

Table 3.10
Templates Packaged with First Publisher

File name	Description
NEWS.PUB	Newsletter template (with seven additional format templates on Program Disk 2)
INVOICE.PUB	Template for an invoice
FLYER.PUB	Template for a flier
LIST.PUB	Template for a list (such as a mailing list, phone list, client list, supplier list, and so on)
BUSINESS.PUB	Template for business stationery and business cards
MENU.PUB	Template for a restaurant menu
CARD.PUB	Template for greeting cards or invitations

The NEWS.PUB template is used to produce newsletters—a common goal with First Publisher users. Because working with baselines to create multi-column formats can be a bit tricky, as you will see in later chapters, First Publisher also includes seven preset format templates you can use as the basis for your own newsletters. Figure 3.21 shows a miniature of each of these templates.

In the following section, "A First Publisher QuickStart," you will learn to create a newsletter, using First Publisher's newsletter template, NEWS.PUB.

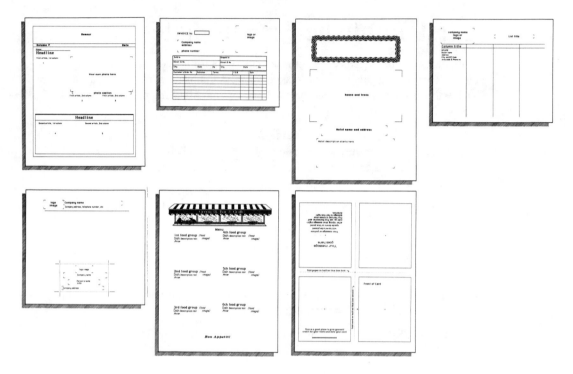

Fig. 3.21. *These templates are provided with each copy of First Publisher. In addition to the templates shown here, seven preset format templates for the NEWS.PUB template are included on Program Disk 2.*

 # A First Publisher QuickStart

In this section, you will take a mini-trip through First Publisher. Rather than follow the journey all the way from idea to printed page, you will skip the beginning, paper-and-pencil planning stage and start right in with a First Publisher template. At other places in this book, you are taught to design and create publications from scratch, so having the procedure for using templates in this location should prove helpful.

In this QuickStart, you will do the following:

❏ Select and load a newsletter template

❏ Get text

❏ Modify text

❏ Add banners

❏ Add headlines

❏ Get clip art

❏ Resize and place clip art

❏ Print the publication

> A reminder before you begin: use backup copies of your First Publisher disks, not the originals. Also, when you save your publication, remember to save it under a name that is different from the name of the template. Otherwise, the template is overwritten by your publication file.

Step 1: *Copying the Template*

First, you need to copy the NEWS.PUB template to your hard disk (or to a formatted data disk in drive B if your system does not have a hard disk). The main templates are stored on the Sampler Disk, and the additional format templates for NEWS.PUB are stored on Program Disk 2. For this exercise, you will need only the Sampler Disk.

To copy NEWS.PUB to your hard disk, follow these steps:

1. Place the Sampler Disk in drive A and close the drive door.

2. Type *copy a:news.pub c:\pub\work* (*Note:* This line assumes that the directory to which you are copying the file is named WORK. Be sure to enter the path and directory name that is correct for your system's configuration.)

3. Press Enter. NEWS.PUB then is copied to the hard disk.

To copy NEWS.PUB to drive B, follow these steps:

1. Place the Sampler Disk in drive A and a blank, formatted disk in drive B.

2. Type *copy a:news.pub b:* and press Enter. 1 File(s) copied appears on-screen. This message indicates that the file has been copied to the disk in drive B.

Step 2: *Starting First Publisher*

Next, you need to start the program. The way you start it depends on whether you have a hard disk or a two disk drive system.

To start First Publisher on a hard disk system, follow these steps:

1. Turn on the computer.

2. Go to the First Publisher directory by typing *cd\pub* and pressing Enter.

3. Type *fp* and press Enter.

To start First Publisher on a two disk drive system, follow these steps:

1. Make sure that the computer is turned on. (The A prompt should be displayed on the screen.)

2. Insert Program Disk 1 into drive A and the Fonts Disk into drive B. (The Fonts Disk will store a backup copy of your work file in the extra space on this disk.)

3. Type *fp* and press Enter.

4. After First Publisher is loaded, remove Program Disk 1 from drive A and insert the blank, formatted data disk on which you copied the NEWS.PUB file. This disk will store the First Publisher documents you create.

Step 3: *Opening a Publication*

When the First Publisher screen is displayed, you are ready to open the NEWS.PUB template file and start building your publication.

To open the NEWS.PUB file, follow these steps:

1. Move the mouse so that the mouse cursor points to the word File in the menu bar. Click the mouse button. (Remember that the term *click* refers to a press-and-release action. The File menu is not displayed until you release the mouse button.) If you are not using a mouse, press F1 to display the options in the File menu.

2. Move the mouse down (or press ↓) until the option **Get publication** is highlighted.

3. Click the mouse button (or press Enter). First Publisher then displays the Get dialog box, which allows you to choose the name of the file you want (see fig. 3.22).

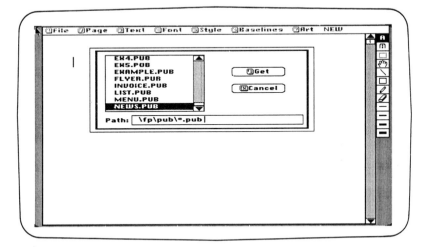

Fig. 3.22. *The Get dialog box.*

4. Move the mouse to the name of the file you want (NEWS.PUB) and click the mouse button; then move the mouse to the Get button (or to Cancel if you have chosen the wrong file), and click the mouse button again. (If you are using the keyboard, use ↑ or ↓ to move the highlight to the correct file name, and F1 to select it.)

After you click the Get button or press F1, NEWS.PUB is displayed on the First Publisher screen (see fig. 3.23).

If This *Weren't* a Template. . .

If instead of using a First Publisher template you were designing your own publication, at this step you would plan out the document by using the **Define page** option on the Page menu. You use this option to set the number of columns, the leading, the margins, and other information pertinent to the format and layout of the page. The template files have these things already done for you.

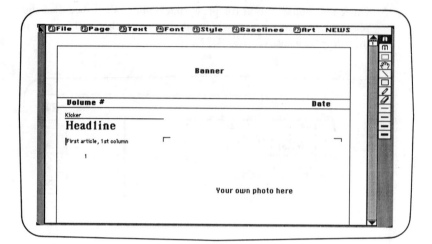

Fig. 3.23. *NEWS.PUB is loaded into First Publisher. (Notice the file name in the upper right corner of the menu bar.)*

Erase Comments Before Using the Template

Before you go any further, take a minute to look closely at NEWS.PUB. At the top of the page, you see the word Banner. Then, as you scan down the page, you can see a variety of notes that the makers of First Publisher inserted so that you would know what goes where.

You need to erase those comments before you add your own text and graphics. To erase the notes on the template (these notes are all written on the graphics layer), first make sure that you are using a *copy* of NEWS.PUB, and then follow these steps:

1. Click the eraser tool (the seventh tool from the top on the graphics tools row on the right side of the screen). If you are using the keyboard, press F9 seven times. The cursor changes to the shape of an eraser.

2. Move the eraser to the notes.

3. Press and hold down the mouse button while you move the eraser over the notes. This procedure erases the words.

Another method of erasing the notes involves using the selection tool to enclosed the items and then pressing Del. Depending on the amount of art you need to erase, this may be the easiest method for you to use. However, if the area you need to erase is not rectangular, you need to use the eraser tool, because the selection tool captures only a rectangular area at one time. If you have used Del to erase the items from the screen, you can recover them by selecting **Paste** (Alt-V). (You can only recover the last item erased.) If you use the eraser, however, the items are gone and cannot be recovered. Later in this chapter, in the section "Adding the Banner," you learn to use the selection tool.

Note: If you prefer, you could leave the comments until you begin working on that particular area. Some users like having the example notes in place so that they can refer to the type size and style used for headlines, kicker lines, and so on.

What Are Baselines?

Now you're almost ready to start making the template a publication of your own. But first, before you get too far into the procedure, you need to learn about baselines.

Baselines, in First Publisher, are lines on which the text is placed. When you are laying out the publication, you plan where you want text to appear, and you modify the baselines accordingly. The Baselines menu offers you a wide range of choices for modifying baselines. The procedures for working with Baselines are explained fully in Chapter 7.

To better illustrate this discussion, display the baselines on the NEWS.PUB template. Make sure that the text tool is selected by clicking the top A in the row of graphics tools on the right side of the screen. Then click the Baselines menu and select **Adjust single** (or press Alt-A). The baselines for the document are then displayed (see fig. 3.24). Use the mouse or the cursor keys to move the display so that you can view the baselines.

The text is inserted when you begin typing, starting at the left edge of the top-left baseline. As you type, the text continues down the left column.

> Text on the text layer must occupy baselines.

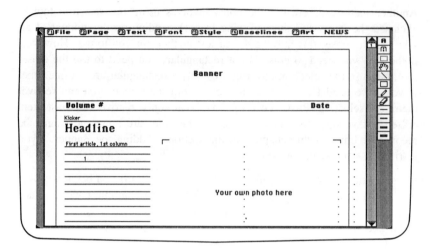

Fig. 3.24. *Baselines for the NEWS.PUB template.*

Graphics text, on the other hand, can be positioned anywhere on the publication. When you are creating a headline, for example, it's much easier to
switch to the graphics layer by selecting the graphics text tool (the outlined
A), and then create the headline by setting the font and style you want and
typing the headline. You then can position the headline wherever you want
by grabbing it with the selection tool and using the hand tool to position it
in the correct location. (For more detailed discussion on each of these tools,
see Chapter 6.)

> Graphics text often is used for headlines and banners. This type of
> text is created on the graphics layer and can be moved anywhere
> on the publication. Baselines are not used for graphics text.

Step 4: *Working with Text*

With First Publisher, you have two options for working with text. You can
type text, which is, in effect, using First Publisher as a word processor, or
you can load into First Publisher a text file created in another program. (For
really fast typists, the typing method may be too slow. If you have a considerable amount of text to enter, you may want to consider exiting First

Publisher, typing the text with your word processing program, and loading the text into First Publisher.) Chapter 1 lists word processors that produce files compatible with First Publisher. (*Note:* The procedure for importing text from another program is explained in Chapter 5.)

Entering Text

For this exercise, you will enter a paragraph of text. When you start First Publisher, the default text type is Geneva, 10-point Normal type. Just to make sure that the typeface, size, and style have not been modified. Check the Font and Style menus by following these steps:

1. Click the Font menu name or press F4.

2. Make sure that the Geneva font is checked. (If not, click Geneva or highlight the item and press F10.)

3. Move the mouse cursor out of the Font menu to close the menu. (If you are using the keyboard, press Esc.)

4. Click the Style menu or press F5.

5. See whether Normal and 10 Points are checked. (If not, select those options as explained in Step 2.)

6. Close the Style menu by moving the mouse cursor out of the menu or by pressing Esc.

The cursor is positioned at the far-left edge of the top baseline. To enter a paragraph, simply type the following (mistakes and all):

This month we begin the process of electing new leasers for 1989.
At the October meeting, we will nominated candidates for the three rotating vacancies on the Board of Directors that go into effect January 15.

As you type, if you make mistakes (that aren't deliberate), you can use the backspace key to ''back up'' over the text you have typed, thereby erasing it.

As you can see, First Publisher ''wraps'' the text automatically, meaning that when one line is full, the program continues to the next line. You don't need to press Enter until you are finished with the paragraph. The page now looks like the one shown in figure 3.25.

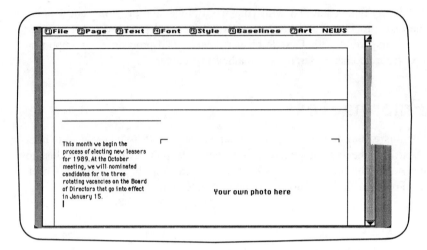

Fig. 3.25. *The page with one paragraph entered.*

Modifying Text

As you have probably noticed, the paragraph in figure 3.25 has a couple of problems. To modify the first misspelling (you need to change *leasers* to *leaders*), follow these steps:

1. Place the mouse cursor between the letter *s* and the letter *e* in the word *leasers*, and click the mouse button. If you are using the keyboard, use the cursor movement keys to move the cursor to that position.

2. Press the backspace key.

3. Type *d.*

That procedure corrects the misspelling. Simple? Absolutely. Remember that you can use this technique to edit as large a text string as you want. If you have a lot of backspacing to do, however, you will find it more efficient to delete the phrase by highlighting it and pressing Del rather than backspacing over the entire phrase and typing another one.

Moving Text

The next step involves removing the word *will* from its incorrect spot in the sentence. *Will* actually goes between *that* and *go* in the last sentence.

1. Place the mouse cursor immediately preceding the word *will*. If you are using the keyboard, use the cursor movement keys to move the cursor to that position.

2. Press the mouse button and drag the mouse to the right (while you keep the mouse button pressed). After the word *will* is highlighted, release the mouse button. If you are using the keyboard method, press F10 and press → several times.

3. When the word *will* is highlighted, press Del. (Or, if you are using the keyboard method, press F10 after the word *will* is highlighted, and then press Del.) The word then is cut from the publication and is placed on the text clipboard (which you cannot see).

4. Place the mouse cursor between the words *that* and *go* in the last sentence. If you're using the keyboard, use the cursor movement keys to move the cursor.

5. Click the mouse button to bring the cursor to that position.

6. Open the Text menu (F3) and select **Paste** (or press Alt-V).

7. Press the space bar to add a space, if necessary.

If you have used other ''cut-and-paste'' programs, you may be accustomed to using the Del key to cut and the Ins key to paste. In First Publisher, the Ins key has another function. When you have a large amount of text to insert, first position the cursor at the point you want the text to begin, and then press Ins—and the remainder of the text on the publication will disappear, allowing you to enter text more quickly. (This increase in speed is due to the fact that when text is present, First Publisher realigns all the text as you type. For example, if you are working in the first paragraph of a publication and there are eight paragraphs on-screen, the program realigns all that text continually while you type. This slows down First Publisher's ability to ''see'' the text you type.)

After you have typed the text, press Ins again, and First Publisher will return and realign the missing text.

Figure 3.26 shows the publication with the corrections in place.

So far, you have learned the basic techniques for working with text and the text clipboard. Next, you will learn about adding banners, creating headlines, and using graphics.

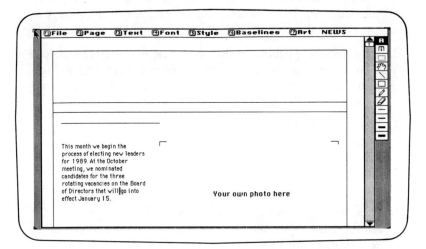

Fig. 3.26. *The sample publication with corrected text errors.*

Step 5: *Saving Your Work*

Saving may seem like a procedure that is usually performed when you are *finished* with something. But if you have ever lost an afternoon's work to a badly timed thunderstorm, you know that not saving a publication until you're finished is courting disaster. For that reason, the steps for saving are included here.

To save your publication, follow these steps:

1. Open the File menu by clicking File or by pressing F1. (You can also save the publication without accessing the menu by simply pressing Alt-S from any point in First Publisher.)

2. Select **Save** or press Alt-S. First Publisher displays the Save dialog box, as shown in figure 3.27.

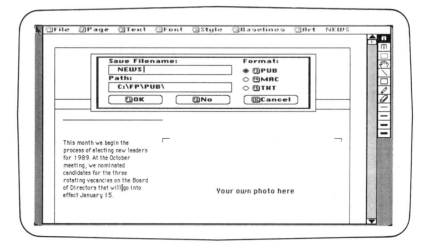

Fig. 3.27. *The Save dialog box.*

3. Make sure that the PUB format is selected. If not, click the radio button in front of the the word PUB, or press F3.

4. Type the name you have chosen for the file. In this case, the name is *indreal* (for Independent Realtor). Be sure to name the file something other than NEWS.PUB; otherwise, the NEWS.PUB template will be overwritten. (*Note:* If you need to specify a path other than the one shown in the Path box, position the cursor in the Path box and type the correct path.)

5. Click OK or press F1. If you have saved a file under that name before, First Publisher displays another dialog box reminding you of that fact and asking whether you want to proceed with the save operation (see fig. 3.28).

That's all there is to saving your files. Remember to save every 15 minutes or so. Some people actually use timers to remind them to save; others stick a well-worn but useful sign above their computers, saying ''Save frequently and often.''

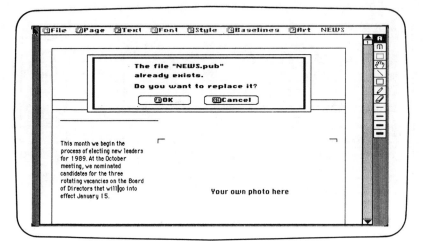

Fig. 3.28. *If you try to save a file under a name used previously, First Publisher asks you to verify the save operation.*

Step 6: *Adding the Banner*

Next, you advance to the graphics layer, where you make your publication look like *your* publication. Remember when you erased the word *Banner* that appeared in the space at the top of the template? You had to use the erase tool because the word was on the *graphics* layer. This type of text is called *graphics text*. The advantage to using graphics text is that you can create it anywhere on the publication and then move it to whatever position you desire. You don't have to worry about baselines, or text flow, or any of the considerations that affect the placement of body text.

To create the banner for your version of NEWS.PUB, follow these steps:

1. Select the graphics text tool (the second A from the top) by clicking it or pressing F9 once.

2. Display the Font menu by clicking the name in the menu bar or by pressing F4.

3. Select **New York** to designate the typeface for the banner.

4. Display the Style menu.

5. Select **Normal** and **36 Points**.

6. Position the cursor about an inch in from the left edge of the publication and click the mouse button. If you are using the keyboard, use the cursor movement keys to position the cursor and then press F10 twice.

7. Type *Independent Realtor* (or a banner of your choosing).

8. Click the selection tool that is directly below the graphics A on the graphics tools set at the far right edge of the screen, or press F9 once. (*Note:* The selection tool, which is the third tool down from the top, is used to capture the images that you plan to move, copy, delete, and so on.)

9. Position the arrow just above and to the left of the banner; then press the mouse button and drag the mouse down and to the right. If you are using the keyboard, press F10 above and to the left of the banner; then use the ↓ and → arrow keys to enlarge the box. Continue expanding the rectangle until the entire banner is enclosed in the dashed rectangle. Then release the mouse button or, if you're using the keyboard, press F10 again.

> If you make a mistake while capturing part of a graphics element with the selection tool, simply release the mouse button and start again. The new rectangle will replace the old one. Only one item can be captured by the selection tool at one time.

10. Select the hand tool. (*Note:* The hand tool, which is the tool beneath the selection tool, is used to move and position images.)

11. Position the hand cursor over the banner, press the mouse button (or F10), and while holding the mouse button down (or F10), move the banner into its place at the top of the publication (centered above the double lines). If you are using the keyboard, move the banner by pressing the appropriate arrow keys. When you are happy with the position of the banner, release the mouse button or press F10 again.

You can eliminate the steps for moving the banner by positioning the cursor and using graphics text to type the banner in the correct place. Because it's difficult to guess how much room 36-point text will take, however, and because you are likely to want to play around with the position of the headlines and banners to produce the best possible effect, the procedure for selecting and moving graphics text is included here as part of the banner procedure. Figure 3.29 shows the publication up to this point.

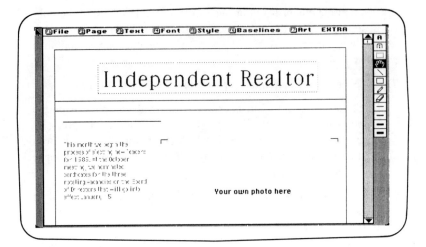

Fig. 3.29. The publication with the banner in place.

You may want to modify the banner once you have it in place. You can select the banner, using the selection tool, and resize it by selecting **Resize** from the Art menu. Because this QuickStart deals with the basics of creating and placing a banner, the procedure for resizing graphics is discussed in Chapter 6.

Now that you have entered and placed the banner, you can modify it, spruce it up, add graphics (covered in a later section), or change it any way you like. If you decide that you would rather try another typeface or that you want to change the name, you can erase the banner by using the eraser tool or by selecting the banner (using the selection tool) and pressing Del.

Step 7: *Adding a Headline*

The procedure for adding a headline is much the same as adding the banner, except on a smaller scale. You're still working with graphics text, which means that you can type the headline virtually anywhere you want on the document and then move it to the desired location.

To add a headline on the *Independent Realtor* newsletter, follow these steps:

1. Select the graphics text tool (second A from the top).

2. Open the Font menu by clicking File or by pressing F4.

3. Select **Helvetica**.

4. Open the Style menu.

5. Select **18 Point** and make sure that **Normal** is selected.

6. Position the cursor at the position you want the headline to go, and press the mouse button or F10. (Remember that you also can use graphics text to type the headline at any position and then move it.)

7. Type the headline, in this case *1989: Year of the Successful Realtor!*

8. If you typed the headline in the correct position, you're done. If you need to move the headline to the right spot, select it by using the selection tool and use the hand tool to move it to the place you want.

You can use this same procedure to add the line called the *kicker* (the small tag line above the main headline on the page—2 1/2 inches on the side ruler and 3/4 inch on the top ruler). The kicker here is Geneva 12-point normal type. A rule has been added to separate the kicker from the headline. (The rule was produced using the line tool, which is found just below the hand tool in the graphics tools row.) Figure 3.30 shows the publication thus far.

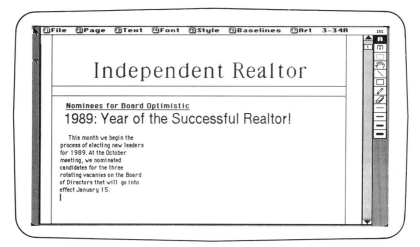

Fig. 3.30. The publication with a banner and headline.

Step 8: *Adding Graphics*

Okay, you have text, a banner, and a headline. Now you need to add graphics. In this section, you will add some artistic touches to your publication by adding clip art.

Selecting Clip Art

One of the nice features First Publisher offers is its own set of clip art—that is, art images you can "clip" from the file and use in your own publications.

For this example, you will clip the image of a cityscape to use in the banner. The clip art is found in the graphics file PERSONAL.MAC. The process of using clip art involves the following steps:

❏ Go to the clip art (MAC) file

❏ Select the art image you want

❏ Save the image as an ART file

❏ Return to the publication

❏ Get the ART file

❏ Resize the graphic as necessary

❏ Position the graphic

The following sections break each of these steps into individual procedures.

Finding the Clip Art File

To access the clip art file you want (in this case, PERSONAL.MAC), follow these steps:

1. Save your publication by selecting **Save** from the File menu or by typing Alt-S.

2. Select **Get graphics** from the File menu.

3. When the Get dialog box is displayed, click PERSONAL.MAC and OK (or highlight the file name by using the arrow keys and press F1).

First Publisher then displays the clip art file. The next step is to select the image you want.

> You cannot get to the clip art files by choosing **Get art** from the Art menu. This ''art'' refers to the art files you create using First Publisher. If you have created an image by using the graphics tools, for example, this file would be accessible with the **Get art** option. Or, after you have selected an image in the clip art file and have used **Save art** to save it in ART format, you can use **Get art** to retrieve the file. If you are selecting an image created in or imported from another program, however, use **Get graphics**.

Selecting and Saving the Art Image

To select and save the art image, you follow these steps:

1. Click the selection tool (or press F9 until the tool is highlighted).

2. Place the arrow cursor above and to the left of the image you want to capture. If you are using the keyboard, use the cursor movement keys to move the cursor to the correct position and press F10 twice.

3. Drag the mouse down and to the right, enclosing the image you want to select. From the keyboard, use the arrow keys to manipulate the rectangle, and when you're finished, press F10. (*Note:* For this example, you need only a portion of the cityscape image. Figure 3.31 shows the captured image.)

4. You then need to save the image to an ART file by selecting **Save art** from the Art menu. If you are using the keyboard, press F7 to open the Art menu and use the ↓ key to move the highlight to the **Save art** option; then press Enter.

5. A dialog box is displayed, asking you to enter a name for the ART file. Use a name that will remind you of the file's contents later. For this example, use the file name CITY. Then click OK or press F1. First Publisher saves the file.

Fig. 3.31. *The captured clip art image.*

Returning to the Publication

Next, return to your publication by following these steps:

1. Open the File menu and choose **Get publication**. (If you have made any modifications to PERSONAL.MAC, you will be asked whether you want to save the file. Choose **No**.)

2. When the Get dialog box is displayed, select the name of your publication file (in this case, INDREAL.PUB). You should see your altered newsletter template on the screen once again.

Placing, Resizing, and Positioning the Graphic

The last leg of this journey requires you to paste the image on the publication, resize it to fit the space allotment, and put it in place.

To place the image, you do the following:

1. Select the hand tool from the graphics tools.

2. Select **Get art** and CITY.ART, and then use the hand tool to position the cityscape in a ''white'' area (where no text or lines appear). Finally, click the mouse button (or press F10).

3. The image is placed on the publication.

To resize the image, you follow these steps:

1. Select **Resize** from the Art menu (or press Alt-R).

2. Position the arrow cursor over one of the four black handles and click the mouse button or press F10. Then move the mouse (or use the cursor keys) to resize the item as necessary. When you move the handles, the size and shape of the image changes accordingly. Resize the cityscape so that it fits to the left of the banner *Independent Realtor*. If you are using the keyboard, when the image is the size you want, press F10. Remove the handles by selecting Alt-R again.

To position the image, you do the following:

1. Select the hand tool.

2. Move the image to the correct position to the left on the banner, using the move procedure described previously.

Figure 3.32 shows the publication with the clip art images pasted in place. Notice that a duplicate image of the item was made (by selecting **Duplicate** from the Art menu when the image was selected) and then the image was ''flipped.'' The option **Flip horizontal** was used to reverse the direction of the buildings. A box was also added (using the box tool) and another image was copied in (this one from PUBLICAT.MAC). These operations are discussed in more detail in Chapter 6.

You are almost finished with the QuickStart tour. Remember that the rest of this book focuses on the various things you can do to enhance your First Publisher documents and make them unique. The last step in this QuickStart involves getting a printed copy of your First Publisher creation.

If you want to view the entire document before you print, you can select the **Show page** option from the Page menu, or press Alt-Z. The entire page is then shown on the screen, but because the image is small, you use this view basically for checking the placement of items on the page. When you are ready to remove the full-page view, press the space bar or click the mouse outside the view box.

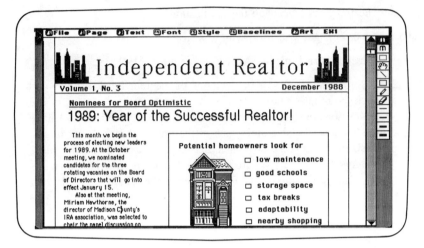

Fig. 3.32. *The completed document.*

Step 9: *Printing the Publication*

When you have finished doing all you can think of doing for your publication (or when you want to check your progress), you are ready to print. The procedure is simple. After you have saved the file, follow these steps:

1. Open the File menu by clicking File or by pressing F1.

2. Choose the **Print** option. First Publisher then displays the Print dialog box (see fig. 3.33).

3. The Print dialog box is explained thoroughly in Chapter 8. For now, you can leave all the options as they are (or, if you want to take the time to print the highest-quality version, click the radio button in front of the **Smoothed** option).

4. Click OK or press F1.

If you're like most people, as soon as you see the publication in print, you will begin to think of other ways to enhance it. For this reason, you may want to print in draft mode most of the time, until you are positively finished with the document. Selecting draft mode saves you time—and printer ribbons. When you go to print the final version, use standard or smoothed

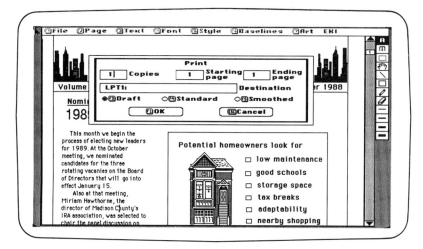

Fig. 3.33. *The Print dialog box.*

mode to give the publication a more polished look. (If you are using Version 2.01, you also have the option of choosing scaled or unscaled printing. For more information, see Chapter 8.) Figure 3.34 shows the finished *Independent Realtor* newsletter.

Chapter Summary

In this chapter, you covered a lot of ground. The first half of the chapter detailed the various First Publisher elements you will use as you create different publications, and the other half took you on a QuickStart that listed the procedures for basic First Publisher tasks. The remaining chapters concentrate on building publications the hard way; starting from scratch rather than using First Publisher templates.

Fig. 3.34. The finished Independent Realtor *newsletter.*

Part II

▼

The Basics: Creating a Publication

Includes

Beginning the Publication

Entering and Editing Text

Creating and Using Graphics

Finishing the Layout

Printing the Publication

4

Beginning the Publication

W hat would happen to the world if no one planned ahead? Bus drivers would get in their buses in the morning and drive around, randomly picking up passengers. Interstate highway systems would *never* get finished (maybe *that's* the problem). Businesses would go bankrupt.

Producing an effective publication that is targeted to the correct audience, that has the right tone and image, that is visually appealing, and that is easy and enjoyable to read takes a certain amount of planning. Whether you plan on a drawing board, in your head, or on paper, the *thinking* stage of the design process is a crucial one. The amount of time you spend planning will, of course, depend on the complexity of the project. If you have been producing a flier by writing it out by hand, you will spend little or no time planning. If you have just been assigned the job of developing a company newsletter, however, you will want to get a basic idea of the type of publication your company wants to see before you sit down at the keyboard and begin creating.

Once you have thought about the text and the type of art you would like to use in a publication, you use First Publisher's **Define page** option on the Page menu as your "think ahead" tool. This option allows you to set the number of columns, the amount of leading, and the margins and gutters for the page. Some First Publisher users prefer to import the text for their publication and *then* use **Define page**. You can follow whichever method is most comfortable for you. If you specify the **Define page** settings before you begin creating the publication, you can change any or all of the settings at a later time.

This chapter begins with a set of planning strategies you can use as you begin to develop your publication. If you are an experienced desktop publisher, you may want to skip ahead to the section ''Opening Publications.'' If you are new to desktop publishing, you should find the ''Designing Your Publication'' section helpful, offering you a wide range of considerations that aid you in producing the product you want. Once you have the project mapped out, this chapter shows you how to open the First Publisher file and begin setting the specifications for that file. The chapter then concludes with the procedures for saving, naming, and deleting files.

Designing Your Publication

No one has to argue the benefits of planning: too many of us have suffered the consequences of not having thought things through. Although your desktop publishing efforts may not be affected severely by omitting the planning stage, you invariably will save time and produce a better product if you carefully plan the publication you want to produce.

The design phase of creating a document can be as lengthy or as short as you would like. For that matter, although this method is not recommended for new users, some people do their best work on-screen, without having put any real thought into the design at all. Other people spend hours—or even days—thinking about the audience, talking to their constituents, conducting their own brands of ''research'' to find out what looks best and why. Most people, however, take 10 to 30 minutes before sitting down at the computer and think about the items listed in the following sections.

Overall Design Tips

Before you read through the tips for individual project types, here are a few general tips you should consider:

> *Consider your audience.* Who will be reading your publication? Make sure that the style of the text and the art you select is geared toward that person. If you are composing a serious newsletter for a society of nuclear scientists, you may want to avoid using cartoon-style graphics and light, too-friendly text. A sophisticated-looking banner, and a serious, factual writing style would be more appropriate for such an audience.

Consider your objectives. If you have inherited the job of producing the company newsletter or of producing attention-getting press releases for the marketing department of your company, you need to consider what goals the materials are intended to meet. Do you want to inform, inspire, or motivate? Will the press release go out to companies evaluating your product or to potential sales prospects? Write down your views on the objectives of the publication, and talk them over with others in the department. Figure 4.1 shows a sample questionnaire that a representative of a desktop publishing firm might use to find and document these objectives.

Keep a folder of styles you like. Whether you produce brochures, fliers, menus, or newsletters, keep samples of other peoples' products. Typeset or not, mimeographed or professionally printed, the idea is not how the product was produced, but whether you can emulate it. This folder also can help when people have trouble deciding on a particular style or format; you can pull out the samples folder and let them show you what they like.

The sections that follow outline planning strategies for individual projects.

Planning Newsletters

First Publisher is used most often to produce newsletters. Figure 4.2 shows two varieties of newsletters.

As you can see from figure 4.2, these two newsletters are drastically different. *Baby News* and *Medical Update* may, on occasion, carry a similar article related to pediatrics, but you can be sure that their audience, tone, and content are drastically different. Even the art in the publications represents a drastically different publishing style. When you begin to plan your newsletter, consider the following questions:

What type of design is appropriate for the audience? Baby News required a light, friendly design, so a two-column design was chosen. *Medical Update*, on the other hand, needed a more professional look, so a more sophisticated layout (three columns on top, two on the bottom) was selected. (*Note:* First Publisher does offer a preset layout for the style used in the *Medical Update* publication. This template is in the file 3TOP2BOT.PUB.)

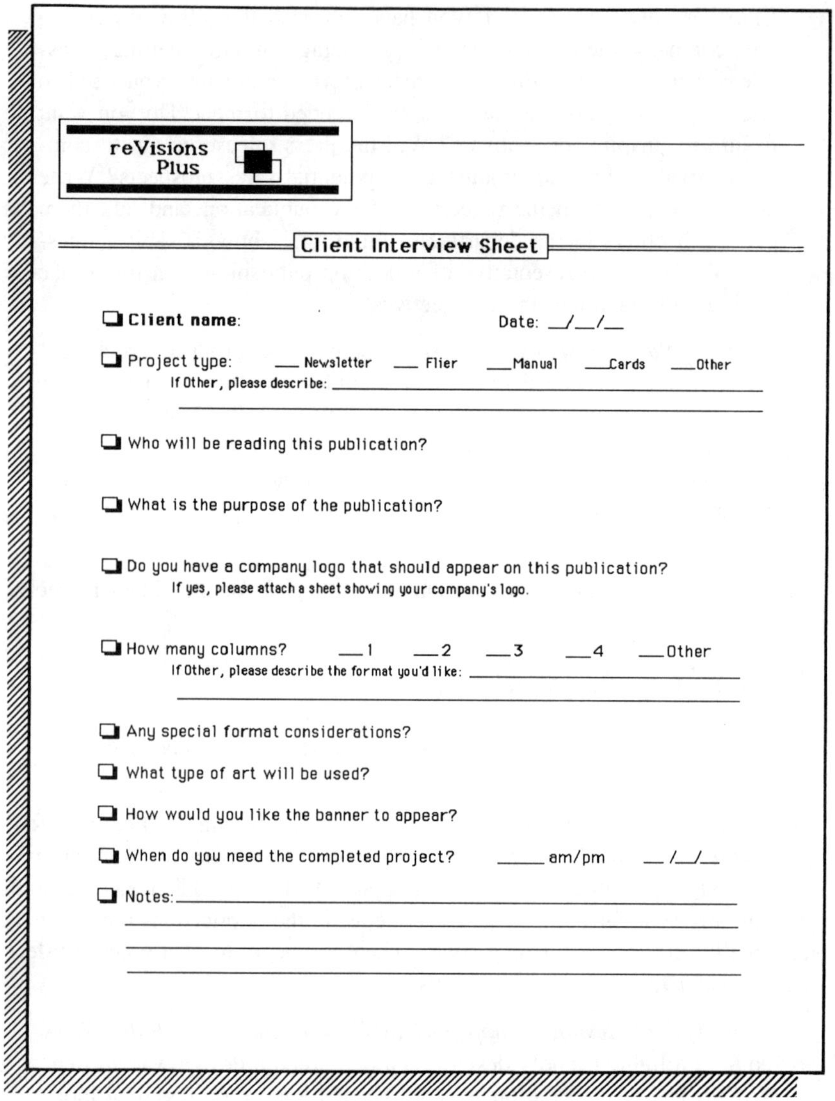

reVisions Plus

Client Interview Sheet

❑ **Client name:**   Date: __/__/__

❑ **Project type:** ___ Newsletter ___ Flier ___Manual ___Cards ___Other
      If Other, please describe: _____
      _____

❑ **Who will be reading this publication?**

❑ **What is the purpose of the publication?**

❑ **Do you have a company logo that should appear on this publication?**
      If yes, please attach a sheet showing your company's logo.

❑ **How many columns?** ___1 ___2 ___3 ___4 ___Other
      If Other, please describe the format you'd like: _____
      _____

❑ **Any special format considerations?**

❑ **What type of art will be used?**

❑ **How would you like the banner to appear?**

❑ **When do you need the completed project?** _____ am/pm ___ /__/__

❑ **Notes:** _____
      _____
      _____
      _____

Fig. 4.1. *An interview sheet.*

Fig. 4.2. *Two newsletter samples.*

∿∿∿ Medical Update ∿∿∿

Volume 23, No. 5   February 1989

Research Shows Surprising Results

New Strategies for Mitral Valve Treatment

Recent research has proven that mitral insufficiency from connective tissue disorders and a variety of other causes are leading physicians to consider mitral valve reconstruction as a viable alternative for patients suffering from mitral disorders.

Seeing the advantages to mitral valvular reconstruction has been slow for many leading physicians.

However, mitral valve reconstruction offers a lower percentage of long-term morbidity and mortality than replacement offers.

The research demonstrates that, if caught early, mitral valve repair is much easier on the patient and is a safer operation to perform.

This procedure has been slow to gain acceptance because accurate methods of obtaining research data have not been available.

> **"Many physicians have had trouble seeing the real value in considering mitral valve reconstruction..."**

Researchers have recently attempted using intraoperative cardiac color-flow mapping as a method of gathering the statistical data they need in order to assess whether or not the procedure is worth the cost and risk--albeit minimal--to patients.

Color mapping is a technique that superimposes on the two-dimensional echocardiogram color that highlights the blood flow velocity and direction. This color mapping allows physicians to determine whether a weak valve does in fact warrant further testing as to the possibility of a mitral valve reconstruction.

This technique also lends itself to other diagnostic procedures as well. When a ventricular clot is suspected, the color mapping procedure can be used to determine whether a clot exists,

continued on pg. 3

Hospital News

Family Service Unit Opens at Mount Sinai

Minnie Mouse Coat, Sure; But Mickey Mouse Work? No Way.

He wears a Minnie Mouse coat and his office is filled with toys and stuffed animals, but for Dr. Howard Levy, life is anything but frivolous. The playful trappings contrast sharply with the tragedy that confronts Dr. Levy with each patient he sees. Dr. Levy is the director of the Pediatric Ecology Unit at Mount Sinai Medical Center in Chicago. It's the first facility in the nation designed to evaluate and treat victims and families of child abuse and neglect.

The unit treats patients from newborn to 14 years old. It offers a relaxed, cozy atmosphere. None of the staff wear uniforms, and the rooms are furnished more like a home than a hospital. The walls are adorned with finger paintings and crayon artwork. "The whole environment here," says Dr. Levy, "is aimed toward warmth."

Sadly, for many of the young patients, the warmth of the unit is the first they have experienced.

The Mount Sinai unit is structured to give each child the attention he needs. One of the best things about it, note the doctors, is the way they take things "at the child's speed." Kids are given time to warm

continued on pg. 2

Medical Update   1   Feb 1989

Fig. 4.2—Continued

How many pages will the newsletter cover? Will you want to repeat this design for subsequent pages? As you design the cover page, think about whether front-page articles will continue on inside pages.

How many articles will be involved? Block out the number of articles, the approximate length, and the planned placement for the articles.

What type of banner does the publication need? Will you be designing the banner or has your company already created it? Will you need to scan the banner from an existing document? Again, as you create the banner, keep the audience in mind. An appropriate, eye-catching banner gives the reader the first impression of a publication and may determine whether your project goes in the In box or gets dumped without a second look.

What kind of art will be involved? Will you be using clip art, scanned photos, or freehand graphics? Is the type of art you need available in computer form or will you need to leave space on your printout to paste in the items before you take the publication to be duplicated?

Planning Fliers and Brochures

Attention-getting fliers are easy to produce with First Publisher. In less than an hour, you can design, create, and print a flier that is ready to be photo-copied or printed and sent out. When you are planning a promotional piece —whether a flier or a fold-out brochure—consider these questions:

What kind of business are you promoting? If the flier is advertising a service business, the text and graphics you choose for the flier should convey that idea. If you are promoting a product or advertising a sale at a local retail outlet, you may want to create a graphic that resembles the product(s).

What is most important about what you're trying to say? A flier is a "hit-'em-fast" type of publication. Much of the communication power must rest on the graphics, and you must choose your words carefully so that you convey the strongest message possible in a small number of words. Figure 4.3 shows two fliers: one is effective, and one isn't.

Fig. 4.3. *You can scan the* Winter's Coming! *flier quickly; the other flier has too much text.*

Maids, Inc.

(313) 776-0420

Let Maids, Inc. take care of everything in your house, from the mildew in your basement to the cobwebs in your attic. From top to bottom, we can clean your house--daily, weekly, monthly, bi-monthly, or on an as-called basis.

With over 25 years of experience in the Minneapolis area, we at Maids, Inc. take pride in the jobs we do. Our services include dishes, laundry, vacuuming, windows, bathrooms--and we're available for larger jobs like spring cleaning, moving preparations, and any other happening that requires a quick, thorough housecleaning.

With a staff of 14 employees, Maids, Inc. can be flexible with the scheduling of your housecleaning appointments. Do you work at night? If you'd prefer a maid drop by when you are out--even if you work odd hours--we can arrange to have one of our maids do the job when it's most convenient for you. Weekends, evenings, and day rates differ, so ask the Maids, Inc. representative about charges when you call.

Now, for a short time only, Maids, Inc. is offering a free "get acquainted" discount. We'll come clean your home for only $15; then, if you sign a 6-month contract, you can "lock in" a price of only $25 per visit.

Fig. 4.3—Continued

What type of graphics should be used to grab readers' attention? For many types of businesses, because sales is people oriented, a friendly-yet-serious image is best. You want the public to think you run a personable business but that you take your work seriously. The graphics you choose should reflect the image you want to portray. A business that makes home-knitted baby booties, for example, could be more relaxed in its business-like portrayal—but generally, buyers want to know that they are paying for a professional product. The graphics you choose for the flier should reflect this professionalism.

Planning Business Cards and Stationery

Probably the most important aspect of business cards and stationery is the company logo. Selection of a logo should be a careful process: choose something that in some way "connects" with the service or product you offer. Don't just select a graphic for art's sake. Putting a penguin next to the company name, *Walter's Cleaners*, will not work: it may be cute, but it will not mean anything to anybody. (If the name is *Pen's Cleaners* or if you're running the *Petite Penguin* restaurant, on the other hand, such a graphic would be appropriate.) Figure 4.4 shows a few sample company logos.

If your company has an existing logo that they are happy with, you can scan the logo so that you can use it in their First Publisher documents. (For more information on scanning images, see Chapter 10.)

When designing your company's business cards and stationery, consider these tips:

Make the design of your cards, stationery, envelopes, and other printed items consistent. Once you have decided on a logo, use that logo on all your printed materials—even your newsletters. You can play on the design if you want, varying it slightly for envelopes, maybe enhancing it for the business cards, but keep the basic elements the same. This consistency will help keep your company's name and symbol in the reader's mind.

Keep the design simple and memorable. Choose a design that doesn't fill up the card or the stationery. Remember that the unprinted space on any document is just as important as the printed space. If readers

Fig. 4.4. *Three sample company logos.*

encounter a piece of material that looks difficult to read, has only a small amount of white space (unprinted space), and has a crowded design, chances are they will not even attempt to read the piece.

Make sure that the stationery doesn't "overwhelm" the printing. Resist the temptation to overdo your stationery. A simple design with the company logo at the top is more effective than a form that includes heavy rules all around the page and combines a heavy-duty graphic element with a company name. You want the reader's eye to be pulled to the typed text, not drawn repeatedly to overwhelming graphics.

Highlight the company name. Use the graphic elements to call attention to the point you really want the reader to remember: your company's name. Make sure that you leave enough white space around the name so that the reader's eye is drawn easily to that point. A cluttered business card may not make it to the Rolodex—it might go straight into File 13.

Handouts for Training

Training handouts require even more planning than the average publication because you have an additional purpose: you hope to teach students something about a particular subject. The design of the document should lend itself to a "quick look" format; readers should be able to tell, based on the design, what on the page is most important for them to read first. Figure 4.5 shows a sample handout.

When you are designing handouts, consider these tips:

Make your class objectives known. Place the objectives—or goals—of your course in an easily identified spot on the handout.

Keep the handout brief, with only enough information to refresh the reader's memory when the handout is read later. If you pack too much text into the handout, the effect of quickly "reminding" the reader is lost. Usually one or two pages is sufficient. The longer the handout, the less likely it is to be used outside of class.

You may want to include space for notes. Depending on the nature of your course and whether you are pressed for space on the handout, you may want to include a spot for notes on one page.

Make the major points easy to find. Use graphics to highlight the most important points on a page. You could use numbered steps, boldface type, or a graphic element such as an icon to draw the reader's eye to the important topics.

Use boxed material to reinforce concepts introduced in the text. Boxed information can be effective in restating, or summarizing, a topic introduced in text or in class. Keep boxed material brief. You may want to consider adding a drop shadow behind the box (the procedure for adding drop shadows is explained in Chapter 6).

Summary of Design Strategies

Before designing your publication, think about the following points:

❏ Your company's expectations

❏ The type of format that will appeal to readers

❏ The purpose of the publication

❏ How many columns you want

❏ What type of graphics you need

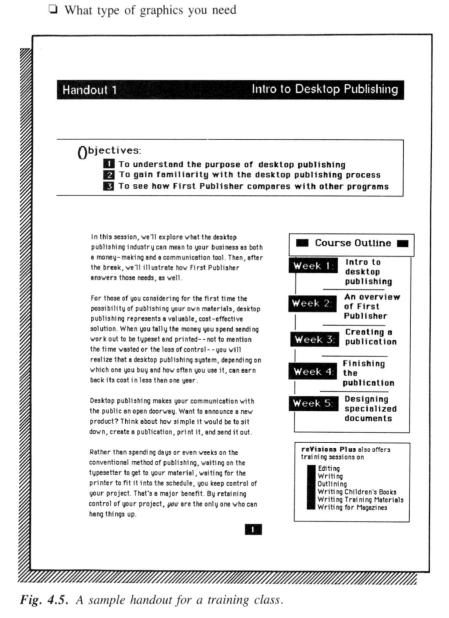

Fig. 4.5. *A sample handout for a training class.*

Then, when you have a clear picture of where you want to go with a publication, you're ready to define the first page of your project.

Like many people, you may find that as you become proficient with First Publisher, you spend less and less time on the planning stage. But if you start with a clear image of where you want to be when you finish creating your First Publisher document, you will have an easier time getting there.

Opening Publications

When you begin using First Publisher to create your project, the first step after the paper-and-pencil design stage involves opening a publication. If you are creating a new publication, you don't need to do anything: First Publisher automatically displays a new, blank screen right after you start the program. As figure 4.6 shows, the word NEW appears in the upper right corner of the screen.

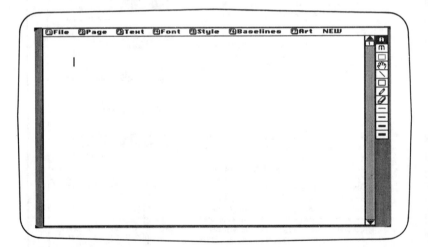

Fig. 4.6. The new file in First Publisher.

If you are going to use an existing publication, you have two options: you can retrieve a publication you have already worked on by selecting **Get publication**, or you can use **Get publication** to choose a First Publisher template. Although for the sake of the discussion in this chapter it is assumed that you want to design a new publication from scratch, the following sections explain each of these two options.

Selecting a File

First, to select a file you have already created, you need to access the File menu. To access this menu, move the mouse cursor up to the word File in the menu bar and click the mouse button. (If you're using the keyboard, press F1.) When the File menu is displayed, move the mouse to highlight the **Get publication** option and click OK. If you're using the keyboard, you can use the down-arrow (↓) key to highlight the option and then press Enter. (You can also skip the menu selections altogether by pressing Alt-G.) The Get dialog box, shown in figure 4.7, then is displayed.

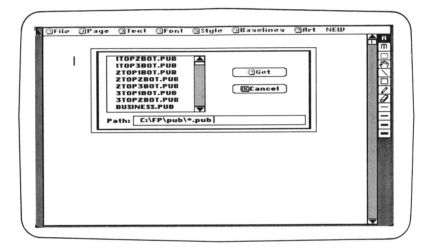

Fig. 4.7. *The Get dialog box.*

Look through the file names shown in the small window on the left side of the dialog box. As you can see, this window also has an elevator bar that you can use to display more files. Notice that the Get button appears gray rather than black; this dimmed appearance indicates that the Get button cannot be used until a file is selected. When you find the file you want, click the file name to highlight it (or highlight it by using the arrow keys to move the highlight bar to that item). Then click the Get button or press F1. If you have chosen the wrong file or decide at this point not to proceed, click the Cancel button, and the screen is returned to the blank file that was originally displayed.

If the file you want is not displayed, it may be in another directory. Check the path designation to see whether you need to type a new path. If you need to review the path concept, refer to Chapter 2.

Working with Different File Types

The type of file you are looking for determines the type of files First Publisher displays in the Get dialog box. For example, when you select **Get publication**, the default path First Publisher searches ends with *.PUB, meaning ''find and display all files that end with the extension PUB.'' Table 4.1 shows the relationship between the selected **Get** option and the file name extension.

Table 4.1
Working with First Publisher Files

When you select	First Publisher looks for the extension
Get publication	PUB
Get graphics	MAC
Get text	TXT
Get art	ART

You can display any other files in those subdirectories by changing the path designation. For example, the path

c:\pub*.pub

means that First Publisher has looked in the PUB directory to find and display the files that end with the extension PUB. If you have stored your publication files in another subdirectory, the window in the Get dialog box may display No matching files were found. This message doesn't mean that no files are in that subdirectory; it means that First Publisher didn't find any files with the extension PUB. To see which files are stored in that directory, you could change the path to the following:

c:\pub*.*

This path says to ''find and display *all* files in the PUB directory.'' Similarly, if you know the extension of the file you want, you can specify that extension, as in the following:

c:\pub*.pcx

(*Note:* The PCX extension is the extension for graphics files created in or converted to PC Paintbrush.)

If you are using a two disk drive system, this procedure is less complicated. The path designation most likely is *b:*.pub*, and the same rules mentioned previously apply for the various file types displayed.

After you click the Get button (or press F1), a dialog box appears, telling you that the file is being read and then formatted (see fig. 4.8). Your file then appears on the screen.

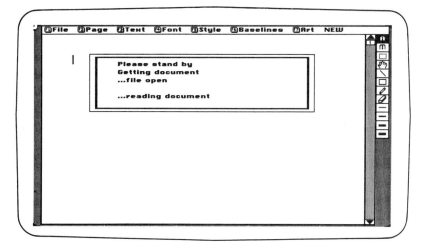

Fig. 4.8. *The "in-process" dialog box.*

Choosing a Template

If you are choosing a template, the procedure for opening a publication is basically the same. But first, if you don't have the template files on your hard disk or if you are working on a two disk drive system, you need to make sure that First Publisher has access to the template you want. Chapter 3 describes the templates available on the Sampler Disk and shows you what each template looks like. The templates from which you can choose are the following:

NEWS.PUB
FLYER.PUB
INVOICE.PUB
LIST.PUB
CARD.PUB
BUSINESS.PUB
MENU.PUB

On Program Disk 2, you will find seven additional newsletter templates that give you a variety of format choices. The newsletter format templates are the following:

1TOP2BOT.PUB
1TOP3BOT.PUB
2TOP1BOT.PUB
2TOP2BOT.PUB
2TOP3BOT.PUB
3TOP1BOT.PUB
3TOP2BOT.PUB

The names of these templates really give away their content; for example, 1TOP2BOT.PUB is a template in which the publication is designed to have one column on top and two columns on the bottom.

These templates, which are new with Version 2.0, are a great enhancement to First Publisher. As you will learn in Chapter 5, working with baselines—the lines on which the text is placed—can be a tricky job. In these templates, the baseline work is done for you; all you have to do is fill in the text and add graphics.

When you have the appropriate disk in the drive or have copied the template files to the hard disk, select **Get publication** from the File menu. When the Get dialog box is displayed, click the template file you want and then click the Get button. (If the template files are in drive B, you need to make sure that the path designation begins with *b:*.) After the "in process" dialog box appears and disappears, the template is displayed.

Remember when you save the file to specify a file name other than the name of the template (NEWS.PUB). Otherwise, the original template file will be overwritten. For more information, see the section "Saving Files" later in this chapter.

Defining the Page

When you are creating a publication "from scratch," you need to tell First Publisher how many columns you want the publication to include, how much leading (white space) you want to appear between each line, and how much room you want allotted to the margins and the gutter (the vertical white space between columns in a publication). The margin and gutter settings are measured in inches; the leading, in points. (A *point* is a standard unit of measurement for type equal to about 1/72 inch.) You use the **Define page** option on the Page menu to specify these settings. Figure 4.9 shows the default settings for the Define Page dialog box. (*Note:* Your margin settings may be different, depending on the printer you are using.)

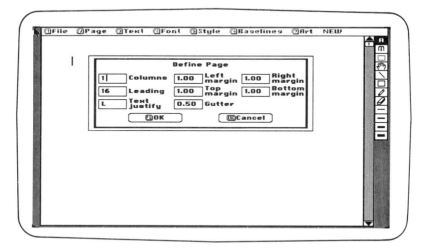

Fig. 4.9. The default settings for the Define Page dialog box.

You can use the settings either as they are, or you can enter new settings. When you want to change a setting, simply position the cursor in the box next to that setting by moving the mouse cursor to that location and clicking the mouse button. If you are using the keyboard, you can use Tab, Enter, or the arrow keys to reach the setting you want to change.

When you have finished modifying the settings, click OK and First Publisher saves the settings for the current publication.

When you use **Define Page** to enter settings for the current page, those settings are also in effect for any pages following the current one. If you add a page following the current page, that new page also is given the settings for the current page. You can select different settings for the new page by selecting **Define page** when that page is displayed on the screen. Doing so will not affect the original page, but any pages you add after that one will take on the **Define page** settings of the modified page.

Setting Columns

The number of columns you select depends largely on the decisions you made while designing the publication. First Publisher allows up to four columns. (However, you can use the templates 2TOP3BOT.PUB or 3TOP2BOT.PUB or create your own similar design to give the appearance that five columns are used. Creating another design involves the manipulation of baselines, which are covered in detail in Chapter 5.)

As figure 4.9 shows, the default setting for columns is 1, meaning that when you type or import text into the publication, the text is placed in one column that extends across the screen.

To change the column setting, simply type the number of columns you want. Figure 4.10 shows two sample publications: one has one column, and one has four columns.

Changing the Number of Columns on an Existing Publication

In First Publisher, you can change the number of columns without losing the text or starting over with the publication. Even after you have placed text and graphics, you can go back to **Define page** and change the number of columns you had specified. Before changing settings, however, remember to save a copy of the publication—just in case you don't like the change.

Because the text and graphics layers are independent of each other, you don't have to worry about text in any way harming the graphics you have already placed.

One additional tip: When you set the number of columns with **Define page**, choose the maximum number of columns you think you might use. If you later decide that you want to use three columns instead of four, for example, you can ''zero out'' the unwanted column. On the other hand, if you choose three columns and then decide you really need four, you have no way to break apart baselines to make another column. (The procedures for modifying baselines are discussed in Chapter 7.)

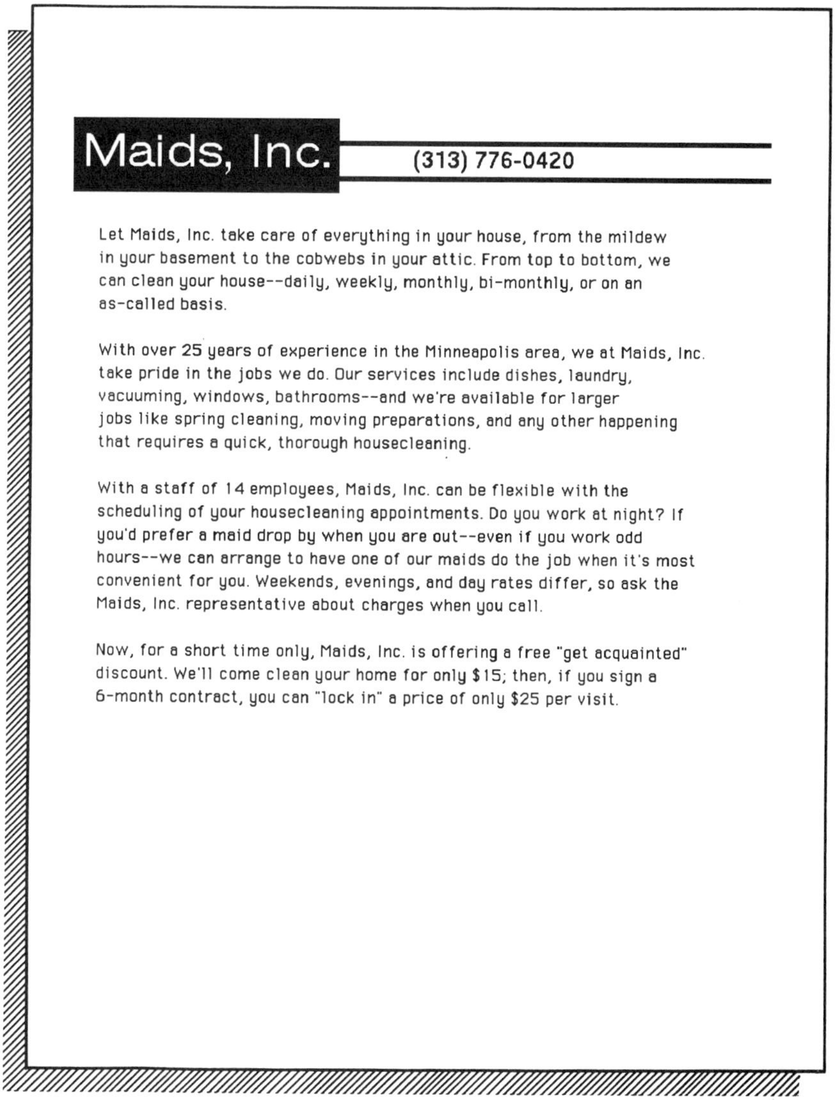

Maids, Inc.

(313) 776-0420

Let Maids, Inc. take care of everything in your house, from the mildew in your basement to the cobwebs in your attic. From top to bottom, we can clean your house--daily, weekly, monthly, bi-monthly, or on an as-called basis.

With over 25 years of experience in the Minneapolis area, we at Maids, Inc. take pride in the jobs we do. Our services include dishes, laundry, vacuuming, windows, bathrooms--and we're available for larger jobs like spring cleaning, moving preparations, and any other happening that requires a quick, thorough housecleaning.

With a staff of 14 employees, Maids, Inc. can be flexible with the scheduling of your housecleaning appointments. Do you work at night? If you'd prefer a maid drop by when you are out--even if you work odd hours--we can arrange to have one of our maids do the job when it's most convenient for you. Weekends, evenings, and day rates differ, so ask the Maids, Inc. representative about charges when you call.

Now, for a short time only, Maids, Inc. is offering a free "get acquainted" discount. We'll come clean your home for only $15; then, if you sign a 6-month contract, you can "lock in" a price of only $25 per visit.

Fig. 4.10. Examples of different column settings.

Applefield Elementary PTO Roster
3rd quarter 1989

Aronsen, Marian.	Culver, Diana	Granger, Peter	Johnson, Mike
1017 N. College	94 Wedgewood	98 Harpington	67 Ellerbee
575-9922	833-5454	833-5555	833-8888
Allen, Renee	Daniels, Marge	Gump, Marcia	Kittle, Dean
456 N. 109th	14 Snodhopper	1415 N. College	333 Wedgewood
832-1811	575-8773	575-5334	832-1414
Andrias, Buffy	DelVerne, Anita	Harlan, Darla	Land, Marcia
34 Teagarden Ln.	76 Linda Ln.	51 N. 198th	517 N. College
832-6767	575-8880	575-9001	575-8880
Brown, Michelle	Dracula, R.J.	Hawthorne, John	Lawton, P.
58 Windfield	31 Halloween Ct.	67 River St.	19 Linda Ln.
833-9898	833-0000	833-9844	575-3472
Butterworth, Lea	Eggbert, Ronald	Hendricks, Shay	Long, David
98 Madagascar	832 N. 108th	2304 Brentwood	67 Harpington
832-4636	832-7744	833-8989	833-7641
Buzzard, Mary A.	Eltzroth, Jeanne	Hooker, Samatha	Lump, Renita
1806 N. 98th	465 N. 197th	48 Windfield	733 Teagarden Ln.
833-4466	833-5656	832-1111	832-4444
Carpenter, L.	Fangard, Elise	Hummingbird, P.	Manx, Kitty
34 Redrose Ln.	45 N. Windfield	4500 N. 103rd	55 Petrie Place
832-5858	833-2133	575-8660	833-7699
Compton, R.	Fenwick, Patricia	James, Danielle	Mellencamp, Joan
576 N. Michigan	688 N. Holston	15 Redrose Ct.	14 Traverse Way
833-7326	832-7878	833-7833	833-4747
Cray, Linda	Freeley, Lisa	Jarvis, Paula	Mitchell, Mona
12 Ellerbee	90 Redrose Ct.	23 Ellerbee	819 Ellerbee
832-2377	832-7666	833-4444	832-1119

Fig. 4.10—Continued

Setting the Leading

The *leading* is the amount of white space that appears between lines. The amount of space between lines will vary depending on the typeface you use in the body of the document. Figure 4.11 shows a flier with 18-point leading. Figure 4.12 shows the same flier with 9-point leading. Both figures have the same typeface and size.

Fig. 4.11. *A flier with 18-point leading.*

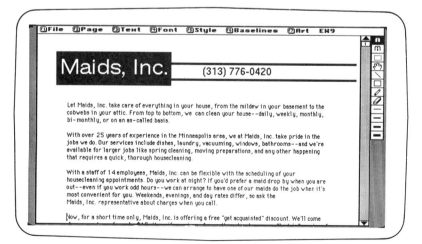

Fig. 4.12. *The same flier with 9-point leading.*

First Publisher accepts leading amounts between 9 and 72 points. If you specify any other amount, you are prompted to correct the entry.

Aligning Text

Also in the Define Page dialog box, you can choose the way text is aligned in the columns. You can specify one of the following, as shown in table 4.2.

Table 4.2
Text Alignment Commands

To specify	Type in the Text Justify Box
Left-justified text	L
Right-justified text	R
Full-justified text	J
Centered	C

If you already know how you want the text to look, you can go ahead and specify the setting you want. (Left-justified, the most common alignment, is the default.) Like the other items on the Define Page dialog box, you can change this setting later if you change your mind.

If you look at other newsletters, you will see that left-justified text is the most common. The text is lined up along the left edge of the column. Right-justified text aligns down the right edge, and full-justified text "fills out" the lines with spaces so that each line extends to the left and right margins. Figure 4.13 shows examples of various justification settings.

Remember that if you select the Centered option, all text *within the columns* will be centered. If what you really want to do is produce a centered heading, you use the **Center** option available in the Baselines menu. (This procedure is explained in Chapter 7.)

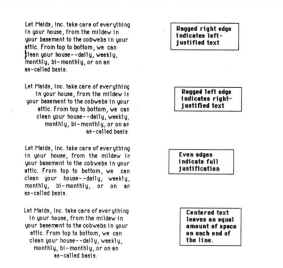

Fig. 4.13. *Examples of justification settings.*

Setting Margins and Gutters

The margins you set for your First Publisher documents depend, in part, on the capabilities of your printer. The defaults that First Publisher assigns to the Define Page settings on your system depend on the printer you specified during the installation procedure.

Figure 4.14 shows the Define Page settings for an Epson FX-286e printer.

You can modify the margin settings to meet the needs of your particular publication. Don't "cut into" the default margin settings if you're trying to pick up room, however. The margins displayed by First Publisher are the *smallest* you should use; if you decrease the amount of space allotted to the margins and then print text or graphics out into that space, the text or graphics may be cut off or distorted.

If you plan to modify the margin settings, do so by increasing the amount of space you give to margin allotment. In other words, enter a larger number in the boxes that display the margin settings. Remember to use decimal settings to indicate the margin size—that is, use 1.75 instead of 1 3/4.

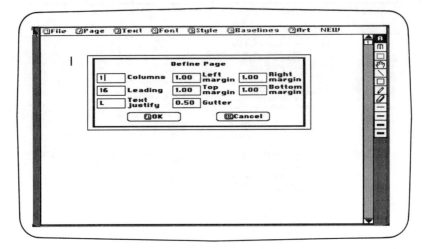

Fig. 4.14. Default Define Page settings for an Epson FX-286e.

It is easier to make room for a banner you add in graphics text by adjusting the top margin at this stage. Otherwise, you must use **Adjust below** on the Baselines menu to move the baselines down to make room for the banner. (More about baselines is explained in Chapter 7.)

Saving Files

As mentioned in Chapter 3, remember to save your work frequently as you develop a publication. You may want to save the publication at obvious steps: after you define the page, after you add text, after you edit text, after you add graphics. Other important times to save include just before you do something drastic that you may not like, which allows you to do away with the modified file and return to the one you liked better.

To save your publication, follow these steps:

1. Open the File menu by clicking File or by pressing F1.

2. Select **Save**. First Publisher then displays the Save dialog box, as shown in figure 4.15. (You can also bypass the menu selections altogether, if you prefer, by pressing Alt-S.)

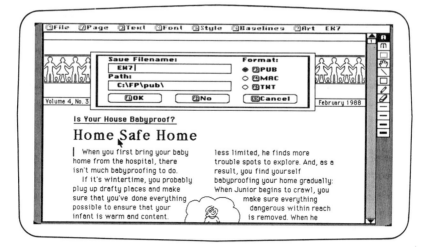

Fig. 4.15. *The Save dialog box.*

3. If you are saving a publication, make sure that the PUB file type is selected. If not, click the radio button in front of the word PUB. If you want to save the page as an art file, click the MAC radio button. If you want to save the page as a text page (First Publisher will not allow you to save the page as text if you have added a graphic element), select the TXT radio button. (If you are using the keyboard, you can press F3 to select PUB, F4 to select MAC, and F5 to select TXT.)

4. Look at the path designation. If necessary, type a new path so that the file will be saved to the correct directory.

5. Type the name you have chosen for the file. First Publisher will accept up to eight letters in a file name. You don't enter the extension; First Publisher assigns the extension for you, depending on which radio button you clicked (PUB, MAC, or TXT). For more information about choosing a file name, see ''Naming Files'' later in this chapter.

6. When you are satisfied with the name and the path designation, click OK or press F1. If you want to stop the save operation, click Cancel (or press Esc) and your current publication is displayed. If First Publisher finds another file that has been saved with the name you specified, the program will alert you to this fact and ask whether the save operation should be continued. If you choose to continue the same operation, the existing file with the name you specified will be overwritten.

Naming Files

Naming files doesn't take an astronomical amount of talent, but if you abide by a few guidelines you might avoid wondering three months from now what a file named *Goofy* contains or why you named publications after the Seven Dwarfs.

Some good, generic rules for effective file naming include the following:

Choose a name that reflects the topic. If you are doing newsletters for several departments, NEWSL.PUB isn't good enough. Suppose that one department is the Technical Research department. You could use that department's initials (TR.PUB) or use a word that will help "tag" the item in your mind, such as TECHRN.PUB. (In this case, the N would indicate a newsletter, as opposed to a flier, invoice, and so on.)

Indicate the status of the file. If you save more than one backup of a file, particularly if you're worried about needing an earlier version to return to, use some identifier to show the status of the files. For example, if you have three versions of TECHRN.PUB, you could show the order in which they were created by naming them TECHRN1.PUB, TECHRN2.PUB, and TECHRN3.PUB. You might want to keep two copies: an early edition and a revised edition. You could name those files TECHRN.PUB and TECHRNR.PUB. The "R" version could be the one modified most recently.

Include a date, if necessary. If time is an element you need to be aware of, be sure to include a date in the file name. If you have done three monthly newsletters for the Technical Research department, you need something to distinguish between the newsletters, such as TRN4-11.PUB. This file name tells you that the file is a newsletter, the *TR* tells you it's for Technical Research, and *4-11* shows the date of the newsletter.

Be careful with Oops files. If you are an impulse saver (as in "Oops, I'd better save this!"), you may be tempted to just give a file any old name. You just want to get the save operation over with and get back to what you were doing. Everyone does a fair amount of that kind of unorganized saving. But as a rule, try to organize your files so that you don't waste a lot of time and disk space. Littering your hard disk with Oops files only leaves a mess that you will have to clean up sooner or later.

First Publisher accepts any characters in a file name that DOS conventions allow. For example, the characters * and ? can be used in DOS command lines (they are called wild card characters), but they cannot be used as part of a DOS file name. First Publisher doesn't allow these characters to be used either. The characters not allowed in a First Publisher (or DOS) file name are the following:

> + = / [ ] " : ; ? * | < >

The following list shows some acceptable file names in First Publisher:

> NZOO8-28.PUB
> LOGOREV.PUB
> #122.PUB
> PUB.PUB

Deleting Files

After you have been using First Publisher for a little while, you may want to clean up your floppy disks or hard disk. You may need to delete a few Oops files or sweep away old versions of finished publications. When you want to delete a file in First Publisher, follow these steps:

1. When a publication *other than* the one you want to delete is displayed on the screen, open the File menu by clicking it or by pressing F1.

2. Choose **Delete file**. A dialog box then is displayed, showing you the names of files in the specified directory. If you don't see the file you want to delete, change the path designation.

3. Highlight the file you want to delete by clicking it or by using the arrow keys to move the highlight to the appropriate file name.

4. Click the mouse button (or press F10).

5. Click the Delete button. As shown in figure 4.16, First Publisher then displays a box telling you the file is about to be deleted. (This message gives you the option to back out of the procedure, if necessary.)

6. Click OK or press F1. The file then is deleted.

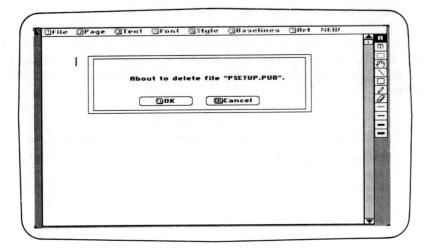

Fig. 4.16. *The Delete dialog box.*

If you are using the DeskMate version, you will notice several differences in the File menu. Instead of the Get publication option, you can choose New for new publications or Open for existing publications. You also have a Save as... option, which enables you to save a copy of the current publication under a different name. Additionally, the Run... option enables you to run other programs without exiting First Publisher.

Chapter Summary

In this chapter, you went through the design process of thinking out the publication and explored the various page definition settings available in the Define Page dialog box. This chapter also explained some basic file operations, including how to change path designations, save and name files, and delete files. Now that you have made some basic decisions about your publication, you are ready for Chapter 5, "Entering and Editing Text."

Entering and Editing Text

N ow that the design phase is out of the way, you are ready to begin creating text for your First Publisher document. In this chapter, you will explore the options on the Text menu, learn about baselines, and find out how to enter, import, and edit the text in your publication.

One major consideration needs some attention before you start creating text, however. Have you decided which fonts you want to use in your document? (The First Publisher *User's Guide* shows examples of all the fonts that are packaged with the program.) If you want to use a font shown in the users' manual that does not appear in the Font menu, you will need to use FONTMOVE to make that font available for your use. If this is the case, turn to Chapter 10 and follow the procedures for using FONTMOVE to add fonts to First Publisher. Then, once the Font menu displays the names of all fonts you want to use, you can begin adding text to your publication.

Methods of Assembling the Publication

At this point in the development of a First Publisher publication, you come to a point of decision: First Publisher can be used in more than one way.

You need to decide which method of using First Publisher seems most natural to you.

The first method, which is the general course of instruction in this book, works well on a hard disk system that allows you to save and retrieve files easily. This book leads you through the steps in the process in the following order:

1. Define page, setting columns, leading, and margins. (*Note:* This procedure was covered in Chapter 4.)

2. Create, enter/import, and edit text in publication (which is already in the correct format of columns, leading, and margins).

3. Create and add graphics to the publication (which already has formatted text in place).

4. Save the publication.

5. Print the publication.

The second method involves creating the various elements as separate files and then merging them. Because the program allows you to save three types of files (art, text, and publication files), you can save the text in a TXT file and the art in an ART or a MAC file and then later use those files in the final publication. This method seems to work best for those users who are importing or entering long blocks of text, who need to retrieve a number of graphics from various files, and who are working with a two disk drive system. The steps involved follow:

1. Enter and edit text and then save text as a TXT file.

2. Create graphics and save as an ART or a MAC file.

3. Define page for publication (set columns, leading, and margins).

4. Pull in TXT file.

5. Pull in ART file (or first clip the art from a MAC file).

6. Save the publication.

7. Print the publication.

Introduction to the Text Menu

You will use the Text menu for most of the text-manipulation tasks you perform in First Publisher. When you are working on the graphics layer of the First Publisher document, four of the five options on the Text menu are disabled; only **Get text** is available for your use. In text mode, **Cut**, **Copy**, and **Paste** are available only if you have first highlighted a text block. Table 5.1 explains the function of each of the options in the Text menu.

Table 5.1
Options on the Text Menu

Option	Description
Get text	Allows you to import text from an existing First Publisher TXT file or a file you are importing from a compatible word processing program
Save text	Lets you save a marked block to disk as a TXT file for later incorporation into a publication
Cut (Del)	Used to remove a marked text block from the document. Use **Cut** with move and delete operations
Copy (Alt-C)	Makes a copy of the highlighted text block and places the copy on the text clipboard
Paste (Alt-V)	Inserts at the cursor position the text currently on the clipboard

An Introduction to Baselines

As you may recall from Chapter 4, *baselines* are the lines on which the text is positioned. Although you will not be modifying the baselines in this chapter (that discussion fits under the heading of ''layout''), understanding why and when you will need to work with your publication's baselines is important.

What Do Baselines Look Like?

If your publication has a one-column format, the baselines resemble the lines on a sheet of notebook paper. If the publication is designed to be two columns, the baselines appear in two-column form. Figure 5.1 shows examples of the baselines in various column formats.

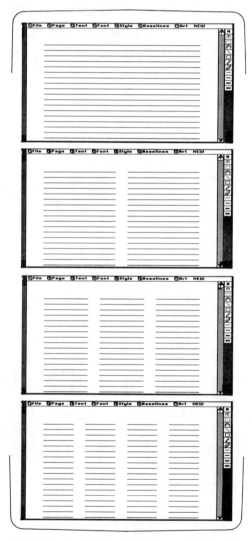

Fig. 5.1. Examples of different baseline formats.

The baselines are not visible until you select an option from the Baselines menu. These options are "toggles," meaning that you click the item once to enable it, and a check mark appears next to the item; then you click the item again to disable it. The option also is disabled if you select one of the graphics tools or make a selection from another option. Table 5.2 explains the options on the Baselines menu.

Table 5.2
Options on the Baselines Menu

Option	Description
Adjust single (Alt-A)	Allows you to shorten or lengthen a single baseline
Adjust column	Allows you to move a column of baselines up or down
Adjust above	Lets you select one baseline and move every baseline in that column above and including the selected one
Adjust below	Lets you select one baseline and move every baseline in that column below and including the selected one
Center (Alt-X)	Centers a baseline (often used to center headings in conjunction with **Adjust single**)
Left justify	Moves the selected baselines so that text will be placed starting at the left edge of each line
Right justify	Moves the selected baselines so that the text extends evenly to the right edge of each line
Full justify	Adjusts baselines so that the text extends evenly to both ends of selected baselines
Change leading	Allows you to change the amount of space between lines (applies to the option selected in the Baseline menu)
Realign text (Alt-T)	Realigns text for the whole page

Why Are Baselines Important?

Unlike some programs, First Publisher does not offer an automatic text flow feature. Instead of clicking the mouse to indicate where you want to place the text, you must manually manipulate the baselines so that your text flows onto them correctly. Once you get used to manipulating the flow of text in this way, you will like the added control you have over the placement of the text.

Suppose, for example, that you are working with a two-column publication and the text you have entered fills both columns. You want to add a box that lists upcoming events for your organization to the bottom right corner of the page (see fig. 5.2). You have created this box as a graphic item, using First Publisher's box and graphics text tools. How will you move the text on the newsletter so that you can fit in the boxed information?

Fig. 5.2. A two-column newsletter and an Upcoming Events box.

Because the Upcoming Events box is a graphic, it resides on the graphics layer. The text you have entered for the newsletter article is on the text layer. First Publisher allows you to position the box right over the text, but the program doesn't "know" that the text needs to be reformatted (see fig. 5.3).

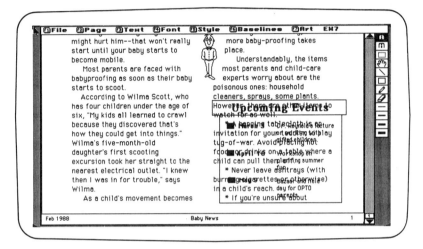

Fig. 5.3. *The newsletter with the graphics item pasted in.*

As you can see in figure 5.3, the bottom corner of the newsletter is a mess. First Publisher allowed you to paste the graphic onto the newsletter, but the text shows underneath. To solve this problem, you can modify the baselines so that First Publisher does not flow text through the area covered by the box or you can use the program's **Picturewrap** feature. (*Note:* The step-by-step procedures for modifying baselines are provided in Chapter 7. This discussion is meant only to give you an overview of the ways in which you may need to modify the baselines of your publications. **Picturewrap** is discussed in Chapter 7, as well.)

To stop the text from flowing into the area, you use the **Adjust below** command to "zero out" the unwanted baselines. (*Note:* Before you use **Adjust below**, you need to make sure that you *do* want to change the baselines of all lines below that point in the column you have selected.) After the specified baselines are canceled out, the baselines look like the ones shown in figure 5.4.

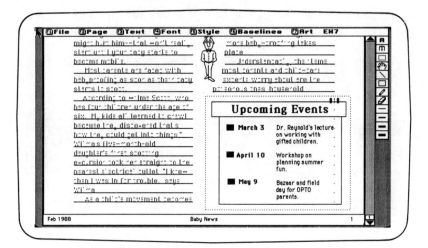

Fig. 5.4. *The baselines of the modified publication.*

Now the text stops before flowing into the Upcoming Events box because baselines no longer exist for the text (see fig. 5.5).

When Will You Work with Baselines?

As the preceding section explains, you use baselines whenever you deal with the text layer of a First Publisher publication. Baselines are not used for text that you enter by using the graphics text tool; that type of text is known as *graphics text*, and First Publisher treats graphics text as if it were any other type of graphic element, like a box, a line, or a piece of clip art.

A few examples of situations in which you might modify baselines include the following:

❑ When you want to run text next to a graphic (closer than the automatic **Picturewrap** feature will go)

❑ When you want to change the leading or justification of a headline

❑ When you want make one article a different width than the rest of the column

❑ When you want to customize the placement of text by lengthening or shortening lines

❑ When you are organizing text flow

Fig. 5.5. The publication after the baselines have been modified.

For more information on the procedures for modifying, canceling, and moving baselines, see Chapter 7.

A Look Back at Page Definition

Chapter 4 introduced the concept of page definition. As you may recall, you use the **Define page** option in the Page menu to define the number of columns, the amount of leading, and the margins for the publication. When you begin each First Publisher session, the **Define page** settings are set to the default one-column specifications. (If you load an existing publication by choosing **Get publication** from the File menu, however, the **Define page** settings assigned to that publication are the current specifications.)

The example used in this chapter and in the chapters that follow assumes that you have set the **Define page** settings to look like the settings in figure 5.6.

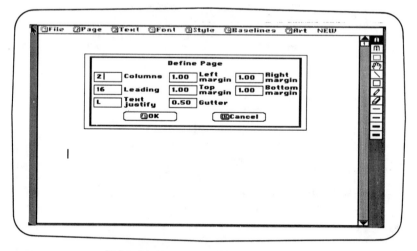

Fig. 5.6. *The **Define page** setting for the example.*

As you can see from figure 5.6, none of the settings on the Define Page dialog box—except the column setting—were modified.

The newsletter used in this example, *DT Publisher*, will be a simple two-column design. The newsletter will be aimed at readers who are new to desktop publishing and are building up their library of information on various products and peripheral devices. For the remainder of this chapter, you will work on page 1 of *DT Publisher*.

Entering Text

As you may already know, First Publisher offers you two methods of putting text into your publication: entering (typing) or importing. This section explains both methods.

> Remember that when you start a new publication by selecting **Start over**, if you were previously working on a different publication, First Publisher keeps the Define page settings for the previous document. If you were working on a three-column publication and now want to begin working on a two-column publication, for example, you need to select **Define page** from the Page menu and specify the settings you want. If you just select **Start over**, First Publisher sets up another three-column design. You also need to set the Define page settings when you begin a publication after starting First Publisher. For more information on using the **Define page** option, see Chapter 4.

Entering Text

Typing text in First Publisher is like typing text in a word processing program, although First Publisher may be a bit slower (depending on how fast a typist you are) and the format of the screen is different. This section explains how to type text directly in First Publisher.

Determining the Specified Font

You can specify the font for the text before you begin entering the text or after you enter it. The default font setting for body text is 12-point Geneva normal. In a later section of this chapter, you will learn to change the font, size, and style of text that has already been entered. For now, check to see what font and style is active in your First Publisher document by following these steps:

1. Pull down the Font menu by clicking the menu name or by pressing F3. The item with the check mark is the current font.

2. Open the Style menu by clicking the menu name or by pressing F4. The selected style (bold, italic, or normal) and size are indicated by check marks.

You also can check the current font and style selected by choosing **Status** from the File menu. If you are using the keyboard, do this by pressing F1 and using the ↓ key to highlight **Status**; then press Enter.

Positioning the Cursor

As you know, First Publisher shows two cursors on the screen. The mouse cursor is the cursor that moves when you move the mouse; the bar cursor is the cursor that marks the position on-screen where text will be inserted when you begin to type. (Of course, if you haven't installed a mouse, the mouse cursor will not appear on your screen.)

When you start a new document, the cursor starts out where any good cursor should: at the leftmost edge of the top left baseline (see fig. 5.7). Note, however, that at this point the baselines are not displayed on the screen. If you don't want to start on that line, press Enter until the cursor moves down the page to the position you want. If, after moving the cursor down, you change your mind and want to move the cursor back up, you can press Del or the Backspace key until the cursor is positioned correctly. (Remember that unless one of the options in the Baselines menu is enabled, the baselines are not visible on the screen.)

If you are working with a publication you created earlier, you can move the bar cursor to whatever position you want either by positioning the mouse cursor at that point and clicking the mouse button or by using the arrow keys on your keyboard to move the cursor. If you are using the keyboard method and you need to access a part of the publication that is located down the page, use Alt-End to move down the page and then use the arrow keys to get to the exact spot. Later in this chapter, in the section "Moving around the Screen," you will learn about the various keys and options for moving the cursors on the screen.

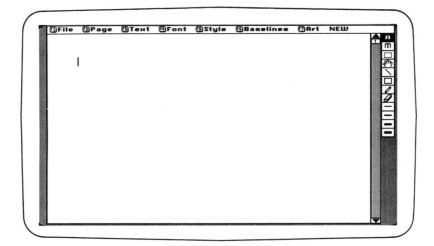

Fig. 5.7. *The cursor position on a new publication.*

Typing the Text

Now that you have specified the font and positioned the cursor, all you need to do is type the text.

As you type, you will notice that the text wraps automatically when you reach the end of the line; you don't need to press Enter to make the cursor go to the next line—the program "senses" the end of the line and wraps the text to the next line. Some programs automatically hyphenate words whenever possible, but First Publisher instead moves the whole word down to the next line. This looks cleaner and causes less awkwardness for the reader.

> Only press Enter when you come to the end of a paragraph. If you press Enter at other times as you're entering text, when the text rewraps, the Enter keystroke will cause a paragraph break where you might not want it.

Press Enter to mark the end of a paragraph, and the cursor moves to the next line. If you want to leave a blank line between paragraphs, press Enter twice when you are ending a paragraph.

If the document you are typing has headings, you can either type the headings in at this stage or paste them in as graphics later. If you plan to include them here, on the text layer, press Enter twice at the end of the last paragraph before the heading (pressing Enter ends the paragraph and leaves a blank line). Then type the heading. Press Enter twice again. You then have the heading on one line with a blank line before and after. Later, you can go back and change the font so that the heading stands out. If you want, you also can modify the baseline on which the heading is positioned so that the heading is centered over the text.

Whatever justification setting you decided on in the Define Page dialog box is in effect now. If you chose left-justified text, the text you type should be lined up along the left edge with a ragged right edge. (*Note:* The word *ragged* indicates that the lines break at the end of a word and that spaces have not been added to make the right edges line up.)

> You choose the alignment for the text by using **Define page** from the Page menu. This option allows you to determine whether the text will be left-justified, right-justified, centered, or full-justified. (For more information on **Define Page**, see Chapter 4.)

If you type quickly, your fingers probably will get ahead of First Publisher. When you get ahead of the program, First Publisher beeps at you, signaling that it is having trouble keeping up with your typing. If the program beeps, stop for a minute and wait until everything you have typed is displayed on the screen. If you want to add paragraph indents to the beginning of each paragraph, press the space bar five times to add five extra spaces before you begin typing a new paragraph.

Figure 5.8 shows the article typed into *DT Publisher*. You don't need to type in the example shown here; this is just for illustration purposes.

Adding Text to the Middle of a Publication

If you are adding text to an existing publication, you will find that adding a sentence in the middle of a document can be an excruciatingly slow process. This slowness is caused by First Publisher's "realign" feature, in which the program realigns all the text on the page whenever text is modified. If you have two full-page columns of text and you modify a sentence in the upper left corner of the page, for example, First Publisher realigns the text *after you add each word*, which causes a great deal of realigning, especially if you are adding 10 or 15 words.

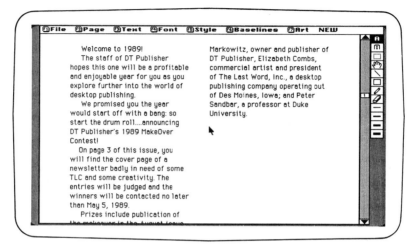

Fig. 5.8. The first DT Publisher *article*.

To get around this problem, position the cursor at the point you want to insert text and then press Ins. All the text beyond the cursor position will disappear, allowing you to enter the text more quickly and allowing First Publisher to skip all that realignment stuff (see fig. 5.9). When you have entered the necessary text, press Ins again and the program returns the text it had hidden (see fig. 5.10). First Publisher automatically realigns the text as it is returned.

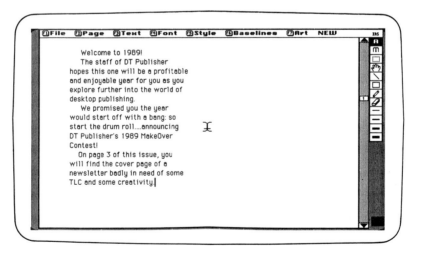

Fig. 5.9. After pressing Ins, text beyond cursor position disappears.

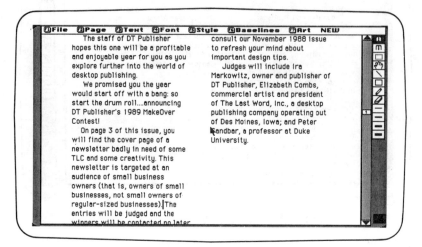

Fig. 5.10. *The publication after Ins was pressed again.*

If you have a large section of text to enter, you also can enter it in a separate text file (by using a word processor or First Publisher) and then import the section at the appropriate point in the publication.

Saving Text

Remember to save your files every 15 or 20 minutes. Typing 1,000 words of an article and then having a power surge that causes your computer to lock up can be an exasperating experience. Granted, this situation will not occur often, but when it does, you will wish you hadn't taken the chance by not saving more often.

The way in which you save the text in a First Publisher publication depends on the method you are using to assemble the project. If you are creating the publication as you go—doing the text entry and the layout at the same time, as in the example in this book—you need to save the file with a PUB extension. If you are working on the file as a text file that later will be incorporated into a publication, as explained in the First Publisher *User's Guide*, you will be saving the file as a TXT file. Figure 5.11 shows the PUB, TXT, and MAC radio buttons. (The MAC button is used when you are saving the file as a graphics file. This procedure is discussed in Chapter 6.)

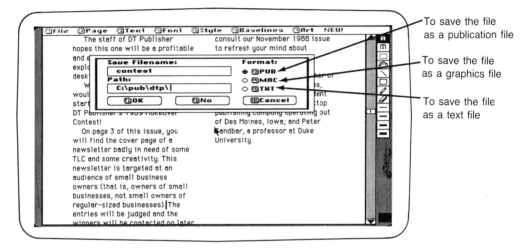

To save the file as a publication file

To save the file as a graphics file

To save the file as a text file

Fig. 5.11. *The PUB, MAC, and TXT radio buttons.*

To save the file to a PUB file by using the menu selections, follow this procedure:

1. Open the File menu by pressing F1 or by clicking the menu name in the menu bar.

2. Highlight the **Save** option by moving the mouse cursor to that point or by using the arrow keys.

3. Select the option by clicking the mouse button (or by pressing Enter). The program then displays the Save dialog box.

4. Enter the name and path of the file you want to save. Make sure that the PUB radio button is checked. Doing so causes First Publisher to add the PUB extension automatically; if you try to type the separator period (.), the program will beep at you.

5. Click the OK button (or press F1), and First Publisher saves the file.

You also can save the file as a text file by following Steps 1 through 3 and then selecting the TXT radio button in Step 4.

> As a shortcut, you can save PUB, TXT, and MAC files in First
> Publisher by using Alt-S. This is a quick way to display the Save
> dialog box and bypass the menu selections necessary to save files.

If you are saving the file as a TXT file by using the **Save text** option,
follow these steps:

1. If you want to save only a portion of the text in the document,
   highlight the text you want to save. If you don't highlight a specific section, all text in the document gets saved.

2. Click the Text menu by pressing F3 or by clicking the menu name
   in the menu bar.

3. Highlight the **Save text** option by moving the mouse cursor to that
   point or by using the arrow keys.

4. Select the option by clicking the mouse button (or by pressing
   F1). The program then displays the Save dialog box.

5. Enter the name you want to use for the file. First Publisher will
   add the TXT extension for you.

6. Check the path designation and modify it if necessary. Then click
   the OK button (or press F1), and First Publisher saves the item as
   a text file.

> If you use the **Save** option in the File menu, you have the option of
> saving the file as a publication, a graphics file, or a text file. Sim-
> ply click the appropriate radio button (PUB, TXT, or MAC). First
> Publisher then will know to attach the correct extension to the file.

Importing Text

With First Publisher, you also have the option of using text that you have
created with other word processing programs. First Publisher can use text
files you create in any of the programs or formats listed in table 5.3.

Table 5.3
Text Files Recognized by First Publisher

ASCII
DCA
Microsoft Word (Version 3)
MultiMate
PFS: First Choice
PFS: WRITE
PFS: Professional Write (Versions 1.0 and 2.0)
Wang PC
WordPerfect (Versions 3, 4.1, and 4.2)
WordStar

> If you don't know which version of the word processing software you have, consult the program's documentation or look for the version number on the opening screen of the program.

If you use a word processor other than the ones listed here, you still can import those files into First Publisher by first saving the file in ASCII format. Consult your word processor's documentation to find out how to save in ASCII format.

If you are accustomed to using a word processor, you already know its advantages: faster typing, flexibility in correcting errors, and automatic formatting. A wide range of features make word processing headache-free when compared with using a typewriter.

First Publisher has additional advantages when you use imported text. When you import a document you have created in a word processor, the obvious benefit is that you save the time required to type the text into the publication. Your word processor probably accepts typing much more quickly than does First Publisher. You also have the option of controlling some of the formatting like bold, italic, or paragraph indents (although the formats that translate will depend on your word processor). First Publisher also has special commands called *FONT* commands that allow you to tell First Publisher what font you want to use while you are still importing the text. (These commands are explained later in this section.)

Here are a few tips to remember when you are preparing to import text:

❑ If you plan to import text for an entire newsletter that consists of several articles, save each article in a file by itself and then import the articles one at a time.

❑ Insert an extra line before and after the headlines in the text file so that the headlines are not run in with the imported text.

❑ Insert First Publisher's *FONT* commands in your word processing document to have the program automatically assign the correct font styles and sizes to the indicated text. (More information about *FONT* commands is included later in this chapter.)

❑ Make sure that the Font menu displays all the fonts you need before you import the text. (If you need to add fonts, read the FONTMOVE procedures in Chapter 10.)

❑ If your word processor has the capability of displaying the formatting codes used, such as hard carriage returns, delete those codes before you import the file. This saves you quite a bit of work in First Publisher, because once the file is imported, you will not be able to see the hard carriage returns or soft hyphens, for example.

To import text into a First Publisher publication, follow these steps:

1. Open the First Publisher file into which you want to import the text. In this case, it is DTP.PUB, the publication file for *DT Publisher*. (You may be working on a TXT file instead.) Also, make sure that you have selected the font style and size you want to use when the file is imported, because if you don't, the incoming text will take on the font you have most recently used or the default font.

2. Position the cursor at the point you want the text to be inserted (see fig. 5.12).

3. Select **Get text** from the Text menu. The Get dialog box then is displayed.

4. Highlight the name of the file you want to import. Be sure to enter the correct path designation.

5. Click the Get button (or press F1) when you have highlighted the correct file. Figure 5.13 shows the completed Get dialog box.

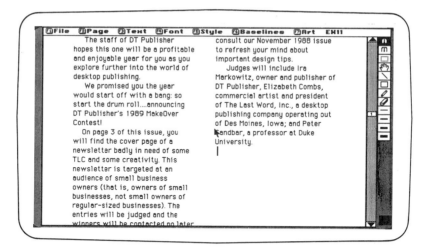

Fig. 5.12. Positioning the cursor where you want to insert the text.

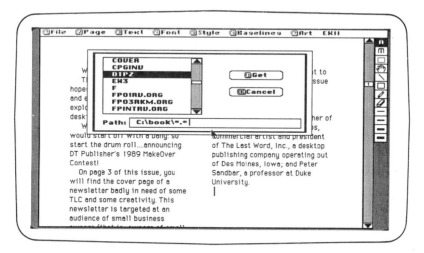

Fig. 5.13. The Get dialog box for importing text.

Some people may think they need to copy the word processing file to the PUB directory where they store their First Publisher publications, but this procedure is not necessary. You can specify a different path in the Path box of the Get dialog box, such as

c:\ws4\tech\trn2-89.txt

This path designation causes First Publisher to look in the Technical Research (TECH) subdirectory of the WordStar 4 (WS4) directory for the text file for the February 1989 newsletter.

After you select the file and the path, a dialog box is displayed that asks from what program or format you are importing (see fig. 5.14). Select the correct format and click OK (or press F1).

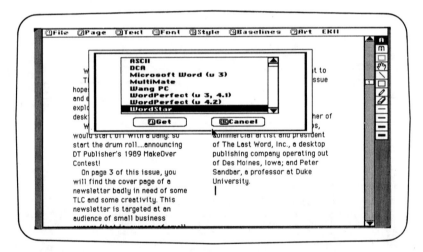

Fig. 5.14. *Selecting the text format.*

If you are unsure of the version of your word processing program, you have three options: start the word processing program and look for the version number on the opening screen, check the program's documentation for the version number, or select the format you think may be the one you need and see what First Publisher does with the file. (If you get an error message, try a different format.)

The cursor then changes to the shape of a clock, indicating that you need to wait while the program reads the file. Another message box then is displayed and tells you that the file is being converted to a file format First Publisher understands (see fig. 5.15).

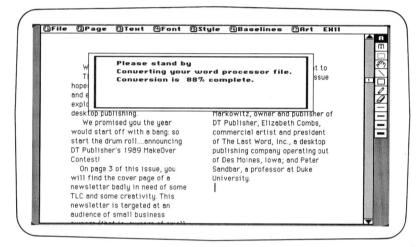

Fig. 5.15. The conversion message box.

The text then is placed on the screen, in the format you specified with **Define page** in the Page menu.

Tabular Material in Imported Text

If you are importing columnar material, such as a table of information within the body text, expect to lose the exact format of the columns when you import the text into First Publisher. The program may keep the table in generally the same format, but the spacing will be different. This spacing difference occurs because First Publisher's columns are not based on a tab concept like word processing and spreadsheet columns.

To save yourself the time of adjusting the spacing First Publisher uses when importing tabular material, you may find it helpful to pull the text in the table flush left, against the left margin. Then, after the file is in First Publisher, you can correct the spacing by positioning the cursor and adding spaces (see fig. 5.16).

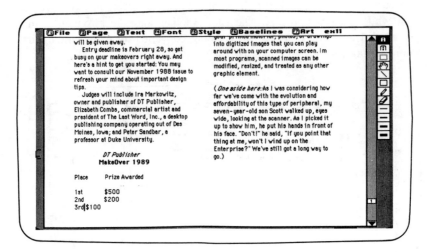

Fig. 5.16. *Fixing a table imported into First Publisher.*

Additionally, if you already have a table in a word processing file that you would like to use in a First Publisher document, you do have a few options for importing the table without losing the format. You can use the method described in the preceding paragraph, or you can do one of the following: use SNAPSHOT and SNAP2ART to take and develop a picture of the table and then import the file as a graphic; import the table as text, save it as a MAC file, and then manipulate the columns as art images; or in the word processing file, format the columns so that they are all in one column against the left edge of the screen; then after you import the file as text, divide the long column into the appropriate columns. (This last option would not work well for a multicolumn, complicated table, however.)

Importing ASCII Text

As you may know, ASCII (American Standard Code for Information Interchange) refers to the method your computer uses to translate binary ones and zeros (which is how the computer "sees" data) into the characters and special symbols you type and see on the screen. ASCII format is supported by most word processing programs; consult your individual word processing program to see whether it supports output to an ASCII file.

Depending on the way you have entered the data in the ASCII file, the format of the file in First Publisher may not be what you expected. Table

5.4 shows how First Publisher reads the carriage return codes (which are inserted each time you press the Enter key).

Table 5.4
First Publisher and Carriage Return Codes

In Your Word Processing File:	In First Publisher:
Where you pressed Enter once	The Enter keystroke was treated as a space and the next line begins next to it.
Where you pressed Enter twice	The paragraph was ended and a blank line was inserted.
Where you pressed Enter once and added a space	The paragraph was ended and added a space and no blank line was inserted.

The procedure for importing an ASCII file is identical to that for importing any word processing file. When you are asked which format or program you are importing from, click ASCII and then click the Get button (or press F1).

First Publisher also has the capability of exporting ASCII files. This means that you can import the text from a word processing program, modify it, save it as a TXT file, and export it back to your word processor as an ASCII file.

Using the *FONT* Commands

First Publisher also offers a feature that allows you to set the font you want for headings and other text *before* you import the file. These commands are called *FONT* commands, and they look like this:

*FONT HELVETICA 18 BOLD*What's Next?

This line tells First Publisher to turn the text following the second asterisk (*) into Helvetica 18-point boldface type. If you do not accompany that line with another line that turns the special font off, the remainder of the text in the document will appear in 18-point Helvetica bold.

You can use *FONT* commands whenever you want to change the font in the document. You could even specify all the fonts you want to use in the document before you import the file, if you want, as long as the fonts you specify can be found in First Publisher's MASTER.FNT file. If you want the body text of the document to appear in Geneva 10-point normal type, for example, you could specify a *FONT* command to carry out those instructions. Then, when you want to add a heading, say, three paragraphs into the document, you could insert another *FONT* command to make the heading Helvetica 18-point bold. You then need to change the body text back to Geneva 10-point normal, so a third *FONT* command could make that change.

Figure 5.17 shows how a WordStar file looks with *FONT* commands embedded. Figure 5.18 shows the First Publisher screen after the file was imported.

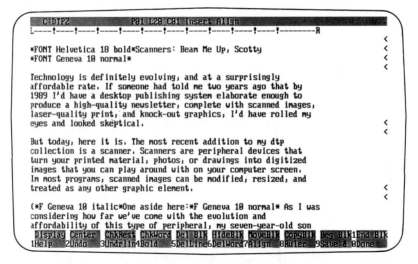

Fig. 5.17. *A WordStar file with *FONT* commands.*

In figure 5.17, the first *FONT* command tells First Publisher to make the body text Geneva 10-point normal; the second makes the heading Helvetica 18-point bold; then the third *FONT* command returns the text to Geneva 10-point normal.

Here are some rules for using First Publisher's *FONT* commands:

❏ Remember to check your MASTER.FNT file to make sure that the fonts you specify in the *FONT* command lines are available.

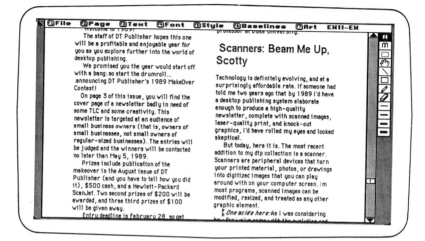

Fig. 5.18. The First Publisher screen after the WordStar file was imported.

❏ If you want only to change the font of a single item or heading and then return to the previous font, remember to use a *pair* of *FONT* commands: one to change the font to the new setting, and one to change the new setting back to the previous font.

❏ Don't include the word *point* after the numeric point size. If you type *FONT Geneva 16 point italic*Hi There!*, for example, First Publisher will tell you that it cannot find "16 point point" type.

❏ Always include both asterisks—one before the word *FONT* and one after the style (bold, italic, or normal).

❏ Don't add spaces after the second asterisk unless you want those spaces to appear on the publication.

❏ Instead of typing *FONT* every time, you can shorten the command to *F* or some other derivative; but don't forget the asterisks.

❏ You can indicate boldface or italic by typing *b* or *i*.

❏ Use *FONT* commands when you are entering a large amount of type in various sizes and styles or when you are unsure of the exact font you want to use.

Working with Overflowed Text

At times, you may have difficulty judging how much text you have in a word processing document and how that text will transfer to First Publisher pages. Because how much text you can fit on one page depends on the font you have chosen and how many graphics you plan to use, you may find that your article takes up much more room than you had anticipated. First Publisher accepts a maximum of 5,000 characters on each page.

Foreseeing this situation, First Publisher developers built into the program an "overflow" feature that can be a real lifesaver. Few things are as disheartening as squeezing a few final lines on the document, only to discover that part of the text is missing. Where did it go? Do you have to type it again? No, First Publisher is preserving it—safely—in an area known as the *overflow area*. This area, like First Publisher's clipboards—is an unseen area, but rest assured that your text hasn't been beamed up into the ozone somewhere.

When you import a long file, First Publisher flows the text automatically to subsequent pages. When you go back and type additional text into the publication, however, some of the text might get "bumped" off the page. For example, suppose that in the *DT Publisher* example, a paragraph was added in the middle of the publication after the rest of the text had been imported. Because the last bit of text couldn't fit on the page, First Publisher placed the text in the overflow area.

To make sure that First Publisher did put the text in the overflow area, select **Status** from the File menu or press Alt-I. First Publisher then displays a message box showing you the number of characters that are being stored in the overflow area for page 1 (see fig. 5.19). You cannot see the actual text; only the number of characters are displayed. To remove the message box, click anywhere on the publication outside the box or press Esc.

Now that you know text is in the overflow area, what do you do with it? You can either leave the text there (it will stay attached to the page but will not be printed), edit the text on the page so that the overflow text will fit (although in this case, this option is not realistic), or move the overflowed text to the next page.

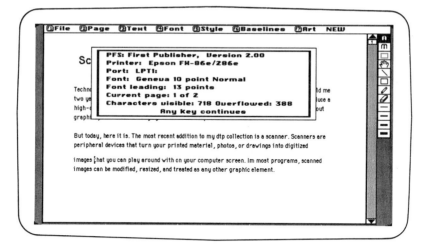

Fig. 5.19. *The last paragraph of the second article didn't fit on page 1.*

Putting Overflowed Text on Another Page

In this instance, because the publication will be several pages long, the best solution is to move the text from the overflow area to another page. Before you can move the text to another page, you must create the page. Although the procedure for adding pages is covered in more detail later in this chapter, it is covered briefly here, with an added "overflow" twist:

1. Pull down the Page menu by clicking the name or by pressing F2.

2. Select **Jump to page**. A dialog box is then displayed asking for the page you want to jump to (see fig. 5.20).

3. Type *2* and click the OK button (or press F1). A second dialog box is displayed, alerting you to the overflowed text and asking how you want to resolve it (see fig. 5.21).

4. Click the button next to the phrase **Move text into clipboard** (or press F3). This command moves the text to the clipboard so that you can paste the text onto the new page.

5. Click the OK button (or press F1) to move to page 2.

6. Position the cursor and choose **Paste** from the Text menu (or press Alt-V). The program then inserts the overflowed text on page 2.

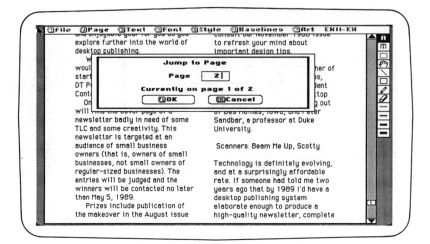

Fig. 5.20. *The Jump to Page dialog box.*

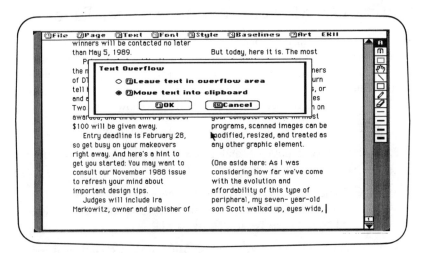

Fig. 5.21. *The dialog box for overflowed text.*

Changing Font Size To Eliminate Overflowed Text

Another solution to the problem of overflow text is to reduce the size of the type in the document. If you are using 12-point type, this type size reduction is a possibility. But if you try reducing the size of any type smaller than 10-point, you may wind up packaging a magnifying glass with every newsletter you send out.

Suppose that you used 12-point Geneva normal type and placed the extra text onto page 2. The procedure that follows shows you how to reduce that type to 10-point type:

1. Highlight the entire page either by positioning the cursor and dragging the mouse down and to the right or by pressing F10 once at the beginning of the text and scrolling to the end of the text by pressing PgDn and pressing F10 again (see fig. 5.22). You also can get to the end of the page quickly by pressing Alt-End.

2. Select **10 Points** from the Style menu. When you release the mouse button (or press Enter), the text is changed to 10-point size (see fig. 5.23).

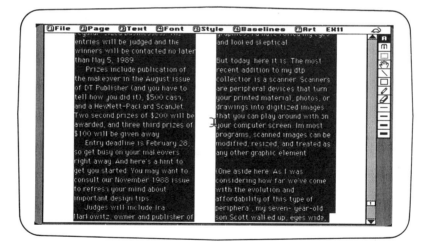

Fig. 5.22. The entire first page highlighted.

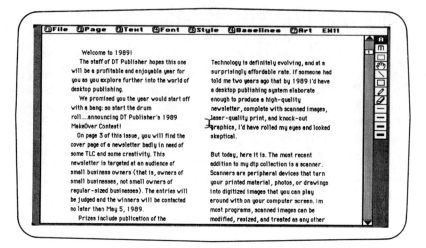

Fig. 5.23. The type reduced to 10 points.

Modifying Leading

The result looks better, but the page still needs some work. Notice the amount of white space—or leading—between the lines. This leading amount is still set for 12-point type. Two methods are available for modifying the amount of leading between lines:

❏ You can use **Define page** to change the leading, but when you select that option from the File menu, any baseline modifications you have made up to that point are lost.

❏ You can use the **Change leading** option in the Baselines menu, and the baseline modifications remain intact. (However, if you originally used **Adjust column** to move the baselines down to make room for the banner, the baselines move back up into the banner after you use the **Change leading** option. Other baseline modifications are not affected.)

To use **Define page** to modify the amount of leading, following these steps:

1. Open the Page menu.

2. Select **Define page**.

3. Change the setting in the Leading box to **13**.

4. Click the OK button or press F1.

After you click OK, the publication is reformatted with 13-point leading.

To use the **Change leading** option in the Baselines menu to change the amount of leading, follow these steps:

1. Open the Baselines menu.

2. Select **Adjust column**.

3. Click on any baseline in the left column. Three black handles will appear on the baseline.

4. Open the Baselines menu again and select **Change leading**.

5. Type *13* in the Leading box.

6. Click OK or press F1. The leading change is then made.

As figure 5.24 shows, this reformatting saves you quite a bit of space and looks much better.

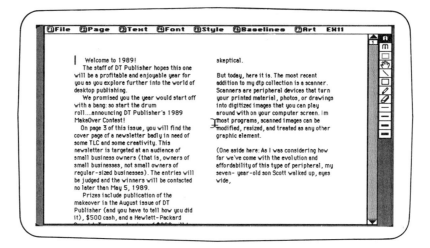

Fig. 5.24. The publication with adjusted leading.

As you can see, you now have room for the overflow text in the lower right column of the publication. But First Publisher doesn't just automatically pull in the text from the second page; you need to pull it over manually.

First, go to the second page by selecting **Jump to page** from the Page menu. Next, highlight the text and select **Cut** from the Text menu (see fig. 5.25). Finally, return to page 1 by using the **Jump to page** command again and paste the text in the correct location by positioning the cursor and selecting **Paste** from the Text menu (see fig. 5.26).

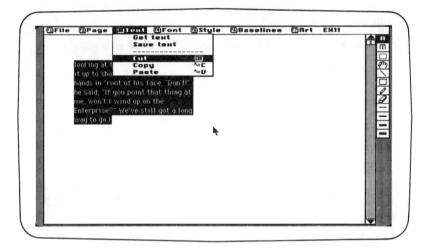

Fig. 5.25. Cutting the text from page 2.

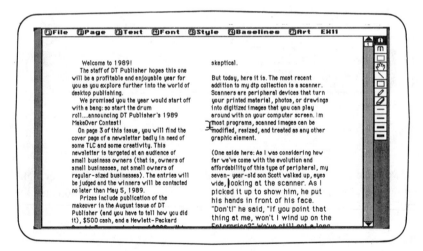

Fig. 5.26. Pasting the text into the available space on page 1.

Now you know how to get text into First Publisher—whether you type it yourself or import it from a word processing file. You have also learned what to do with overflows and special format problems. In the next section, you will learn to edit what you have entered.

Editing Text

Few people type everything accurately 100 percent of the time. In fact, many people back up and correct every fourth or fifth word: which can be really discouraging when you're faced with a 10,000-word document. Thankfully, First Publisher has the capacity to allow for correcting mistakes. In this section, you will learn how to maneuver around the page and how to select, add, move, copy, and erase text.

Moving around the Page

If you have been dabbling with First Publisher up to this point, you have no doubt discovered ways to move the cursor around the page. When you begin editing and fine-tuning your text, it becomes even more important that you be able to get quickly to the parts of the document you need.

When you are working on the text layer of a First Publisher document, you have a set of keys available that do not have the same function on the graphics layer.

As you learned in Chapter 3, you can use the keyboard to work with First Publisher, you can use the mouse, or you can use a combination of the two. Most people use the keyboard for operations that require a quick keystroke or two and use the mouse (if one is available) for operations that would take longer from the keyboard—such as working with graphic items, moving the cursor, and selecting options—or that would not be possible at all, such as drawing curves freehand.

Chapter 3 also explained the elevator bar and how you can move through the document by clicking the bar relative to the part of the publication you want to display. You also can click the arrows located at either end of the elevator bar, although this method is slower than the others.

Table 5.5 shows the various keys you can use to get around in a First Publisher publication.

Table 5.5
First Publisher Editing and Cursor-Movement Keys

Keystroke	Moves the cursor to the position
Home	Beginning of the current line
Ctrl-Home	Beginning of the page
PgUp	Up one screen
Ctrl-PgUp	Up a fraction of one screen
PgDn	Down one screen
Ctrl-PgDn	Down a fraction of one screen
End	End of the current line
Ctrl-End	End of the text on the page
↑	Up one line
↓	Down one line
←	Left one character
Ctrl ←	Next word to the left
→	Right one character
Ctrl →	Next word to the right
Ctrl-N	Next column
Ctrl-P	Previous column
Shift +	Next page
Shift -	Previous page

Selecting Text

The next step in editing First Publisher text involves learning how to select text. *Selected* text is the text that is highlighted on the screen. Figure 5.27 shows a section of selected text.

You need to select text for many operations: when you need to move, copy, or delete text, you need to be able to tell First Publisher what text you want to manipulate.

To select text by using a mouse, follow these steps:

1. Position the mouse cursor at the start of the text you want to select.

2. Press the mouse button to move the bar cursor to that point.

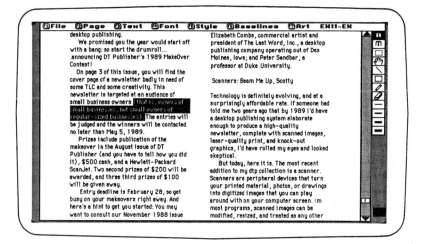

Fig. 5.27. Selected text.

3. Press the mouse button and drag the mouse to the end of the text you want to select. The text then is highlighted, appearing as white text in a black (or gray) block. Remember that you can use the cursor-movement keys shown in table 5.5 to maneuver around the screen.

4. Release the mouse button.

The text is now selected, ready for you to use in whatever operations are necessary.

If you are using the keyboard instead of a mouse, highlight text by following these steps:

1. Press F10 once to anchor the highlight.

2. Use the arrow keys to move the cursor to the end of the text you want to highlight. Remember to use the cursor-movement keys if they will help you get to your destination more easily.

3. Press F10 again to indicate the end of the selected text.

Correcting Misspellings

Correcting errors in your publication requires another ultra-minor surgery. When you identify an error in spelling, punctuation, or whatever—few persons write text an editor would love—you simply need to position the cursor and use the Backspace key to delete the character(s). For example, if you have entered the text

Mary had a little lamb. Its fleece was white as snow.
And everywhere that Mary went, that lamb was sure to gop.

All you need to do is position the cursor between the letter *p* and the period (.) and press the Backspace key. Another method of getting rid of that pesky *p* is by positioning the cursor immediately in front of the letter and pressing Del. You also could highlight the item you don't want and then press Del.

Copying Text

At times, you will want to copy sections of text. Perhaps you have included a lead for an article on page 1 of your newsletter, but now you're considering moving the lead to page 3. You can copy the lead to that point just to see how it looks; then, if you change your mind, you can delete that paragraph and still have the original intact on page 1. To copy a block of text, you simply do the following:

1. Select the text to be copied.

2. Open the Text menu by clicking the menu name or by pressing F3.

3. Select **Copy** or press Alt-C.

The text you selected then is copied to the text clipboard. Remember that you can copy only one item to the clipboard at a time; any text you had stored on the clipboard previously is now erased.

> Remember that First Publisher has two clipboards: one for text and one for graphics. Each clipboard can store only one item at a time.

Pasting Text

After copying text, the next step is pasting it. The paste operation is actually the opposite of the copy or the move operation. In those operations, you take text and place it on the text clipboard; in the paste operation, you take text from the clipboard and place it in the publication. To paste an item from the text clipboard, follow these steps:

1. Position the cursor at the point you want the pasted text to be inserted.

2. Open the Text menu by clicking the menu name or by pressing F3.

3. Select **Paste** or press Alt-V.

The text item in the clipboard is now pasted at the cursor position. (*Note:* If the **Paste** option on the Text menu is gray, no text is on the clipboard.)

After the paste operation, the text clipboard is not "empty." That particular text item remains on the text clipboard until it is replaced by another item or until you exit First Publisher.

Moving Text

Moving text is only slightly different from copying text. Copying, of course, *copies* the selected text to the clipboard, leaving the original text intact on the publication. Moving, on the other hand, *removes* the original from its place on the document and places the item on the text clipboard. Although First Publisher has no actual "move" command, you can combine **Cut** and **Paste** to get the same effect:

1. Select the text to be moved.

2. Open the Text menu by clicking the menu name or by pressing F3.

3. Select **Cut** or press Del.

4. Position the cursor in the place to which you want to move the text.

5. Select **Paste** from the Text menu or press Alt-V.

The item then is copied to the indicated position, and all text following that position is reformatted. After the **Cut** operation, the text is realigned to fill the gap left by the movement of the text.

Erasing Text

When you want to erase text, follow these steps:

1. Select the text you want to erase.

2. Open the Text menu by clicking the menu name or by pressing F3.

3. Select **Cut** or press Del.

> Every time you **Cut** something from a First Publisher document, the program actually removes it only as far as the text clipboard. If you want to recall it, you can use the **Paste** option. Otherwise, the item will be erased when the next item is copied to the text clipboard or when you exit First Publisher.

Working with Pages

The last section in this chapter deals with the topics of adding and deleting pages. First Publisher makes it easy for you to manipulate the pages of your publication as you work.

One thing is a bit surprising about using the "pages" commands; from their names, you may not be able to tell what they do. For example, you would expect **Jump to page** only to take you to a page that's already been created, when, in fact, it can create pages as well. You would think you would use the **Insert page** command to add a page to the end of the publication, but the command actually inserts a page *before* the current one. Table 5.6 lists the "page" commands and their functions.

Table 5.6
First Publisher's "Page" Commands

Command	Function
Jump to page	Adds a page if it has not been created and takes you to the new page
Insert page	Adds a page *before* the current one
Delete page	Deletes the page you specify

Adding Pages

When you begin creating your publication, you may not know how many pages it will require. When you import large text files, First Publisher creates the pages automatically. You also can specify the number of pages you want when you set the **Define page** settings, or you can add to or delete pages at any time. Remember that the **Define page** settings you specify for the first page also apply to all subsequent pages, unless you modify those settings.

To add one or more pages to your First Publisher document, follow these steps:

1. If you haven't saved the file recently, save it now.

2. Open the Page menu by clicking the menu name or by pressing F2.

3. Select **Jump to page** or press Alt-J. A dialog box is displayed, asking for the page number you want to reach and telling you which page is now displayed.

4. Type *2* and click the OK button. Page 2 of the publication then is displayed. Notice that the number in the elevator box is now 2 (see fig. 5.28).

> You may want to check the status of the file to see whether you have any text stored in the overflow area that should be pasted on the new page. To check the status, select **Status** from the File menu or press Alt-I.

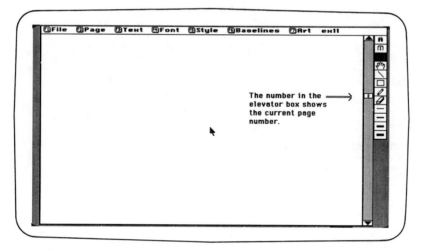

Fig. 5.28. *The page number shown in the elevator box.*

Inserting Pages

The **Insert page** command is a little different from the **Jump to page** command. Suppose that you are working on a booklet for the regional sales meeting and you just ran across a handout of sales tips from a recent training session. You want to incorporate the information from that page (it is already in a text file) into the First Publisher document you are creating, but you need to reserve the last page of the document for the addresses and phone numbers of each sales manager in the district. With **Insert page**, you can insert a blank page immediately preceding the last one and then use First Publisher's text import features to bring the sales tips onto that page.

To use this **Insert page** option, do the following:

1. Save the file if you haven't already done so.

2. Select **Insert page** from the Page menu. The Insert Page dialog box is displayed (see fig. 5.29).

3. Enter the number of the page *before which* you want the page to be inserted.

4. Click OK or press F1.

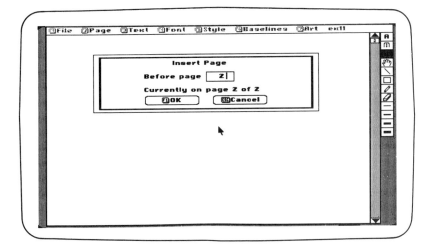

Fig. 5.29. *The Insert Page dialog box.*

Deleting Pages

When you change the size of the type you're using or you decide to scrap an article that had taken up a considerable amount of room, you may find yourself with an extra page or two in your publication.

To delete pages, follow these steps:

1. Save the file if you haven't recently done so.

2. Select **Delete page** from the Page menu. A dialog box is displayed, telling you which page is the current page and asking for the number of the page to be deleted.

3. Enter the number of the page you want to delete.

4. Click the OK button or press F1.

When you delete one or more pages in a document, First Publisher automatically renumbers the remaining pages. If you are working on a four-page document and you delete page 3, for example, the original page 4 becomes the new page 3. If you want to keep the same page numbering, you need to use **Insert page** to fill the vacancy left by the **Delete page** command.

Chapter Summary

In this chapter, you learned all sorts of procedures related to entering, importing, and editing text. Also explained were the steps for adding, deleting, and inserting pages; correcting misspellings; changing font size and style, and using automatic *FONT* commands. In the next chapter, you will add artistic touches to your First Publisher publications by working with graphics.

Creating and Using Graphics

A publication without graphics is just a bunch of type. That's a bold statement, perhaps, but it's true. Whether it's part of your job to produce professional-quality press releases or to create snazzy advertising material, chances are that you use First Publisher in order to integrate text and graphics to produce a visually appealing document.

Throughout this book, the word *graphics* is used to describe any element created on the graphics layer of a First Publisher publication. (If you do not know what the graphics layer is, refer to "Working with the Graphics Layer" later in this chapter.) Therefore, any of the following are accurately called graphics:

Clip art
Free-hand art
Art imported or screen-captured from other programs
Banners created as graphics text
Headlines created as graphics text
Scanned images
Rules
Boxes

Although there's no rule that you *must* use graphics in a First Publisher document, you are certainly missing an opportunity if you don't. First Publisher makes using graphics ultrasimple; they even packaged 175 clip art images with the program, and more than 2,500 additional First Publisher clip art images are available separately.

As you will see in this chapter, the graphics capabilities of First Publisher offer quite a bit of flexibility in enhancing the design of your document. For nonartists, First Publisher offers—packaged with the program—five ''sheets'' of clip art you can use in your own publications. First Publisher's graphics tools give you the ability to draw boxes, rules, and free-hand drawings. Additionally, you can import graphics from other programs like Windows Paint, PC Paintbrush, Publisher's Paintbrush, and LOGITECH Paintshow®.

Why Use Graphics?

Whether or not you decide to use graphics in your publication, you should be aware of the reasons that most publishers—desktop and otherwise—feel graphics are a necessity in their publications.

Artwork breaks up the page for the reader, giving the impression that the information presented is assembled in bite-sized chunks. Research has shown that readers avoid reading a page that is nothing more than line after line of text: They will read something they feel is ''manageable,'' something that they can pick up and put down as necessary, something that doesn't require a 40-minute block of time.

Along a similar line, artwork gives the reader's eye a rest. Too much text is hard on the eyes as well as the brain. Particularly when you're reading about something light, like the latest PTO elections or the success of the Peach Festival, a few pictures help break up the monotony of Geneva 12-point type.

Graphics can add information to the page and help reinforce what is said in the text. A graph, for example, can portray in one image the dramatic success of the Apple Fair, while it might take paragraphs to textually compare the results of the Fair in the last three years. One rule of thumb, however: Although a picture might be worth a thousand words, don't use it *instead* of a thousand words. Never use a graphic to explain what should be said in the text. The most effective publications *say* it with words and *show* it with graphics—not one or the other.

Some graphics are just plain fun. On publications that warrant it, cartoons or light-hearted graphics can make the project more appealing and enjoyable. Remember to consider your audience; a *Pet Pals* newsletter might be able to use cartoons, but a serious report about a diplomat's fact-finding mission to the Inuvik Region probably would not.

Lastly, use the graphics you choose to draw attention to a specific article or element within an article. Because everything in our lives competes for our attention—the boss, the kids, the bills, TV, school, grandparents, the dog —sometimes we need to be ''courted'' into spending time reading an article that we might otherwise toss aside. If you receive a newsletter that has an article about a recent high school football game, you might throw it out without a second look. However, if there were a graphic image of a grandstand full of fans waving pennants madly on a crisp October afternoon, you might pause a moment to look at that picture. And then, when the thought ''I wonder what they're so excited about'' crosses your mind, you're hooked. You may not read the entire article, but the graphic did spark your interest.

A Few Rules
for Choosing Graphics

Before you get started using First Publisher's graphics tools and the clip art images supplied with the program, take a few minutes to review the following rules for creating effective graphics:

Don't overwhelm the page. One well-placed, well-planned graphic element makes a more favorable impression than six cluttered ''what-the-heck-let's-put-this-here'' graphics. Think about the type of graphic element you want to use, and then limit yourself to only one or two graphics per page.

Make sure the graphic ''connects'' to the text. Make sure that the graphic fulfills a purpose. Obviously, in the example of the newsletter that showed a picture of an enraptured crowd at a football game, a picture of an ice cream cone would be inappropriate. (Occasionally, advertising uses a purposely misplaced graphic of this sort. The idea is to make you wonder ''Why is this here?'' and then spend more time looking at the item. In the text there may be some sort of vague connection. Unless you are using First Publisher to create wacky party invitations to send to your friends, stay away from this misleading gimmick.)

Use enough white space to showcase the image. Although most people don't think about it, the white space they see on the page is as important as the text and graphics. White space helps display graphics, set off text columns, and improve the look of headings. Size your graphics so that they allow an appropriate amount of white space as a border; don't make them so large that they look scrunched against the text.

Adding Graphics to Your Publication

As you may recall, Chapter 5 explained that there were different ways to assemble a First Publisher document. Some users prefer to create each element—text and graphics—in separate files and then merge the files to form the document. Other users "build" the publication as they go by first designing the publication, then entering or importing text, then adding graphics, and then fine-tuning the layout. This book takes the second, "building-block" approach to creating a document.

If you are using clip art items in your publication, you can use the building-block approach with no problem. However, if you want to create your own graphic items, such as shadow boxes, free-hand art, or other items not available in First Publisher's clip art library, you should open a new file and create your graphics there.

Creating graphics on the graphics layer of a publication that already includes text can be unnecessarily confusing and distracting. It's better to start with a clean slate, and then later copy the art you create into the First Publisher document. (To display a blank screen, select **Start over** from the File menu. Procedures for saving art are explained later in this chapter in the section "Saving Images.")

The Differences between MAC and ART Files

Many users new to First Publisher are a bit foggy about the difference between MAC and ART files. What are they, and when do you use them?

MAC files are the clip art files that come with First Publisher or that you create yourself. Additional MAC files are also available from Software Publishing Corporation or other vendors. The graphics in these files must be cut and saved as individual ART files before they can be used in a publication. In other words:

❏ MAC signifies a file that stores many graphics elements.

❏ ART indicates an individual art image that can be pasted in a publication.

You can create your own MAC files; First Publisher gives you the option of selecting the MAC radio button when you select **Save** from the File menu. But, if you cannot use MAC files directly in your First Publisher documents (you must save the art to an ART file to use it in the document), why would you want to save art to a MAC file?

If you are working on a page that is a compilation of various graphics—perhaps you are trying several twists of an old company logo—you could save that file as a MAC file so that you have all the logos together. Later, if you decide to use one version, you can select and save that individual item as an ART file and paste it directly into your document.

> If you are trying to preserve the column format of a table you're importing, try importing the file as an ASCII file and then saving the First Publisher file as a MAC file. You can then modify the table as a graphic image and not need to worry about text wrap or formatting problems.

Table 6.1 reviews all the files you use, create, and save in First Publisher and shows you on which menus they are found.

Working with the Graphics Layer

If you are working through this book sequentially, you have already found out about the layers in a First Publisher publication. The program "sees" each document on-screen as a combination of two layers: text and graphics. On the text layer, as you might expect, you enter and edit text by using the text tool (the text tool is at the top of the tools row) and by selecting options in the Text and Baselines menu. On the graphics layer, you create and modify graphic images by using the tools available on the right side of the screen and by working with the options available in the Art menu.

Table 6.1
Files Used in First Publisher

File Type	Options for Retrieve/Save	Found on
Publication files (PUB)	**Get publication**	File menu
	Save (as PUB)	File menu
Text files (TXT)	**Get publication**	File menu
	Get text	Text menu
	Save (as TXT)	File menu
	Save text[1]	Text menu
Graphics files (MAC)	**Get graphics**	File menu
	Save (as MAC)	File menu
Art files (ART)	**Get art**	Art menu
	Save art[1]	Art menu

[1] You must select a block of text before using **Save text**; an image must be selected before you can use **Save art**.

When you select one of the tools *below* the text tool, or when you select one of the options on the Art menu or when you get graphics, First Publisher automatically changes to the graphics layer. If you have entered text on the text layer, the text becomes illegible. If no text exists on the text layer, there is no noticeable difference on the screen when First Publisher changes to the graphics layer. When you return to the text layer, any graphics on the screen look the same as when you worked on the graphics layer. This means that the only difference in the appearance of the two layers on the screen occurs when you select a graphics tool or option to enter the graphics layer; the text on the text layer of the screen then becomes unreadable.

Figure 6.1 shows how the publication looks on-screen when the selection tool (which is a graphics tool) is selected. Notice that the characters on the text layer are not clearly defined.

Introduction to the Art Menu

You will use the options on the Art menu for manipulating the graphics items individually. This menu offers several options (such as **Rotate**, **Magnify**, and **Invert**) that are not available in other desktop publishing programs. Figure 6.2 shows the choices available on the Art menu, and table 6.2 explains each of the options. The key or key sequences placed in parentheses in table 6.2 can be directly used instead of accessing the Art menu and then selecting that option.

Fig. 6.1. *The text layer becomes unreadable when the graphics layer is in use.*

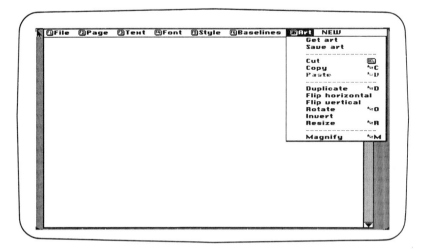

Fig. 6.2. *The Art menu.*

Table 6.2
Options on the Art Menu

Option	Description
Get art	Retrieves individual ART files so that you can place them in the current publication
Save art	Saves the selected art image
Cut (Del)	Removes selected art from the First Publisher document and places it on the graphics clipboard. If you cut another graphic, the first item on the clipboard is overwritten.
Copy (Alt-C)	Copies selected art and places copy on the graphics clipboard. If you copy another graphic, the first item on the clipboard is overwritten.
Paste (Alt-V)	Places the art item from graphics clipboard to the indicated position in the document
Duplicate (Alt-D)	Creates a duplicate image and places the duplicate on the page, without using the graphics clipboard
Flip horizontal	Flips selected image horizontally
Flip vertical	Flips selected image vertically
Rotate (Alt-O)	Rotates selected image 90 degrees
Invert	Turns the white area within the selected area to black, and vice versa
Resize (Alt-R)	Allows you to change the size of the selected image
Magnify (Alt-M)	Magnifies selected area of art image so that you can work with the graphic pixel-by-pixel

In sections later in this chapter, you will use each of these options. For now, the familiarity with the choices provided by this table is sufficient.

Introduction to the Graphics Tools

Whether you use clip art or create your own graphics, you have the option of using First Publishers graphics tools, located on the right side of the screen, to enhance your publications. Figure 6.3 shows the position of the graphics tools.

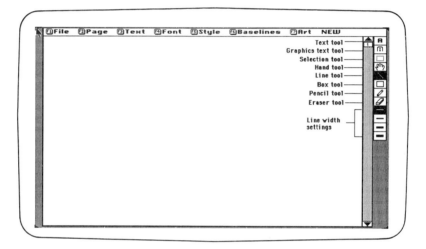

Fig. 6.3. *The graphics tools.*

At the bottom of the tools row are four individual line settings—offering four different line widths. You can select these widths to change the look of boxes and lines drawn with the other tools on the graphics tools row. Table 6.3 explains each of these tools.

The four items shown at the bottom of the tools row are not actually tools; they are the line widths available for use with the line, box, and pencil tools.

You can select any of the items in the tools row by moving the mouse cursor to that particular tool and clicking the mouse button or by pressing F9 to move to each tool in turn. Pressing Shift-F9 selects the text tool, located at the top of the tools row.

In the sections that follow, you will learn to work with each of these tools.

**Table 6.3
The Graphics Tools**

Tool	Name	Description
	Text tool	Used to enter and edit text
	Graphics text tool	Used to enter and edit text on the graphics layer. (*Note:* This text is treated as a graphic element and cannot be manipulated from the text layer.)
	Selection tool	Used to select a graphic image for various operations such as cut, copy, move, resize, rotate, invert, and flip operations
	Hand tool	Used for placing or moving a graphic element
	Line tool	Used for drawing straight lines
	Box tool	Used for drawing boxes on the graphics layer
	Pencil tool	Used for drawing lines or images "by hand" and for manipulating and editing drawings pixel-by-pixel
	Eraser tool	Used for erasing graphic elements

The Text Tool

Because the text tool is not a graphics tool, it technically shouldn't be covered in this chapter. However, the text tool will be covered for the sake of completeness.

The text tool is active whenever you enter or edit text. When First Publisher initially is loaded, this tool is the active tool.

(*Note:* When a tool is *active*, or in use, its image is inverted, meaning that what usually appears white is now black, and items usually black are white. So, when the text tool is active, the black A on a white background becomes a white A on a black background.)

When the text tool is selected, First Publisher displays the text layer. To switch to any of the graphics tools, click that tool with the mouse or press F9 to cycle through the tools until the one you want is highlighted. To return to the text layer and the text tool, press Shift-F9.

> If you have been working in graphics mode (on the graphics layer) and you want to redisplay the text layer so that you can see how your modifications look, press Shift-F9.

The Graphics Text Tool

You will use the graphics text tool often as you create banners, information boxes, and other text items you would rather paste down than type in. Graphics text is just that; text treated as a graphic, meaning that you can resize, rotate, invert, and perform any operation on the text that you could perform on any other graphic in First Publisher.

Banners and the Graphics Text Tool

The banner, or name, of your publication is one of the most important design elements you create. The banner is one of the first things a reader sees and it should make a statement about your publication.

When you use the graphics text tool to create a banner for your publication, First Publisher provides flexibility that other programs cannot offer. Suppose that you create the banner in 36-point Helvetica, the largest type your setup can offer, but that still isn't big enough. Because the text is *graphics* text, you can select and resize it, stretching it to fill whatever space you need to fill (see fig. 6.4).

First Publisher does a great job of smoothing the edges of resized graphics —but you can magnify the item and work with the individual dots, or pixels, comprising it if you want to fine-tune the text of the banner. You can do this using the **Magnify** option on the Art menu.

The graphics text tool also opens the door to creativity. Because you can treat text as graphics, you can come up with unique designs for your banners, playing on the name of your organization, or working up a company logo. Figure 6.5 shows examples of banners created with the graphics text tool.

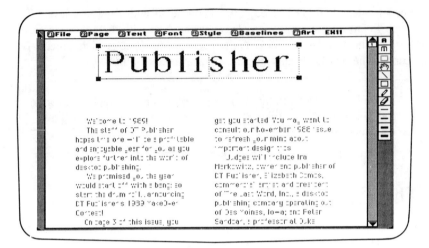

Fig. 6.4. Stretching the banner created with graphics text.

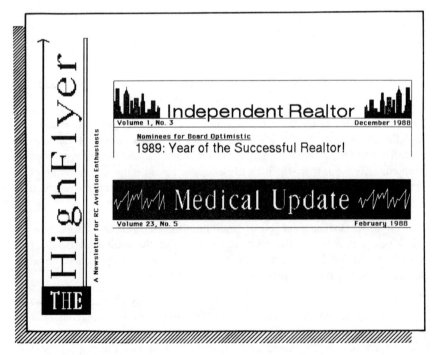

Fig. 6.5. Examples of banners created with the graphics text tool.

Headings and the Graphics Text Tool

When there are headings in the publication, you have two choices: you can enter the headings as text on the text layer (and adjust the individual baselines so the text flows correctly), or you can leave space on the text layer and paste in the headings as graphics text. Some prefer the latter method, but you should use the method with which you are most comfortable.

When you create headings using the graphics text tool, the procedure is identical to the procedure for creating banners: select the graphics text tool, specify the font and style you want, and type the text. Because the text entered is a graphic element, you can "grab" it using the selection and hand tools (covered later in this chapter) and move it to any point in the publication. Figure 6.6 shows two headings that were created as graphics text.

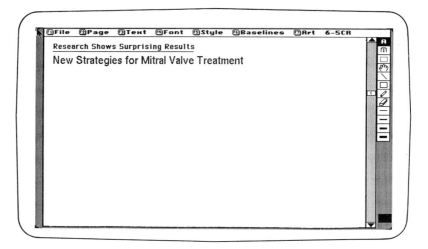

Fig. 6.6. Headings can also be created as graphics text.

The Selection Tool

You use the selection tool to "grab" items—or portions of items—to be used in another operation. Whether you want to move, copy, cut, resize, magnify the item, or perform any other operation on the Art menu, you must select it first.

To use the selection tool, follow these steps:

1. Choose the selection tool by clicking it or by pressing F9 until the selection tool is highlighted.

2. Position the mouse cursor at the upper-left corner of the item you want to grab. If you are using the keyboard method, use the arrow keys to move the cursor to the correct position on-screen, and press F10. (Actually, you can start with *any* corner of the image, but this book consistently uses the method described here.)

3. With the mouse, press the mouse button and drag the mouse down and to the right so that the entire element is enclosed in the flashing rectangle. On the keyboard, use the ↓ and → keys to enlarge the box.

4. Release the mouse button (or press F10). The image is enclosed in the rectangle and has been successfully selected.

You can now perform various operations on the selected image. *Note:* If you leave any part of the image outside the selection rectangle, that part is not included when you work with the selected image. This can be beneficial if you only want to select part of an image. If you want to redefine the selected area, reposition the cross-hair cursor at the upper left corner of the image and repeat Steps 3 and 4 so that all or part of the image is enclosed.

Releasing the Selected Image

First Publisher doesn't automatically "know" when you are finished using a selected image. Once you have moved the image or performed an operation on that image, you must release the item from the selection tool. Otherwise, the item continues to flash and be redrawn on the screen each time you use an option or another tool, which can be distracting and time-consuming.

Even when you switch to another tool or change to the text layer, the selected item remains selected. Although the flashing rectangle doesn't show on the text layer, the contents of the selected area will "flash" when you make any modifications on the screen. To release the item, select the selection tool again, position the mouse cursor away from the selected item, and click the mouse button (or press F10). This releases the image and, in effect, turns the selection tool off, because you are not selecting another image.

Figure 6.7 shows how you can use the selection tool to select an image.

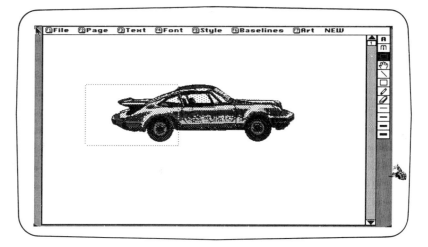

Fig. 6.7. *Use the selection tool to select an image or part of an image.*

The Hand Tool

The hand tool is often used to move images around on the page. This tool must be used with the selection tool; you cannot move an image before you tell First Publisher what it is you want to move.

To use the hand tool, follow these steps:

1. Make sure that the image you want to move has been selected with the selection tool. Refer to ''The Selection Tool'' in this chapter for instructions on selecting an image.

2. Position the hand tool anywhere on the selected image. If you are using the keyboard, use the arrow keys to move the hand to the desired location.

3. Press and hold the mouse button (or press F10).

4. Move the item to the desired position by using either the mouse or the arrow keys.

5. Release the mouse button (or press F10).

First Publisher automatically selects the hand tool for you when you use options like **Get art** or **Paste** from the Art menu. When you use those options, the program knows that you must position the art on the screen, so the hand tool is automatically chosen. After positioning the hand tool where you want the item to be pasted, you click the mouse button, and the art appears where the hand tool has indicated it is to be positioned. Because the item is still selected and the hand tool is still active, you can use the mouse cursor to move the item around on the screen after it is pasted (see fig. 6.8).

> First Publisher's rulers are helpful for controlling the exact place-
> ment of graphics. If you are using a CGA card, the rulers appear
> distorted, but if you use the rulers to place a graphic two inches
> from the top and two inches from the left edge of the page, the
> graphic is printed in that position.

Fig. 6.8. The effects of using the hand tool.

The Line Tool

The line tool, predictably, is used to draw lines. Whether you want to add rules, close up a gap in a box, or connect the dots, the line tool finds the straightest road to your destination.

To use the line tool, follow these steps:

1. Select the line tool by clicking it or by pressing F9 until that tool is highlighted.

2. Position the cursor at the point on-screen where you want the line to begin by using the mouse or by using the arrow keys.

3. Press and hold the mouse button (or press F10).

4. Drag the mouse in the direction you want the line to go. Notice that you can move the line in any direction; it is not "pasted" down until you release the mouse button. If you are using the keyboard, use the arrow keys to draw the line.

5. When the line is the length you want, release the mouse button (or press F10).

Because First Publisher offers a WYSIWYG ("what-you-see-is-what-you-get") screen, you can tell when you have gotten the straightest line possible by watching it carefully on the screen. This can be a difficult call, especially if you draw a line the length of the page to serve as a border. If you draw a diagonal line, move the angle of the line until the "stair-step" increments look even.

> When you draw lines the length of the screen, or whenever you need to draw a straight line, you can use the **Use Grid** option on the Page menu to turn on an invisible grid that controls the movement of the cursor. For more about the **Use Grid** option, see Chapter 7.

If you don't like the way the line turned out, you can use the eraser tool to erase the line. You can also get rid of the line by using the selection tool to select the line and using Cut (or Del key) to remove it.

You can also select different line widths for the line tool. To find out more about changing the line width, see "The Line Width Settings," later in this chapter.

The Box Tool

If you like to use squares, then you will use the box tool to create boxes of all sizes. Bullet boxes, drop shadow boxes, boxes to enclose a publication message or secondary article—a box, used effectively, can add greatly to the design and readability of your page. In the "Applications for the Graphics Tools" section of this chapter, you will learn a few box tricks. For now, here's how to use the box tool:

1. Select the box tool by clicking it or by pressing F9 until that tool is highlighted.

2. Use the mouse or the arrow key to position the cursor at the place on-screen where you want the upper left corner of the box to appear.

3. Press and hold the mouse button (or press F10).

4. Drag the mouse down and to the right, until the box is the size you want. If you are using the keyboard, press ↓ and → to enlarge the box.

5. Release the mouse button (or press F10).

You can also specify different line widths for boxes. These width settings are discussed in "The Line Width Settings," later in this chapter.

Then, after you select the box, you can perform any modification on it that you want, including resizing, copying and pasting, flipping, or inverting. Figure 6.9 shows a publication in which boxes were used for several different elements.

The Pencil Tool

The pencil tool is for the daring desktop publisher. Anyone who has ever sketched a half-decent doodle will be tempted to use this tool. It *is* fun, but it can also be discouraging. Use the pencil tool when you want to draw something "by hand" to incorporate in a publication.

The pencil tool is invaluable for editing art images, especially when used with the **Magnify** option on the Art menu. You can use the pencil tool to smooth the edges of a hand-drawn graphic or to fine-tune the lines in a scanned or screen-captured image.

To use the pencil tool, follow these steps:

1. Select the pencil tool by clicking it or by pressing F9 until that tool is highlighted.

2. Position the pencil cursor on the screen where you want to begin drawing.

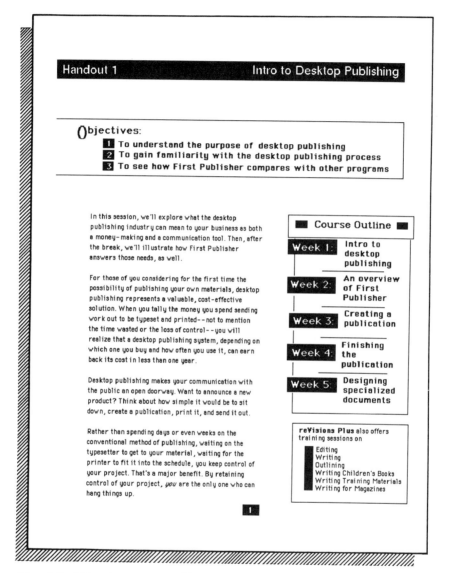

Fig. 6.9. *Using boxes in a publication.*

3. Press and hold the mouse button as you draw (or press F10).

4. Draw the desired image using the mouse to direct the pencil on the screen. Remember to keep the mouse button pressed as you draw.

5. Release the mouse button when you are finished drawing (or press F10).

Like the line and box tools, you can adjust the width of the line drawn by the pencil tool. Refer to "The Line Width Settings," later in this chapter.

Because First Publisher doesn't have every tool you might need, you may have to use the pencil tool at different points in your publishing projects. Here are a few tips to make using the pencil tool less frustrating:

❑ Draw the item larger than necessary and then use the **Resize** option on the Art menu to reduce the size of the image. Reducing the size may smooth out the edges of the image and make the graphic look more professional.

❑ If the item includes straight lines or boxes, use the **Use Grid** option on the Page menu to guide you as you draw the item free-hand.

❑ If you are drawing the item while referring to a photo or picture, use **Show rulers** on the Page menu to give you an idea of how accurately you are copying the item.

❑ Use **Magnify** on the Art menu to get a closer look at the pixels of the image. You can then use the pencil tool to change black pixels to white and white pixels to black, if necessary, to give the image a smoother look.

❑ Save the image several times as you work. One little change may enhance or ruin the image. Also, when you're dealing with pixels, one slip of the eraser tool and you may be back to square one.

Figure 6.10 shows two items drawn with the pencil tool. The first one is shown at actual size, and the second was resized to enhance the sharpness of the lines.

The Eraser Tool

If you're like most people, very soon after you begin using First Publisher's graphics tools, you will get to know the eraser tool. Few people do everything right all the time. The eraser tool allows you to erase an image or part of an image.

To use the eraser tool, follow these steps:

1. Select the tool by clicking it or by pressing F9 until the tool is highlighted.

Fig. 6.10. *Two items drawn with the pencil tool.*

2. Position the cursor (which now resembles a white box) at the place on screen where you want to begin erasing.

3. Press and hold the mouse button (or press F10).

4. Drag the cursor over the item you want to erase by using the mouse or the arrow keys.

5. When the item is erased, release the mouse button (or press F10).

You can also use the eraser tool as a ''spot'' eraser; that is, instead of dragging the cursor over an item, place the cursor over the item and then click the mouse button repeatedly. When you drag the mouse, you can easily erase a part of the image you want to keep. The spot eraser method makes you a little more accurate when you are doing some risky erasing.

Make sure that you have saved a copy of the image before you begin erasing. After you use the eraser to remove an image, the image is gone. If you haven't saved the image and you decide that you really shouldn't have erased that item, your only recourse is to re-create it. Save the image as art by selecting the image and choosing **Save art** from the Art menu (if the graphic will be incorporated in a publication later), or by pressing Alt-S and saving the file as a PUB or MAC file.

Figure 6.11 shows the effects of the eraser tool.

Fig. 6.11. *The effects of using the eraser tool.*

The Line Width Settings

The four line width settings, located at the bottom of the graphics tools row, aren't really *tools*; they are settings used by the line, box, and pencil tools.

When you enter First Publisher, the first line width (1-point width) is the default setting used. For most purposes like drawing boxes, rules, and separator lines, this width is sufficient. In other cases, when you are concerned about adding a "designer" touch to the publication, you may want to experiment with other width settings.

The available line widths are the following:

—   1 point

—   2 point

—   3 point

—   4 point

To select a different line width, follow these steps:

1. Make sure the tool you plan to use is selected. The line, box, or pencil tools are affected by changing the line width.

2. Click the line-width setting at the bottom of the graphics tools row that you want to use. Alternately, press F9 until the desired line-width setting is highlighted (or press Alt-F9).

3. Draw the image.

> If you use one of the heavier line widths and then reduce the size of the image, the heavy lines may appear to "fill in" the image. To avoid this, use a lightweight line when you plan to reduce the size of an image.

Applications for the Graphics Tools

Now that you know how to use the graphics tools, what can you do with them? This section explains how to put the tools to good use in creating items you can use repeatedly in your publications. Remember to save the images after you create them so you can use them again in your publications. The procedure for saving images is explained in "Saving Images," later in this chapter.

Creating a Side Banner

To create a side banner in First Publisher, do the following:

1. Start with a blank screen. (Select **Start over** from the File menu after saving the previous file.)

2. Select the graphics text tool.

3. Select the font and style you want to use. (In figure 6.12, 36-point Helvetica was chosen.)

4. Position the cursor anywhere on the screen by using the mouse or by using the arrow keys and pressing F10 twice. (You can move the banner later.)

5. Type the name of the publication.

6. Use the selection tool to select the banner (be sure to enclose the entire name in the flashing rectangle).

7. Choose **Rotate** from the Art menu. First Publisher rotates the banner so that the right end of the name is pointing upward.

8. Use the hand tool to move the banner to the correct position on the page. If you are using the keyboard, select the hand tool by pressing F9 until the hand tool is highlighted. Then use the arrow keys to move the cursor to the banner and press F10. Use the arrow keys again to move the banner and press F10 again when the banner is positioned properly.

9. Select **Show page** from the Page menu to get an idea of how the banner is positioned.

   You can also further enhance the banner, if you like, by inverting the banner name. Because the banner is still selected, you can choose **Invert** from the Art menu; First Publisher turns all the white space inside the flashing rectangle to black, and vice versa. Figure 6.12 shows an example of a side banner.

Creating Rules

Rules may be the most subtle of all graphic elements. Rules correctly used tend to be transparent in that they add to the design and overall "feel" of the page, but they are not so obvious that they draw attention to themselves.

You will want to use different rules in different places on your document. If you opt to use separator lines between columns, the separator line should be the lightest line available: 1 point. If you want to include a medium-weight line that shows where one article stops and another begins, use a 2-point or 3-point line.

To create a "designer" rule to function as part of a logo, follow these steps:

1. Save the publication, if you haven't already done so.

2. Select the line tool and make sure that the default (1 point) line width is selected.

3. Position the mouse cursor far enough to the left that you can draw the entire line.

4. Press and hold the mouse button (or press F10).

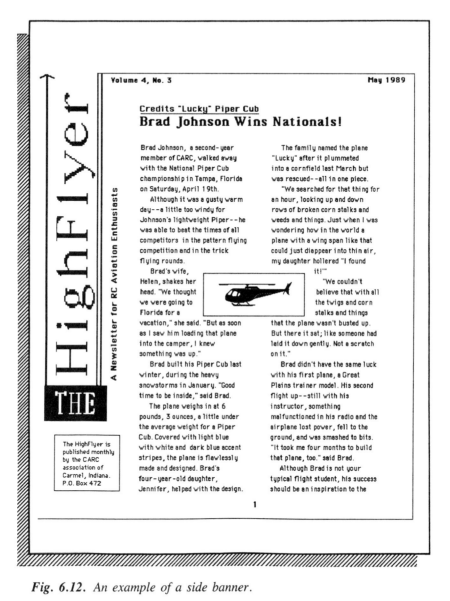

Fig. 6.12. *An example of a side banner.*

5. Drag the mouse to the right (or press →), until the line is the length you want.

6. Release the mouse button (or press F10).

7. Select the 3-point line width by clicking it or by pressing F9 until that line width setting is highlighted.

8. Position the cursor immediately under the left edge of the 1-point line.

9. Press and hold the mouse button while dragging the mouse to the position directly beneath the right edge of the 1-point line. If you are using the keyboard, press F10 and use the arrow keys to move the cursor to the correct position.

10. Release the mouse button (or press F10).

The lines just drawn complement each other. You may want to use the selection and hand tools to select and move the second line closer or farther from the first. Figure 6.13 shows an example that uses these rules (the example is the banner for the newsletter *DT Publisher,* which was started in Chapter 5.)

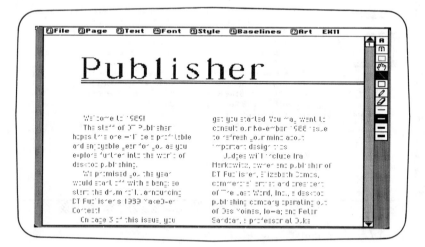

Fig. 6.13. *Using the rule in the* DT Publisher *banner.*

Making Shadow Boxes

A shadow box is a box that gives the appearance of having a shadow behind it—a two-dimensional image. Using this shadow technique can give your publications a "polished" look that a simple line box cannot provide. To create a shadow box, follow these steps:

1. Select the box tool by clicking it or by pressing F9 until the tool is highlighted. (Make sure that the default line width is selected.)

2. Position the cursor anywhere on-screen by using the mouse or using the arrow keys.

3. Press and hold the mouse button while dragging the mouse down and to the right. If you are using the keyboard, press F10 and press ↓ and → to enlarge the box.

4. When the box is the size you want, release the mouse button (or press F10).

5. Select the heaviest line width setting (4 point) by clicking it or by pressing F9 until the setting is highlighted.

6. Select the line tool.

7. Position the cursor a little to the right of the lower left corner of the box. (Place the crosshair cursor directly on the bottom line of the box. When you release the mouse button, the line will appear beneath the box's bottom line.)

8. Press the mouse button and drag the cursor to the bottom right corner of the box. If you're using the keyboard, press F10 and use → to move the cursor to the right corner of the box.

9. Release the mouse button (or press F10). The thick line should appear after the mouse button is released.

10. Position the cursor on the right edge of the box, a little lower than the top right corner.

11. Press the mouse button and drag the cursor to the bottom right corner of the box, meeting the first thick line. Using the keyboard, press F10, and use ↓ to move the cursor to the bottom right corner of the box.

12. Release the mouse button (or press F10). The second thick line should appear.

13. Use the eraser tool, if necessary, to "trim off" any extra length on either of the thick lines.

Figure 6.14 shows the finished shadow box.

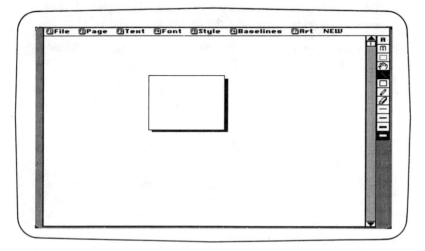

Fig. 6.14. *A shadow box created with the box and line tools.*

Saving Images

Remember to save the images you create at various times during your work session. If you are working on a publication and bring in graphics, save the file as a PUB file. (The procedure for saving PUB files is covered in Chapter 5.) If you are creating your own "clip art" file, you can save the file as a MAC file. If you are working on a graphics file that you plan to import into a publication, as is done in this chapter, save the file as an ART file.

To save the file as an ART file, first use the selection tool to select the single image you want to save. (Remember that ART files are used in their entirety.) Then, choose **Save art** from the Art menu. A dialog box is displayed, asking you to enter a name for the file (see fig. 6.15). Type a name for the image you are saving, and check the path designation shown at the bottom of the dialog box. (You don't need to enter an extension for the file name; First Publisher attaches the ART extension automatically.) If you want to change the directory to which the file will be saved, do so now. When you have entered all the necessary information, click the OK button or press F1.

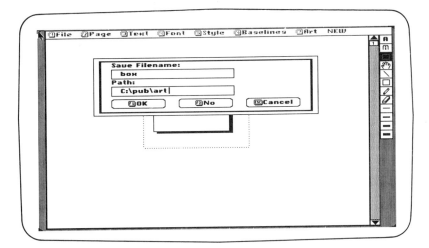

Fig. 6.15. *The Save dialog box.*

If you entered a file name that has already been used, First Publisher alerts you to this and asks whether you want to overwrite the existing file with the new one (see fig. 6.16). If you are simply modifying an earlier version of the file and want to overwrite it, click OK or press F1; if you accidentally entered the wrong file name, cancel the operation and start again.

Using First Publisher's Clip Art Files

As you have probably learned already, First Publisher deals with files a little differently than other programs you may be familiar with. With First Publisher, you can save files as publication files (PUB), text files (TXT), or art files (ART). When you retrieve those files, you must use **Get publication** from the File menu to get PUB files, **Get art** from the Art menu to retrieve ART files, and **Get text** from the Text menu to get TXT files.

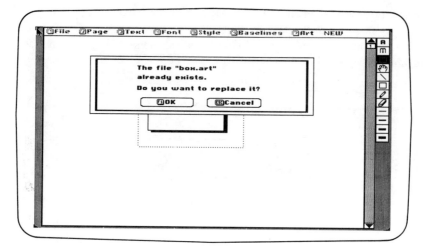

Fig. 6.16. *A message box warns you of overwriting a file.*

Another option available on the File menu, called **Get graphics**, retrieves graphic files. These files have the extension MAC. Most users, at some time or other, try to get graphics using **Get graphics.** What those users discover, when a full page of clip art is displayed, is that what they really wanted was to get a *piece* of art from the *graphics page*. To do that, the user would have to select the desired piece (using the selection tool) and save it using **Save art** from the Art menu. Then, to retrieve it and put it in the document, they would select **Get art** from the Art menu.

The following are the differences between **Get graphics** and **Get art**:

Get graphics, on the File menu, gets the clip art files packaged with First Publisher and gets graphics from other compatible programs (PCX files, MSW files, and so forth) that are compatible with the program. *Note:* You also can save MAC files you create or import.

Get art, on the Art menu, retrieves individual ART images that you can paste in your publications. This option can also retrieve files from PFS: First Choice or from files you have saved as ART files.

Before you can use the clip art images that are packaged with First Publisher, you must save the individual image as a separate ART file. The next section explains how to display, cut, and paste clip art items into your First Publisher document.

What's in the Clip Art Library?

Before you learn how to cut and paste from First Publisher's clip art files, you should know what's available. First Publisher comes with five files of clip art; each file contains one page of art elements. These files are

BUSINESS.MAC
HOLIDAYS.MAC
LEISURE.MAC
PERSONAL.MAC
PUBLICAT.MAC

These clip art files come packaged on the Sampler Disk and are examples of the art in other clip art libraries available from Software Publishing Corporation. First Publisher is the only leading desktop publishing program to come equipped with these "freebies," and for many people, the built-in clip art library more than accommodates the graphics needs of their projects. (*Note:* The makers of First Publisher also offer many other clip art files, available for $39 each.)

Figure 6.17 shows the clip art packaged with First Publisher.

Using Clip Art in Your Publications

Now that you have identified the art you would like to clip, you need to know how to clip it. To use clip art in your publications, you must

❏ Access the appropriate clip art file

❏ Select the art you want to clip

❏ Save the clip art as an ART file

❏ Open your publication

❏ Retrieve the ART file

❏ Position or resize the art to fit the publication

The following sections explain how these steps are done.

Fig. 6.17. *The clip art files available with First Publisher.*

Accessing the Clip Art File

Suppose that you want to clip the small Victorian house from the PUB-LICAT.MAC file. To do so, you must first open the PUBLICAT.MAC file by selecting **Get graphics** from the File menu. The Get dialog box then is displayed, showing you the names of all the MAC files in that subdirectory. (*Note:* If you receive a message saying no matching files were found, check the path designation and change it if necessary to the directory where the MAC files are located.)

Highlight the file PUBLICAT.MAC by clicking it or by using the ↑ and ↓ keys to move the highlight. When the desired file name is highlighted, click the OK button or press F1.

First Publisher then displays the file on the screen. Figure 6.18 shows that only a portion of the page can be shown on-screen at one time.

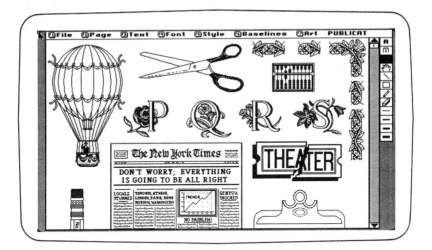

Fig. 6.18. *The default display of PUBLICAT.MAC.*

Selecting the Clip Art Image

To select the small Victorian house, move the display so that the house is within ''grabbing'' distance. Move the mouse cursor to a point about half-way down the elevator bar. Click the mouse button. The page is scrolled up, and the house is now within reach of the selection tool.

Choose the selection tool by clicking it or by pressing F9 until that tool is highlighted. Then, using the technique described earlier in this chapter, select the house by enclosing it in the flashing rectangle.

Saving the Clip Art Image

Because an art image has been selected, options on the Art menu that had previously been disabled now become available. Choose **Save art** from the Art menu. A Save dialog box displays, asking for a name and path designation for the file. Enter a name that will help you recall the item at a later date (such as SMHOUSE). Remember that you don't need to enter the ART extension; First Publisher does that for you.

Opening Your Publication

Next, you need to open the file in which you want to paste the clip art. If that document is a publication, select **Get publication** from the File menu. If that file is to be a new file, select **Start over** from the file menu.

Suppose that the clip art is to be used in a newsletter called *Independent Realtor* (see fig. 6.19). This document, which was created previously, was retrieved with the **Get publication** command.

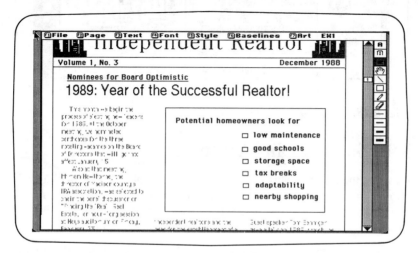

Fig. 6.19. *The* Independent Realtor *newsletter.*

Bringing the Art into the Publication

Next, you need to bring the art you just saved into the publication. To complete this final step, select **Get art** from the Art menu. You then use the arrow keys or the mouse cursor to indicate which ART file you want; click the mouse button or press Enter to select the file. After you click the Get button (or press F1), First Publisher automatically selects the hand tool, allowing you to indicate the position on-screen where you want the image to be placed (see fig. 6.20). After you position the hand and click the mouse button (or press F10 twice), the art is copied to the publication.

Once the image is placed in the publication or the file, you are ready to make any necessary modifications. These are discussed in the next section of this chapter.

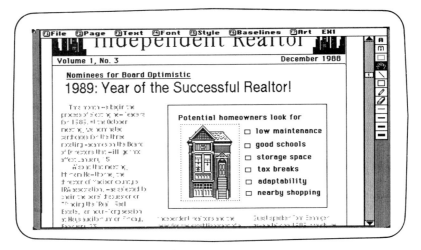

Fig. 6.20. *When you select **Get art**, First Publisher selects the hand tool.*

Working with Art

In this section, you will learn to use the other options on the Art menu; options for working with images once you have placed them in a PUB, MAC, or ART file.

Using the Graphics Clipboard

When a graphics image is cut, copied, or pasted, the operation involves the use of the graphics clipboard. As you may recall, First Publisher has two clipboards: one for text, and one for graphics.

When you use the **Cut** option on the Art menu, First Publisher removes the item from the file, but leaves it on the graphics clipboard. If you decide you don't want to erase the item after all, you can select **Paste** and First Publisher will return the item you deleted. Remember that the graphics clipboard stores only one item at a time, however; if you use **Cut** or **Copy** to place another item on the clipboard, the first item is overwritten.

When you use **Copy,** First Publisher places a copy of the selected item on the clipboard. When you use the **Paste** option, the program pastes the contents of the clipboard onto the publication, and a copy of the item remains on the clipboard, meaning that you can paste the same item several times, if you want.

Cutting and Pasting Art

You often may need to cut and paste an art element. Suppose, for example, that you want to move the house graphic to another part of the publication.

To cut the picture from the publication, you follow these steps:

1. Select the house picture by using the selection tool.

2. Select **Cut** from the Art menu or press Del. The selected element is then cut from the document and placed on the graphics clipboard.

When you are ready to paste the item, position the cursor where you want the image to reappear and select **Paste** from the Art menu or press Alt-V.

Moving Art

Moving an image is actually a cut-and-paste operation in disguise. When you want to move an image from one position in a publication to another position, follow these steps:

1. Select the art to be moved with the selection tool.

2. Choose **Cut** from the Art menu or press Del. This removes the art from the page and places it on the clipboard.

3. Move the cursor to the position you want to paste the art.

4. Select **Paste** from the Art menu or press Alt-V.

The art is then moved to the appropriate spot.

Duplicating Art

Duplication is another name for copying. So why have a **Copy** and a **Duplicate** option? The **Duplicate** option reduces the number of keystrokes involved; it can save you the trouble of dealing with the graphics clipboard or overwriting another piece of art on the clipboard.

For example, suppose that you are using shadow boxes to help highlight some important points in your publication. Instead of selecting a box, copying it with **Copy,** pasting it with **Paste,** and then positioning it, you can use the following steps to duplicate the image:

1. Select the image.

2. Choose **Duplicate** from the Art menu or press Alt-D. The item is immediately duplicated and placed on the document. You can then move the item to the correct position on the page and click the mouse button (or press F10) to paste the image in place.

Flipping Art

First Publisher's "flipping" feature can be a lifesaver if you create your own hand-drawn graphics. For example, suppose that you are drawing a beach ball—not an easy task considering that First Publisher has no circle tool. After you have drawn half of the ball, you can ensure that the ball is symmetrical—and make the job easier, to boot—by using the **Copy** and **Flip** options to make a copy of the first half, flip the copy, and paste it down next to the first half (see fig. 6.21).

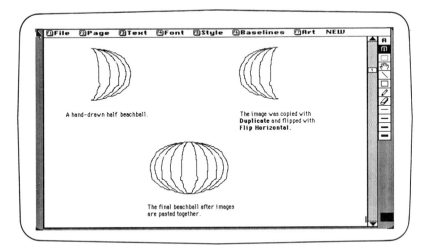

*Fig. 6.21. Using **Flip horizontal** to finish the beach ball.*

First Publisher can flip images horizontally or vertically. Figure 6.22 shows how each of these options work.

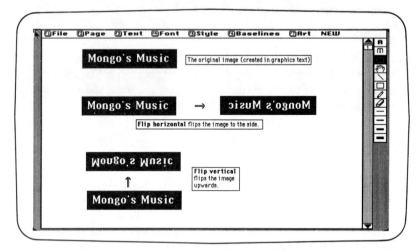

Fig. 6.22. *Examples of using* **Flip horizontal** *and* **Flip vertical**.

Rotating Art

The **Rotate** option is a favorite of many First Publisher users and one of which other desktop publishing programs cannot boast. **Rotate** gives you the option of turning art in 90-degree increments. Whether you use the **Rotate** option to make side banners or to take some of the work out of your graphics chores, you will find this option a big advantage of First Publisher's graphics capabilities.

Figure 6.23 shows examples of how **Rotate** can be used.

Inverting Art

Although First Publisher doesn't have the capacity to create gray tones —that is, shades of gray between black and white—the program can turn a white page black (and vice versa). The **Invert** option allows you to invert the color of a selected image. By inverting the appearance of a banner, for example, you can create a dramatic, professional look for your publication.

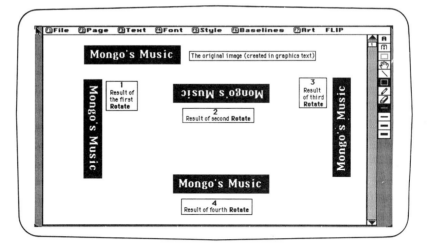

Fig. 6.23. *Examples of the **Rotate** option.*

When you use **Invert**, the color of everything within the selected area is reversed. If the area you invert is surrounded by a rectangle, after the inversion, the rectangle appears white.

To use the **Invert** option, follow these steps:

1. Use the selection tool to select the area you want to invert. Remember that *everything* black within the selected area will become white. You do not have to enclose the area to be inverted in a rectangle drawn with the box tool; when you select it, the boundaries are defined.

2. Choose **Invert** from the Art menu or use the cursor keys to move the highlight to that command and press Enter.

The selected area then is inverted. Figure 6.24 shows the effect of the **Invert** option.

If you don't like the way the inversion turned out, you can change the section back by selecting **Invert** again before performing any other operation.

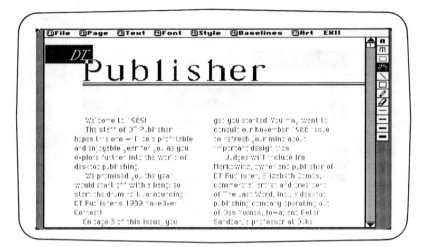

*Fig. 6.24. The effect of the **Invert** option.*

Resizing Art

The ability to resize art is an important one in First Publisher. You can use **Resize**, for example, to fit a graphic item into a defined space, to reduce the size of a drawn item in order to enhance its clarity, or to size letters as you want them for headings and banners. To use **Resize**, follow these steps:

1. Use the selection tool to select the item you want to resize.

2. Choose **Resize** from the Art menu or press Alt-R. Four black "handles" appear on the corners of the selected graphic.

3. Position the mouse cursor over the handle you want to move. If you're using the keyboard, use the arrow keys to move the cursor to the handle you want.

4. Press and hold the mouse button while you drag the mouse in the direction you want to resize the item (see fig. 6.25). From the keyboard, press F10 and use the arrow keys to enlarge the box.

5. When the item is the desired size, release the mouse button (or press F10).

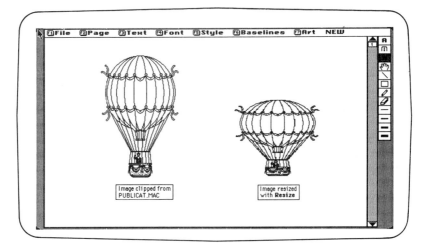

Fig. 6.25. *Using **Resize** to change the size of an image.*

Magnifying Art

The **Magnify** option is used with the pencil tool. This option, which works as a toggle, enables you to get a closer look at a selected image. When it is selected, you can see the dots, or pixels, that make up the graphic image. To use **Magnify,** follow these steps:

1. Select **Magnify** from the Art menu or press Alt-M. The cursor changes to the shape of a miniature magnifying glass.

2. Position the magnifying glass in the center of the area you want to see.

3. Click the mouse button (or press F10). The screen then displays a close-up view of the individual dots, or *pixels*, that actually make up the picture (see fig. 6.26). In the upper left corner of the screen, you see a miniature version of that section of the graphic, so that if you make changes on the image, you can see how it looks from a larger perspective. Notice that the cursor has been changed to the shape of a pencil.

4. If you want to edit the graphic in this form, you can use the pencil to turn black pixels to white or vice versa. Simply click the individual pixel to change its color. You can erase an entire area of

pixels by clicking on a black pixel and dragging the pencil through that area, keeping the mouse button pressed. If you are using the keyboard, press F10 each time you want to turn a pixel on or off.

5. When you are ready to return to the larger, "macro" view, click the box in the upper-left corner or disable **Magnify** by pressing Alt-M.

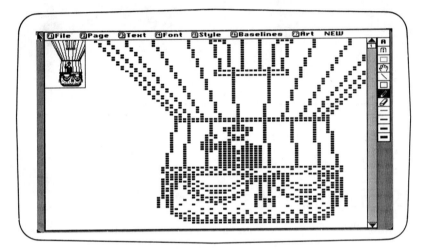

*Fig. 6.26. Use **Magnify** to provide a close-up view of an image.*

> Use **Magnify** when you have hand-drawn a graphic and need to smooth out the edges.

Importing Graphics

Now you have exhausted the graphics resources built into First Publisher. Still, other options are available for getting graphics into the program. You can import graphics from other graphics programs by using basically the same procedure you use to retrieve MAC files. First Publisher can use graphics files from the following paint programs:

PC PaintPlus
PC Paintbrush
Windows Paint
LOGIPAINT
LOGITECH PaintShow
Publisher's Paintbrush

First Publisher can work directly with PCX files, such as those produced by PC Paintbrush and Publisher's Paintbrush. Other paint programs may be compatible with First Publisher as well, if they come equipped with a transfer utility that converts the file into the PCX form readable by First Publisher. (Many paint programs, like LOGITECH PaintShow, have this utility. Check your paint program's documentation for specific instructions.)

Additionally, many public-domain conversion routines are available on bulletin board systems like CompuServe®. Be sure to check these routines carefully before you use them to make sure that they are free of bugs and are compatible with First Publisher.

Adding Art from Other Programs

In this section , you will take a quick look at three popular paint programs and how they are used with First Publisher. Once you have created an image with those programs, how can you use it in First Publisher?

If the file is in a format compatible with First Publisher, follow these steps to turn the graphics file into usable art:

1. Start First Publisher.

2. Select **Get graphics** from the Art menu and highlight the file you want to import. This option brings to First Publisher the entire page—the whole file—you created in the paint program. When the Get dialog box is displayed, make sure that the path designation is specified correctly. (*Note:* If you don't see the file you want or you cannot recall the file's extension, type *.* after the directory name in the path box, such as *c:\fp\pub*.*. This displays all files in the PUB subdirectory.)

3. Choose the selection tool.

4. Select the entire image (or any portion of it that you want to use separately) by clicking in the upper-left corner and dragging the

mouse down and to the right until the desired portion of the graphic is enclosed in the flashing rectangle (see fig. 6.27). If you are using the keyboard, use the arrow keys to move the cursor to the upper left corner and press F10. Then use ↓ and → to enlarge the box, and press F10 again.

5. Choose **Save art** from the Art menu. The Save dialog box is displayed.

6. Enter a file name that will help you identify the file later. Change the path designation, if necessary, so that the file is stored in the correct directory. (Remember that First Publisher automatically assigns the ART extension.) Also, if you are working from a clip art disk, be sure to save your art to the correct directory or you will wind up saving it to the clip art disk.

7. Click the OK button or press F1. The art is saved under the specified ART file name, and you can use it in your First Publisher documents.

Clip art can take up a lot of room on a hard disk. If you are worried about preserving memory, use the clip art files from the floppy disks.

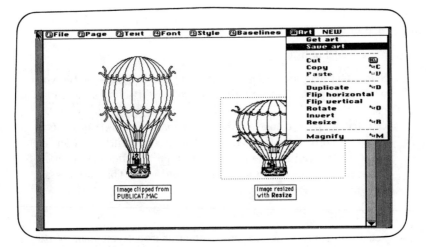

Fig. 6.27. Saving the graphic as an ART file.

Windows Paint

Microsoft Windows Paint is a paint program popular with many users of desktop publishing software. Figure 6.28 shows the workscreen on which you create graphics in Windows Paint. This program complements the graphics areas in which First Publisher needs an extra boost—by providing several additional graphics tools and shading capabilities.

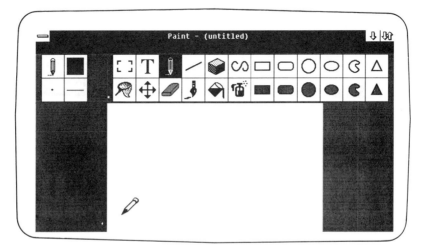

Fig. 6.28. *The workscreen of Windows Paint.*

PC Paintbrush

PC Paintbrush is another popular paint program directly compatible with First Publisher (see fig. 6.29). When you create a file with PC Paintbrush, you can use the art directly—even though the files end with PCX—by selecting the file with the **Get graphics** command on the File menu. (Before you can paste the image as art into your publications, however, you need to capture and save the image as an ART file.) Although PC Paintbrush is somewhat limited, many users find that this paint program offers them everything needed to enhance their First Publisher graphics. The makers of PC Paintbrush, ZSoft™, also produce Publisher's Paintbrush, which offers more features and saves to a PCX file.

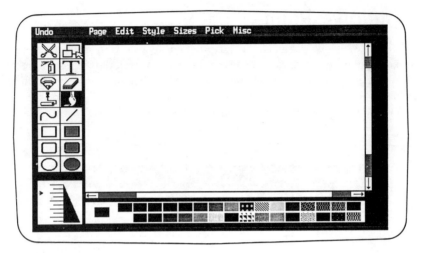

Fig. 6.29. *The opening screen for PC Paintbrush.*

LOGITECH Paintshow

LOGITECH Paintshow is a full-featured paint program that comes with the LOGITECH mouse. This program, which was used to produce all the hand-drawn graphics in this book, offers a wide variety of tools and various paint patterns from which to choose. In figure 6.30, the shapes were painted in various patterns. When this image was converted to a format readable by First Publisher (through the use of a routine called TIF2PCX, which is packaged with LOGITECH Paintshow), the patterns were brought without difficulty into the publication (see fig. 6.31).

Rules for Scanned Images

Later in this book, you will learn how to use a scanner to bring in digitized images. For now, just remember that First Publisher can use images scanned at 72 dpi (dots per inch), so you must use a scanner that can be set to 72 dpi. (If you own a scanner, the product manual explains whether this is possible. If you are taking your picture to a scanning service to be scanned—many printing houses and even some instant copy services now have this capability—ask an employee whether their particular scanner is capable of scanning at this setting.)

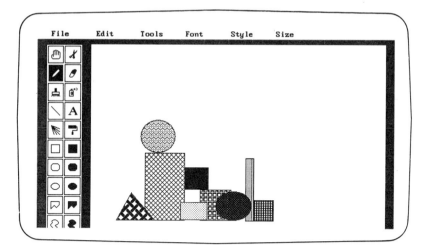

Fig. 6.30. *A graphic being ''painted'' in LOGITECH Paintshow.*

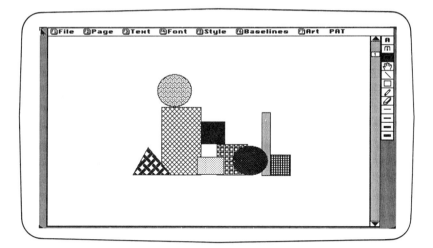

Fig. 6.31. *The item transfers correctly to First Publisher.*

The scanned image must be stored in a graphics file compatible with First Publisher or that can be converted to a compatible format (see the list of compatible paint programs shown earlier in this section). Remember that First Publisher ''sees'' a scanned image the same way it sees every other graphic element. Once the scanned image is imported into First Publisher, you can modify, resize, invert, and flip it, just like any other graphic image. Chapter 10, "First Publisher Special Features," explains the procedure for using scanned images in your First Publisher publications.

Chapter Summary

In this chapter, you learned all about the graphics tools and options available in First Publisher. Tips and applications were provided that will help you add creative touches to your publications. Additionally, you learned how to use First Publisher's clip art library, add graphics to your publications, and modify art elements. This chapter concluded with an overview of importing art and digitized images. The next chapter puts it all together by teaching you how to finish the layout.

Finishing the Layout

This chapter shows you how to pull into a finished product all the elements with which you have been working. If you have been trying the examples throughout the book, you probably have already been making decisions about which methods of using First Publisher you will adopt and which methods you will modify.

Built-in flexibility is one of First Publisher's best features: you have the flexibility to put your publication together any way you want. For example, you may want to produce a simple three-column report that has one heading at the top and your company's name at the bottom. You can simply set the **Define page** settings for three columns, place the text, and change the fonts of the heading and the footer. For some projects, you may not need to work with graphics or the graphics layer at all. In another case, you might want to produce an advertising flier that has no text on the text layer; the flier is just a piece of artwork, a border, and a few lines pasted in as graphics text. Whatever you need to produce, First Publisher allows you to assemble the project in the manner most comfortable for you.

In this chapter, after a brief review of the publishing process to this point, you will work with baselines to complete the text layer. Then you will explore the Page menu, complete the graphics layer, and learn about the Picturewrap feature and realigning the text. This chapter concludes with information for fine-tuning the publication by adding rules and boxes.

Reviewing the Publishing Process

Because First Publisher is such a flexible program, you have several ways to go about setting up a publication. This book has taken the following approach:

design + text + graphics + layout = publication

As you may recall, Chapter 4 provided design tips and explained the use of the **Define page** option of the File menu. Chapter 5 talked about typing or importing text and showed you how to edit the text once it was brought into a First Publisher document. Chapter 6 explained the various graphics tools and options, and discussed a few paint programs that are compatible with the program.

For some projects, you may not have to finish the layout as a separate step. If you started with a new publication, defined the page, pulled in text, and added art and rules while still working on that publication, for example, you were preparing the layout as you worked. But if you created the text and art files separately, you need to define a publication and then import and position the text and the art. This process is known as *layout*. Figure 7.1 shows the difference between the two approaches of assembling a publication.

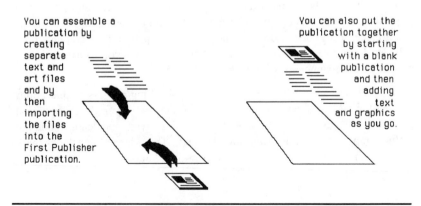

You can assemble a publication by creating separate text and art files and by then importing the files into the First Publisher publication.

You can also put the publication together by starting with a blank publication and then adding text and graphics as you go.

Fig. 7.1. Two approaches for assembling a publication.

You can set the page specifications by using the **Define page** option in the File menu at any time during the creation of a publication. If you have opted to create your text and art files separately and are now planning to merge them in a publication file, you may be working with this option for the first time. If so, read Chapter 4 to find out how to choose the specifications for your publication.

As you may recall, in Chapter 5 you created the *DT Publisher* newsletter, which served as an example of typing and importing text. In Chapter 6, you modified the newsletter further to add a banner, using graphics text. In this chapter, you complete the layout phase for that same newsletter. Figure 7.2 shows how the *DT Publisher* example appeared at the end of Chapter 6.

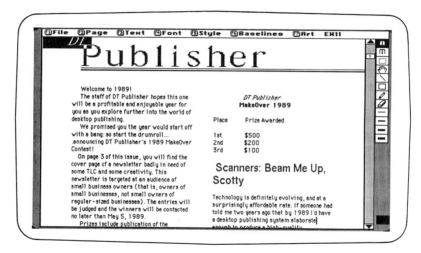

Fig. 7.2. The DT Publisher *example in its current state.*

Finishing the Text Layer

You need to do several things to *DT Publisher* before it can be called a finished publication. The first step is "finishing" the text layer of the newsletter. For this example, finishing the text layer means that you need to do the following things:

- ❏ Add headlines
- ❏ Change the font style and size of headlines
- ❏ Modify baselines so that headings and text are placed correctly on the page

The sections that follow explain each of these procedures.

Creating and Positioning Headlines

When you are adding headlines to the document, you have another decision to make. You can add a headline by

❏ Importing the headline with your word processing file

❏ Typing the headline in its correct position on the document

❏ Adding the headline as graphics text

Importing Headlines

You may remember that when the example shown in figure 7.2 was origi-nally imported from a WordStar file, a *FONT* command was used to change the font and size of the headline. Using a *FONT* command isn't necessary, although doing so does save you the time of respecifying the font later. But, if you prefer, you can import the heading in the same type size and style as the body text and then change the font later.

To change the font, style, and size of existing text, follow these steps:

1. Make sure that the text tool is selected.

2. Position the mouse cursor immediately to the left of the text you want to select.

3. Press the mouse button (or F10) and drag the mouse (or press the right-arrow key) to the right until the entire headline is high-lighted.

4. Open the Font menu and select the font you want to use (see fig. 7.3). The newly chosen font immediately goes into effect.

5. Open the Style menu and select the style and size, if necessary.

6. Move the cursor off the window, and the selected text is changed to the newly specified size and style.

Remember that your headlines should be of a uniform font; don't have three different headlines in three different fonts. As a general rule, use only one or two typefaces in a publication. For variety, you can change the size and style of the font you have chosen.

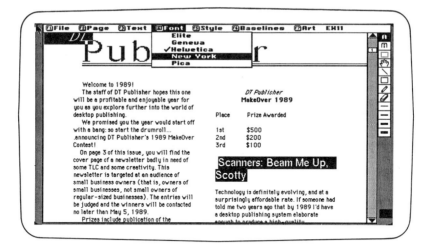

Fig. 7.3. *Changing the font, style, and size of existing text.*

Typing Headlines

You also can enter headlines on the publication by typing them in place. Suppose, for example, that you want to add the heading *Deadline Instructions* in the middle of the first article. (This item is a subheading that is subordinate to the main article heading, so it should appear in a smaller type size than the main headline. You add the main article headline later in this chapter.)

To type a heading in the publication, do the following:

1. Make sure that the text tool is selected. (The text tool is the tool at the top of the tools row, located on the right side of the screen.)

2. Position the cursor at the end of the paragraph after which you want to enter the heading.

3. Press Enter twice to add another blank line.

4. Select **New York** from the Font menu.

5. Select **Bold** and **14** from the Style menu.

6. Type *Deadline Instructions* and press Enter.

The headline should now be sandwiched between two blank lines and displayed in the correct font. Figure 7.4 shows the result.

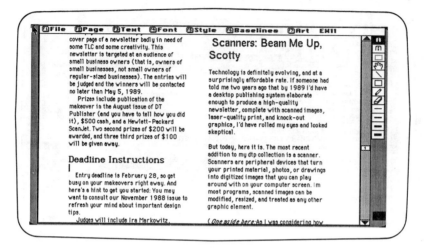

Fig. 7.4. *Typing a headline.*

Adding the Headline as Graphics Text

Your last option for adding headlines is the easiest of all: adding the headline as graphics text. If you decide to use the graphics text tool to enter the headline, remember to specify the font, size, and style first. First Publisher does not allow you to highlight and change typed graphics text as you can regular text on the text layer.

The beauty of using the graphics text tool to enter headlines is that you don't need to worry about baselines (which are discussed in the next section) or positioning the text. You simply type the text anywhere on the publication, select the text with the selection tool, and use the hand tool to push the text to the correct location.

The down side of using the graphics text tool to enter headlines is that the text will print as graphics text, so it will not take advantage of built-in fonts or cartridge fonts on dot-matrix or DeskJet printers. Also, headlines created in graphics text print in lower resolution on laser printers than headlines created with regular text. Therefore, if the banner you are creating does not require large or unusual sizes, you will get a better print quality if you use regular text for the banner and headlines. You can smooth out the graphics text by using the **Magnify** option on the Art menu and by using the pencil tool to modify individual pixels.

When you are using graphics text, you cannot highlight and change the font, size, or style of text by changing the selected items in the Font and Style menus. To change the font of graphics text, you must erase the text, select the font specifications you want, and reenter the text.

To enter a headline as graphics text, follow these steps:

1. Make sure that the graphics text tool is selected (second tool from the top of the tools row).

2. Anchor the cursor by clicking (or pressing F10) anywhere on the screen (preferably somewhere with a great deal of white space so you can easily see what you're doing).

3. Select **Helvetica** from the Font menu.

4. Select **24 points** from the Style menu.

5. Type *Happy New Year!*

6. Select the selection tool by clicking it (or pressing F10) or by pressing F9 until the tool is highlighted.

7. Capture the headline in the selection tool's flashing rectangle by clicking (or pressing F10) at the upper left corner of the headline and dragging the mouse down and to the right.

8. Select the hand tool.

9. Position the hand tool over the headline. Then push the mouse button and drag the headline to the correct position on-screen (see fig. 7.5).

10. At the appropriate position, release the mouse button.

Note: In order to make room for this heading, the baselines in the left column were moved down. The steps for this procedure are included later in this chapter.

You can add a ''kicker'' line, a small headline that leads into the larger headline, by using the same graphics text technique. Usually, a small rule is used to separate the kicker from the main heading (see fig. 7.6).

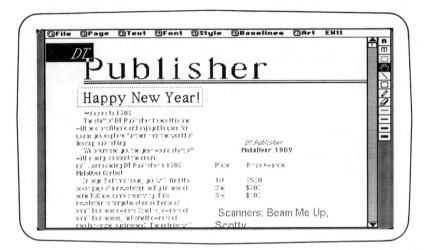

Fig. 7.5. Moving the graphics text headline to the correct position.

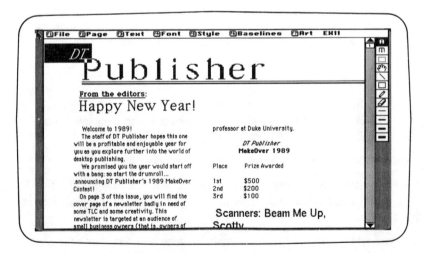

Fig. 7.6. A kicker line in graphics text.

Modifying Baselines

Positioning headlines on the text layer is not quite as simple as positioning graphics text. Earlier chapters introduced you to baselines, but until this phase, your involvement with baselines has probably been limited. In earlier versions of First Publisher, baseline modification was more difficult. With Version 2.0, however, most of the heavy-duty baseline modifications have been done for you. In earlier versions of First Publisher, for example, if you wanted to create a newsletter that had two columns on the top and three on the bottom, you had to zero out the baselines by hand. In Version 2.0, one of the seven available templates already has the baselines set in this format (2TOP3BOT.PUB).

Although you don't need to do any major changing with Version 2.0, you might modify baselines for the following reasons:

❑ You need to make room for graphic elements so that the text doesn't overlap the graphic

❑ You want to move the baselines down to make room for the banner

❑ You want to change the flow of text

Reviewing the Baselines Menu

You use the Baselines menu whenever you need to change the format of the text on the text layer. Table 7.1 provides an overview of each menu option.

Table 7.1
Options on the Baselines Menu

Option	Description
Adjust single (Alt-A)	Allows you to adjust one single baseline
Adjust column	Allows you to move a column
Adjust above	Lets you select one baseline and move every baseline in that column above and including the selected one

Table 7.1—*Continued*

Option	Description
Adjust below	Lets you select one baseline and move every baseline in that column below and including the selected one
Center (Alt-X)	Centers a baseline (often used to center headings)
Left justify	Moves the selected baselines so that text is placed starting at the left edge of each line
Right justify	Moves the selected baselines so that the text extends evenly to the right edge of each line
Full justify	Adjusts baselines so that the text extends evenly to both ends of selected baselines
Change leading	Allows you to change the amount of space between lines
Realign text (Alt-T)	Realigns text that has been affected by the baseline modifications

As mentioned earlier, the baselines in the *DT Publisher* example were moved down to make room for the banner. Figure 7.7 shows how the baselines looked before they were moved. The baselines appear closer together than they would appear on a default document because Geneva 10-point type with 13-point leading has been specified. Remember that baselines are displayed only when one of the options in the Baselines menu is active.

Moving Columns with the Adjust Below Option

To move down baselines in the left column, select **Adjust column** from the Baselines menu. In this case, you need to zero out the baselines that would interfere with the banner. The procedure for "zeroing out" baselines is explained in the next section.

When **Adjust column** is active, the baselines on the document appear. Select the top baseline in the left column by clicking it (or by using the

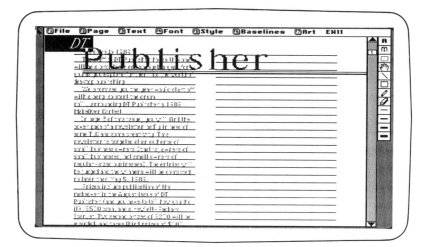

Fig. 7.7. *The baselines before modification.*

arrow keys to move the cursor to that position and pressing F10 twice). Three handles appear on the baseline; one on each end and one in the middle. Position the mouse cursor on the handle in the middle of the baseline, press the mouse button, and drag the handle down until it covers the fourth baseline from the top.

The baseline should look as though it is moving. If only the handles seem to be moving in tandem with the mouse, you are not moving the baseline—you are simply selecting different baselines as you drag the mouse. If your baseline isn't moving, release the mouse button, position the cursor on the top baseline, and start again. Figure 7.8 shows how a baseline looks when it is being moved.

Because the columns of *DT Publisher* need to be even, repeat this procedure to move the right-hand column down to the same place on the publication. Although the text is ''fuzzy'' when you are manipulating baselines, when you turn off the active baseline option, the text once again becomes readable.

Figure 7.9 shows the newsletter after the baselines have been adjusted.

Fig. 7.8. *Moving a baseline.*

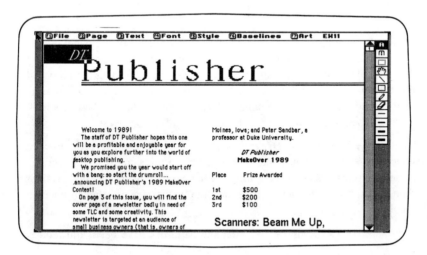

Fig. 7.9. *The newsletter after the baselines have been moved.*

Once you have started making baseline changes, don't use the **Define page** option unless you have made some serious mistakes and want to start over. Choosing **Define page** erases any modifications you have made to the baselines and returns them to the column format specified.

Canceling Baselines

When you are working with baselines, you will need to cancel, or "zero out," a baseline on the publication. For example, suppose that after you move the columns down, you notice that the text extends too far down the page. You can use **Adjust below** to zero out the baselines at the bottom of the page.

To zero out the baselines at the bottom of the newsletter, do the following:

1. Select **Adjust below** from the Baselines menu.

2. Move the mouse cursor to the top baseline you want to remove and click the mouse button. (If you are using the keyboard, use the cursor keys to move the mouse cursor to the appropriate baseline and press F10 twice to select the baseline.) The handles appear on the baseline.

3. Position the cursor on the handle nearest to the gutter. (The gutter is the white space between columns.) In this example, click the rightmost side of the bottom-left baseline.

4. Press the mouse button (or F10) and drag the baseline to the left, in effect pulling the baseline back over itself. This "cancels" or "zeros out" the baseline. (If you are using the keyboard, press F10 once and use the left-arrow key to move the baseline to the left.) If the baseline isn't growing shorter as you move the mouse, you didn't select the outside handle. If you notice that the operation isn't working, release the mouse button and start again.

5. Release the mouse button (or press F10). The baseline has been zeroed out so that text will not flow to that baseline.

Zeroing out baselines is important in controlling the text flow of your publication. Suppose, for example, that you want to place two articles on page one of a newsletter. Five basic steps are required. They are the following:

1. Choose **Define page** and specify a two-column format.

2. Select **Adjust below** from the Baselines menu and zero out both columns starting at the center of the page. (Only the top half of the page should show baselines at this point.)

3. Import the first article. The text flows into the available baselines in the top half of the page.

4. Select **Adjust below** from the Baselines menu and reverse the zeroing out procedure, returning the baselines to their original length.

5. Import the second article. The text flows into the only available baselines, which are located in the bottom half of the page.

> Remember that you can use any of the first four options on the Baselines menu when you want to move, shorten, lengthen, or zero out baselines.

The zeroed-out baseline looks like a white H in a black box. After you move to the next baseline, the H turns to a small black dot, indicating that the line has been canceled. You can reverse the zeroing-out procedure by clicking the dot until the H appears; then click the H and pull the line back to its original position.

> To restore zeroed-out baselines, you may need to pull the handle farther toward the edge in order to separate the three handles. Once separated, it's much easier to grab the outermost handle and pull the baseline back into place.

As you can see, zeroing out a baseline does not actually remove it but simply makes the baseline too small to hold even one letter. Whether you zero out baselines at the start, the middle, or the end of a page or document, text automatically "skips" the canceled line and flows to the next available baseline. Figure 7.10 shows the newsletter after the bottom baselines have been canceled.

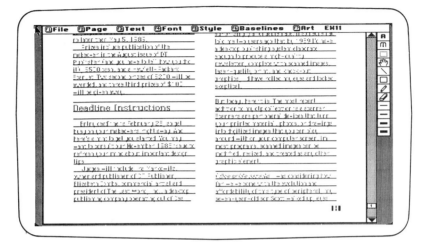

Fig. 7.10. *The newsletter after the bottom baselines have been zeroed out.*

Modifying Individual Baselines

In some instances, you need to be able to manipulate individual baselines. Suppose, for example, that you want to cut a piece of clip art from one of the available clip art files and paste the art between the columns of *DT Publisher*.

First Publisher allows you to cut and paste art on the graphics layer without modifying the baselines at all; but if you don't move the baselines, the text and the graphic will overlap, leaving you with an unreadable mess.

You also have other options for formatting text around a graphic. You can use First Publisher's **Picturewrap** feature (available on the Page menu) to cut out a rectangular block into which text will not flow. Additionally, you can use **Adjust below** or **Adjust above** to move and align baselines to allow room for art. In this example, the text "runs around" a graphic, so **Adjust single** is used here.

To move the baselines so that the text is arranged around the art, follow these steps after you place the art on the publication:

1. Select **Adjust single** from the Baselines menu or press Alt-A.

2. Move the mouse cursor to the baseline you want to modify (in this case, the fifth baseline from the top).

3. Select the baseline by clicking it or by moving the cursor to that position and pressing F10.

4. Shorten the baseline by dragging it back to the appropriate position. (If you are using a keyboard, press F10 and use the arrow keys to move the baseline as far as necessary.)

5. Release the mouse button (or press F10).

Figure 7.11 shows how the publication looks after the baselines on the left side of the page have been adjusted to make room for the art.

Fig. 7.11. DT Publisher *after the baselines have been adjusted.*

Rather than modify the baselines to make room for an image, you can select **Picturewrap** to "block out" a section of the publication so that text doesn't enter that area. You can use **Picturewrap** before or after you place graphics. (For more information, see "Using Picturewrap" later in this chapter.)

Changing Baseline Alignment

As you may recall, you set the text alignment when you define the page (using **Define page** on the File menu). The Baselines menu has a few additional commands that allow you to change the alignment of the text on individual baselines. These commands are the following:

Center
Left justify
Right justify
Full justify
Change leading

You may want to use these baseline alignment settings, for example, when you want to center a heading, create a particular design by aligning the text on the right side of the column, or add white space around a specific line to call attention to it.

The last option, **Change leading**, will be discussed first. You use this option when you want to change the amount of white space that surrounds a particular baseline. Perhaps, for example, you think the *Scanners* headline has too much leading. To correct that situation, you should first delete the extra blank lines that you added by pressing Enter. To erase the blank line above the heading, position the cursor at the beginning of the headline (just to the left of the S in Scanners) and press the Backspace key. The text then moves up one line. Use the Backspace key also to remove the blank line that follows the heading.

To change the leading of the baseline, first select **Adjust single** from the Baselines menu or press Alt-A. When the baselines appear, click the baseline that includes the *Scanners* headline. Next select **Change leading** from the Baselines menu. After you select that option, the dialog box shown in figure 7.12 appears.

Position the cursor in the specification box. The box shows either 16—the default value—or another setting you specified in the Define Page dialog box or in other **Change leading** operations. (For this example, a setting of 25 was entered to get the appropriate spacing.) When you have entered the setting you want, click the OK button or press F1. Figure 7.13 shows the results of the new leading specification.

The remaining options on the Baselines menu deal with the alignment of text on the baselines. Before you can select these options, you must have selected one of the first four items in the Baselines menu. In other words, before you can change the alignment for baselines, you must select the baseline(s) that will be affected. Figure 7.14 shows how the **Center**, **Left justify**, **Right justify**, and **Full justify** options affect text on baselines.

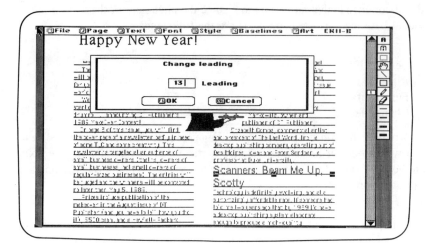

Fig. 7.12. *The Change Leading dialog box.*

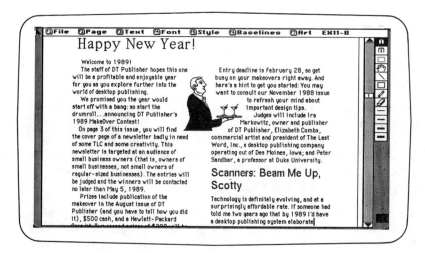

Fig. 7.13. *The results of entering a new leading setting.*

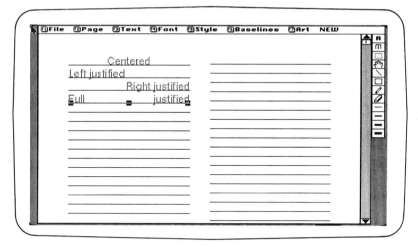

Fig. 7.14. *Using the baseline alignment options.*

Are You Finished with the Text Layer?

When you think you are just about finished with the text layer of the publication, ask yourself these questions:

❏ Are you happy with the font, size, and style you have selected for body text?

❏ Have you edited the text?

❏ Have you inserted and modified headings as necessary? (If you plan to insert headings as graphics text, skip this question.)

❏ Have you modified the baselines so that the text doesn't collide with the graphics?

❏ Are you satisfied with the way the text is laid out on the page?

Completing the Graphics Layer

The next step in finishing the publication involves polishing off the graphics layer. What still needs to be done?

❏ Finishing the banner

❏ Using the grid and rulers to align graphics and text

❏ Adding images

❏ Fine-tuning the display

❏ Adding headers and footers

These procedures require the combined use of the graphics tools and the Page menu. Table 7.2 highlights the commands on the Page menu.

Table 7.2
Options on the Page Menu

Option	Description
Define page	Allows you to set margins, columns, and leading information about the page
Picturewrap	Wraps text around a graphic (Alt-W) element
Show rulers (Alt-L)	Displays rulers on the screen, enabling you to make your layout as accurate as possible
Use grid (Alt-U)	Locks the movement of the cursor into a particular "grid" pattern, enabling you to ensure a clean, precise look for your publication
Set grid size	Lets you modify the size of the grid so that the movement of some tools is still restricted, but within a different variance
Jump to page (Alt-J)	Moves the display to the page you specify
Insert page	Inserts a page before the current page
Delete page	Deletes the current page
Show page (Alt-Z)	Displays the entire page (*Note:* This command produces a "thumbnail" view of the entire page. Although you can see the general layout, you cannot read the text.)

Finishing the Banner

The main part of the banner, the word *Publisher*, was created as graphics text in Chapter 6. The *DT* was added later in that chapter as an example of inverted graphics text. But the banner hardly looks finished.

When you are creating your publication's banner, consider the audience of the publication. Let this consideration guide your choice for the font, size, and graphics used in the banner. To add a modern look to the banner of *DT Publisher*, add a clip art selection to the publication. First save the publication, then open the BUSINESS.MAC clip art file, and capture the image by using the selection tool and the **Save art** command. Then return to the publication, select **Get art**, and select the clip art file you just saved. The program automatically changes to the hand tool, and you then click the mouse (or press F10) to paste the item on the publication. You can move the item to the correct place or resize, invert, or modify the image as needed. (For more information on working with graphics, see Chapter 6.) Figure 7.15 shows the results to this point.

Fig. 7.15. The results of the banner modification.

You may want to use the **Magnify** option, available on the Art menu, to smooth the edges of an image or to help blend it with another graphic. In the *DT Publisher* example, the clip art symbol was positioned next to the banner name; then the image was smoothed with the **Magnify** option.

Using the Grid To Align Elements

You may want to draw the outline of your publication by adding rules on all four sides. Additionally, some publishers like the look of rules used to separate columns of text. (See "To Rule or Not To Rule" in this chapter.) To draw the top rule, you simply select the line tool and draw a line from the left side of the screen to the right. You hopefully will wind up with a straight line, but if you get a "crimp" in the line, or you release the mouse button before you have positioned the end of the line properly, you have to erase the line and start again. To ensure that the lines you draw are straight, you can use First Publisher's *grid* feature.

The grid helps you position both text and art on the graphics layer. Use the grid when you are positioning graphics, when you want to align a headline so that it is even with corresponding text, or when you are trying to align two graphic elements on a page. The grid feature is particularly useful when you are drawing rules the length of the page, when you are aligning two or more graphic elements, or when you are aligning text and graphics. Another use for the grid arises when you are working with multipage documents. If you are copying headers or footers so that they appear in the same position on each page, use the grid to ensure the accuracy of the position.

To turn on the grid, select **Use grid** from the Page menu or press Alt-U (see fig. 7.16). When the grid feature is activated, small dots appear 1/4 inch apart in a grid pattern on-screen, as shown in figure 7.17. (*Note:* This is the default specification for the grid size.)

When the grid feature is active, you can use the Shift and arrow keys to move the cursor in grid increments. To move the cursor one grid increment in a specific direction, press Shift and use the arrow keys in the manner to which you are accustomed (↑ for up, ↓ for down, ← for left, and → for right).

Fig. 7.16. *Selecting* **Use grid**.

Fig. 7.17. *The grid pattern displayed on the screen.*

You can change the size of the grid by selecting **Set grid size** from the Page menu (see fig. 7.18). The available size increments for the grid range from 0.12 inch to 1 inch. Figure 7.19 shows the grid set to the smallest available setting (0.12). You can set the vertical and horizontal grid sizes independently, if you prefer.

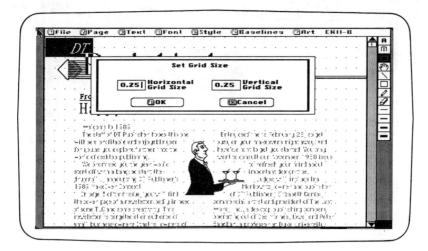

Fig. 7.18. *Selecting* ***Set grid size***.

Fig. 7.19. *Using the smallest grid size.*

For the *DT Publisher* example, suppose that you need to draw one rule across the top and one rule the length of the publication. To create these rules, follow these steps:

1. Select **Use grid** from the Page menu or press Alt-U. The small dots showing the grid size are displayed on the screen.

2. Choose the line tool from the graphics tools.

3. Position the cursor at the left edge of the publication.

4. Press the mouse button (or F10) and drag the line across the width of the publication. Notice that as you drag the line, it "snaps" to the grid lines (see fig. 7.20).

5. At the right edge of the publication, release the mouse button (or F10). You have now completed the first line.

Fig. 7.20. The grid restricting the movement of the line.

If the grid size is set too large, you may wind up drawing the rule farther away from the edge than you would prefer. To fix this problem, you have two options: you can change the grid size by selecting **Set grid size** from the Page menu; or you can draw the second rule with the grid width as is and then turn off the grid, capture the rule with the selection tool, and move the rule to the appropriate position.

Using Rulers To Place Elements

You can use rulers also to align elements and to help you make sure that you place certain elements in the same position on every page. Suppose, for example, that you want to position a page number in the bottom right corner of every page. You can display rulers by selecting **Show rulers** from the Page menu or by pressing Alt-L (see fig. 7.21). A horizontal ruler is displayed across the top of the screen, and a vertical ruler is displayed on the left edge of the screen (see fig. 7.22). The ruler is marked in 1/4-inch increments. After you judge where on the page the page number is to be positioned, you can place the number in that exact spot on every page.

Fig. 7.21. *Selecting the* **Show rulers** *option.*

When you want to remove the rulers, select **Show rulers** (or press Alt-L) again.

Adding Graphics

Next you need to add graphics to the *DT Publisher* newsletter. Again, you have two options: you can create the image here, on the publication; or you can create the art in another file and then import that art into the publication. For this example, assume that you created the art in another file and are now importing the art into the current publication. (For more information on creating and saving art, see Chapter 6.)

Fig. 7.22. *Displaying rulers with First Publisher.*

The image must be in an ART file before you can bring it into your First Publisher document. If you saved the image in a MAC file or imported the image from another document, you first need to turn the image into an ART file that First Publisher can cut and paste. To turn an image in a MAC file into a piece of art available with the **Get art** command, follow these steps:

1. Save the current publication.

2. Select **Get graphics** from the File menu.

3. Choose the name of the file you need and click OK (or press F10).

4. When the MAC file is displayed on the screen, choose the selection tool from the graphics tools.

5. Grab the item you want to save as an ART file.

6. Select **Save art** from the Art menu.

7. Enter a name for the ART file and click OK (or press F10). The image is then saved as an ART file.

8. Select **Get publication** from the File menu and return to the previous publication.

Now the art image is available to you when you choose **Get art** from the Art menu. When you select that option and the file name of the art image, the program changes the cursor to the hand tool, indicating that you should click the mouse button (or position the cursor and press F10) where you want the image to be placed. You then can move the image around the publication as necessary.

When you use a clip art image in First Publisher, you must first save it as an ART image and then import the art by using the **Get art** command (available in the Art menu). Don't try to place a graphic in your publication without first saving it as an ART file, or First Publisher will display an error message.

Figure 7.23 shows an image after it has been imported into the *DT Publisher* example.

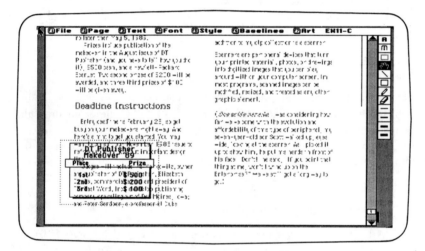

Fig. 7.23. *An image imported into* DT Publisher.

Next the document needs a little fine-tuning. As you can see, the graphics and text overlap. You can solve this problem either by modifying some of the baselines or by using First Publisher's **Picturewrap** feature.

Fine-Tuning the Display with Picturewrap

The **Picturewrap** feature allows you to block out a section of the publication and prevent text from flowing into that area. As you read in an earlier section, you can modify the length of individual baselines to control how closely text is positioned to an image. The **Picturewrap** option allows you to protect a square of space for the graphic.

You can use **Picturewrap** before or after you place graphics. In fact, you can use this feature to block out a section for a graphic you haven't even created yet. To use **Picturewrap**, do the following:

1. Choose the selection tool from the graphics tools.

2. Select the area on the publication you want to reserve.

3. Select **Picturewrap** from the Page menu or press Alt-W (see fig. 7.24). When the option is selected, a check mark appears next to it.

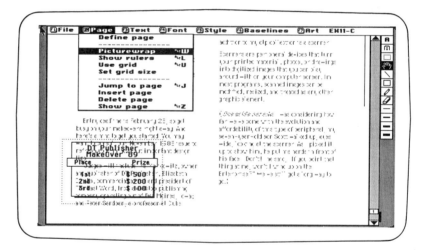

Fig. 7.24. *Selecting **Picturewrap** from the Page menu.*

First Publisher then realigns all text automatically, reserving the area you marked with the selection tool. Whether or not you have an image within that selected area, First Publisher does not flow text into the area, as demonstrated in figure 7.25.

If you turn on **Picturewrap** before you place an image, First Publisher automatically formats the text in a square surrounding the image area. When you want to disable the **Picturewrap** feature, select the option or press Alt-W again.

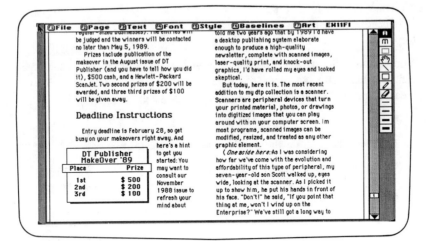

Fig. 7.25. *The effects of using the* **Picturewrap** *option.*

When you are finished using the **Picturewrap** feature, remember to turn it off by selecting it again or by typing Alt-W. If you don't disable the feature and you bring in another image, First Publisher will picturewrap that image also, even if it's not in the place you intended it.

> If you have placed a graphic over text without **Picturewrap**, you can reflow the text by turning on **Picturewrap**, realigning the text, and turning off **Picturewrap** by typing Alt-W.

Adding Footers

If you are creating a newsletter, like the example in this chapter, you may want to add footers to your publication. As you probably know, a *footer* is a line (or lines) at the bottom of a publication that are printed on every page. Often, these lines include the name of the publication, the month, and the page number.

You add the footer as graphics text because of its low position on the page. (Baselines do not extend that far down the page.) Figure 7.26 shows the footer for the *DT Publisher* newsletter.

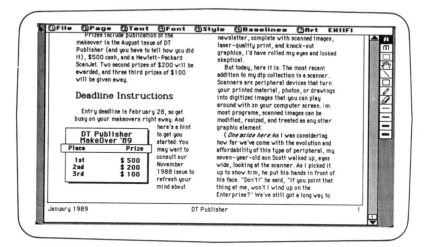

Fig. 7.26. The footer for DT Publisher.

To Rule or Not To Rule

Another important consideration for the design of your document involves whether you want to draw lines around the publication and between columns. Rules in a publication should add—quietly—to the design, not overwhelm or detract from it. Too many rules in a publication steal the reader's attention from the text. You want to use only enough to give the publication an orderly, organized look.

Figure 7.27 shows several examples of rules. In the first example, the publication is entirely bordered by rules. The second example shows a publication that has rules separating the columns, and the third has two rules used as design elements in the center of the page. Choose the style that best fits your audience and your expectations.

Fig. 7.27. *Several examples of rules in publications.*

Medical Update

Volume 23, No. 5   February 1989

Research Shows Surprising Results
New Strategies for Mitral Valve Treatment

Recent research has proven that mitral insufficiency from connective tissue disorders and a variety of other causes are leading physicians to consider mitral valve reconstruction as a viable alternative for patients suffering from mitral disorders.

Seeing the advantages to mitral valvular reconstruction has been slow for many leading physicians.

However, mitral valve reconstruction offers a lower percentage of long-term morbidity and mortality than replacement offers.

The research demonstrates that, if caught early, mitral valve repair is much easier on the patient and is a safer operation to perform.

This procedure has been slow to gain acceptance because accurate methods of obtaining research data have not been available.

> **Many physicians have had trouble seeing the real value in considering mitral valve reconstruction..."**

Researchers have recently attempted using intraoperative cardiac color-flow mapping as a method of gathering the statistical data they need in order to assess whether or not the procedure is worth the cost and risk--albeit minimal--to patients.

Color mapping is a technique that superimposes on the two-dimensional echocardiogram color that highlights the blood flow velocity and direction. This color mapping allows physicians to determine whether a weak valve does in fact warrant further testing as to the possibility of a mitral valve reconstruction.

This technique also lends itself to other diagnostic procedures as well. When a ventricular clot is suspected, the color mapping procedure can be used to determine whether a clot exists,

continued on pg. 3

Hospital News

Family Service Unit Opens at Mount Sinai

Minnie Mouse Coat, Sure; But Mickey Mouse Work? No Way.

He wears a Minnie Mouse coat and his office is filled with toys and stuffed animals, but for Dr. Howard Levy, life is anything but frivolous. The playful trappings constrast sharply with the tragedy that confronts Dr. Levy with each patient he sees. Dr. Levy is the director of the Pediatric Ecology Unit at Mount Sinai Medical Center in Chicago. It's the first facility in the nation designed to evaluate and treat victims and families of child abuse and neglect.

The unit treats patients from newborn to 14 years old. It offers a relaxed, cozy atmosphere. None of the staff wear uniforms, and the rooms are furnished more like a home than a hospital. The walls are adorned with finger paintings and crayon artwork. "The whole environment here," says Dr. Levy, "is aimed toward warmth."

Sadly, for many of the young patients, the warmth of the unit is the first they have experienced.

The Mount Sinai unit is structured to give each child the attention he needs. One of the best things about it, note the doctors, is the way they take things "at the child's speed." Kids are given time to warm

continued on pg. 2

Fig. 7.27—Continued

Fig. 7.27—_Continued_

Adding Boxes To Highlight Information

Another graphic touch you see often in newsletters and magazines are *callout boxes*, boxes that include synopsized information, tips, or quotes. These boxes tell the reader the high points of the article and possibly get the reader interested in reading the article. Used wisely, these boxes also add a sophisticated look to the publication.

Specific instructions for creating shadow boxes are included in Chapter 6. When you place the text in an information shadow box, make sure that you select a different size or style for the text. Generally, staying with the same typeface is best, but you should vary the style or the size of the type. The image added earlier in this chapter was a drop shadow box with a title bar overlay. In figure 7.23, this box was created as graphics text and then imported into the document.

Are You Finished with the Graphics Layer?

When you think you are just about finished with the graphics layer of the publication, ask yourself these questions:

❏ Do you like the way the text is arranged?

❏ Does the banner reflect the style you want?

❏ Did you add rules, boxes, and graphics to enhance the layout?

❏ Did you leave enough white space on the publication? (Does it look too crowded?)

❏ Do the images you have chosen help communicate the text's message?

Chapter Summary

In this chapter, you learned how to finish the text layer and the graphics layer and how to fine-tune your publication by adding rules, boxes, and footers. You also learned how to control the layout of text and graphics by using **Picturewrap** and by modifying baselines. In the next chapter, you will print the publication you have created.

8

Printing the Publication

Something is very rewarding about seeing your creation in print. Anything you create on-screen is just a screen image until you have a copy you can hold in your hands.

This chapter explores the procedures for printing your First Publisher publications. First Publisher is a WYSIWYG (What You See Is What You Get) program, which means that your on-screen creations resemble the output you receive from your printer. The image you see on your screen may vary from the final output depending on the resolution of your monitor, however. If you are using a CGA monitor, for example, the printed output may be slightly different than what you see on-screen; the output may be closer to the screen representation if you're using an EGA monitor. If the placement of the graphics is an important consideration for your work, be sure to turn on First Publisher's rulers even though they appear distorted on the screen. (Enable the rulers by selecting **Show rulers** from the Page menu.)

You will learn the hardware and software information you need to know to use dot-matrix and laser printers. After you learn to set up your MASTER.FNT file, you will learn the procedure for using soft fonts, when to use the various print modes, and how to evaluate your printed product. This chapter also includes tips that can help your printing go more smoothly and save time.

Reviewing Printer History

Today, many kinds of printers are available for personal computers. Just a few years ago, printers with the print quality of just a typewriter cost up to $1,000. Now, less expensive printers can produce output to rival that of professional typesetting systems.

With the current version of First Publisher, you cannot output text directly to a Linotronic typesetting system or other electronic typesetter; at present, the best quality you can get is output from a laser printer, which can print publications at 300 dpi. First Publisher also can produce a clean, professional-looking publication on dot-matrix printers. Before you go any further, stop and review the definitions of a few terms:

Dot-matrix printer refers to the type of printer that places text and graphics on a page by printing a pattern of dots.

Laser printers use laser technology to produce images in a manner similar to photocopying machines.

Resolution refers to the number of dots per inch in a printed (or on-screen) image. The more dots, the higher the resolution. An image printed at high resolution (such as 300 dpi) looks much smoother, less jagged than an image printed at 120 or 72 dpi, which are the resolutions of most dot-matrix printers.

Bit-mapped is a term used to describe text or an image that is actually a pattern of dots.

Soft fonts are fonts on a disk that are available for some laser printers. These soft fonts can be downloaded—or copied—to the printer when a publication is printed.

When First Publisher was introduced, laser printers weren't as common-place as they are today. Unlike other programs, First Publisher takes care of the many users who don't have a laser printer but who need to produce quality publications on dot-matrix printers. The program takes the dot-matrix printer user seriously and addresses the problem of producing high-quality output on a low-resolution machine.

First Publisher is packaged with a master font file, called MASTER.FNT, which contains all the dot-matrix fonts available in the Font and Style menus when you first install the program. Extra fonts also are available in a file called EXTRA.FNT. These are not in the MASTER.FNT file because not all computers have enough memory for all the fonts. Chapter 10 explains the FONTMOVE program, which is used to move fonts in and out of First Publisher. A Laser Support Disk contains the fonts supported by your particular brand of laser printer. First Publisher also supports downloadable fonts (also called *soft fonts*) for the Hewlett-Packard series of laser printers. The procedures for using soft fonts with First Publisher are explained later in this chapter.

Using Dot-Matrix Printers

Probably the biggest problem with dot-matrix printers is their low resolution. Because most dot-matrix printers produce either 72 or 120 dots per inch (most laser printers produce output at 300 dpi), the characters and graphics on a dot-matrix printer can be a bit jagged. If you look closely, you can see the individual dots that make up the pattern of the letter or image.

To help alleviate this problem, First Publisher includes a smoothing feature with the print routine. This feature "polishes" rough text by smoothing the jagged edges of characters and graphics. Figure 8.1 shows a publication printed in standard mode; figure 8.2 illustrates the difference the smoothing feature can make when the same publication is printed with that mode selected. Smoothing is discussed in more detail in the "Using Smoothed Mode" section of this chapter.

First Publisher supports the widest range of printers available with any desktop publishing program, so you will more than likely find yours listed. Table 8.1 lists the dot-matrix printers that are tested and are sure to be compatible with Version 2.0 of First Publisher. If your printer is not on the list, check your printer's users' manual to see whether the printer can emulate one on the list.

If your printer isn't on the list, you may still be able to use the printer. To find out whether your printer can emulate a printer compatible with First Publisher, check the printer's users' manual or call the printer's manufacturer.

If the printer can emulate a printer usable with First Publisher, simply enter the number next to that printer's name when you run the Printer program.

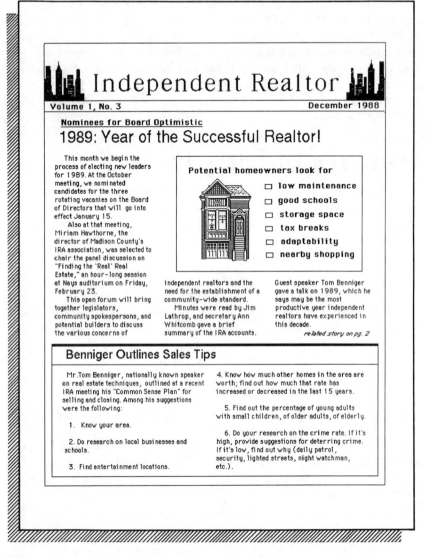

Fig. 8.1. *A publication printed in standard mode.*

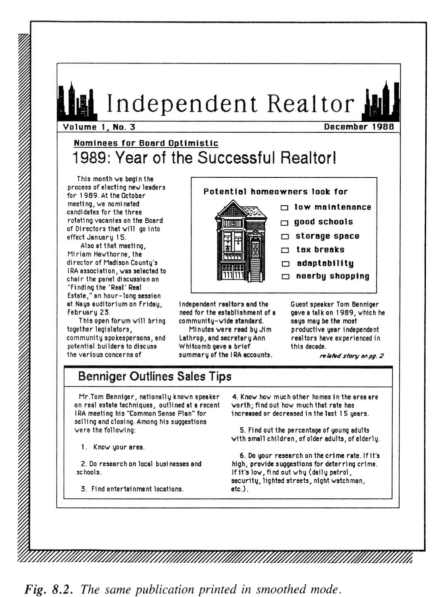

Fig. 8.2. The same publication printed in smoothed mode.

Table 8.1
Dot-Matrix Printers Compatible with First Publisher

Manufacturer	Models
EPSON	EX, FX, JX, LX, MX, RX, LQ
Hewlett-Packard	QuietJet, QuietJet Plus, ThinkJet
IBM	Graphics, QuietWriter II, ProPrinter, ProPrinter XL, ProPrinter II, ProPrinter XL24, ProPrinter X24
NEC	P5, P5XL, P6, CP6, P7, CP7, P9
OKIDATA	Microline Models 92, 93, 182, 183, 192, 193, 292, 293, 294
Panasonic	1080, 1090, 1091, 1092, 1093, 1592, 1595
Star Micronics	Gemini 10X/15X, NR-10/15, NX-10/15, NB24-10/15, NB-15
Tandy	DMP 130, 430, 2110, 2200
Texas Instruments	855
Toshiba	P321, P341, P351, P351C, P1340, P1350, P1351

Using Laser Printers

First Publisher also comes with a Laser Support Disk. On this disk, you will find the high-resolution fonts that work with your laser printer (providing you have one of the printers listed in table 8.2). First Publisher supports all Hewlett-Packard LaserJet soft fonts and several cartridges that you can purchase separately (see table 8.2).

Although First Publisher supports soft fonts for Hewlett-Packard's LaserJet printers, the program does not support DeskJet soft fonts.

Table 8.2
Laser Printers Compatible with First Publisher

Manufacturer	Models
Apple	LaserWriter, LaserWriter Plus, LaserWriter II
Hewlett-Packard	LaserJet, LaserJet+, LaserJet Series II[1], DeskJet[2]

[1]First Publisher supports all Hewlett-Packard LaserJet soft fonts and font cartridges B and F.

[2]First Publisher supports cartridges A, D, E, F, G, H, J, P, and Q. The DeskJet is not a laser printer but is recognized as such by the First Publisher program.

Using First Publisher Print Modes

First Publisher gives you the option of printing output at three different quality levels: draft, standard, and smoothed. You select the mode by clicking the box in front of the mode you want in the Print dialog box (see fig. 8.3).

The time required to print the publication and the quality of the printout vary greatly depending on which mode you choose. With the release of Version 2.01, Software Publishing Corporation also gave users another choice that influences the print time and quality of the printouts. Now users can choose whether they want publications to be printed in scaled or unscaled mode. Table 8.3 gives you an idea of when you might use each of these print modes.

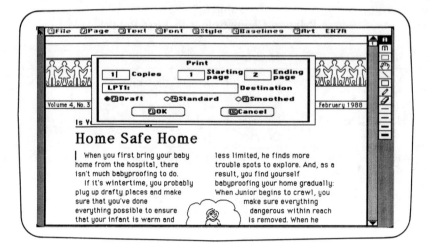

Fig. 8.3. The Print dialog box.

Table 8.3
Using the Print Modes

Mode	Use
Draft	Use this mode when you want to print quickly a rough draft of a working layout.
Standard	Use this mode when you need to see how the text and graphics work together on the publication, but you are not ready to print in smoothed mode. (On some printers, standard mode may produce better looking characters than smoothed mode.)
Smoothed	Use this mode when you want to print the final version of the publication. (If you are unhappy with the formation of any of the characters, try printing the document in standard or unscaled mode.)

Table 8.3—*Continued*

Mode	Use
Scaled	Use this mode when you need to print a document in the exact proportions it is displayed on-screen. Use this feature, for example, when you are printing a publication that includes a map, a diagram that must be accurate, or items that must be true to size, such as business cards or mail-in business reply cards. Scaled mode can be used with draft, standard, or smoothed mode.
Unscaled	Use this mode when printing the publication in the exact on-screen proportions is not necessary. Some printers produce better looking characters in unscaled mode, so if you are having trouble with the formation of text (particularly in smaller fonts), try printing in unscaled mode. Unscaled mode can be used with draft, standard, or smoothed mode and can make a substantial difference in lowering print times. This mode can generally be used for printing all publications that do not require printing to screen specifications, such as most newsletters, fliers, business reports, proposals, press releases, and announcements.

Using Draft Mode

Usually, you use draft mode when you are creating a publication. Draft mode print is not high quality; it is meant to give you a "rough draft" of your publication. Figure 8.4 shows an example of a publication printed in draft mode on an Epson FX-286e printer.

You can print faster in draft mode than in standard or smoothed mode, which is the major advantage of draft mode. To date, no other low-priced desktop publishing program offers draft mode as a printing choice. When the publication in figure 8.4 was printed with Version 2.0, the print time was five minutes. When it was printed with Version 2.01 in unscaled mode, the print time was two minutes.

In all modes, the print time will vary, depending on how much text and how many images are used in the publication and on the capabilities of your

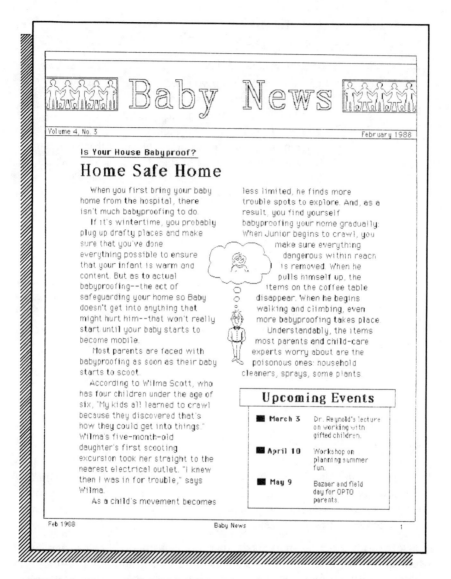

Fig. 8.4. *A example of draft mode.*

printer. Because fonts and images are complex formulas that your printer must interpret, the publications will take longer to print than, say, average word processing files.

Using Standard Mode

Standard mode prints in denser type, filling in more dots and improving the definition of characters. You could use standard mode when you're almost finished with a publication and you want to send a copy to several departments for approval. Figure 8.5 shows a publication printed in standard mode (also on the Epson). Printing this publication in standard mode with Version 2.0 took 28 minutes; Version 2.01 in standard, unscaled mode produced the document in 6 minutes.

Printing with Version 2.0

If you have upgraded to Version 2.0 from Version 1.0, you may have noticed a considerable slowdown in the printing process. This speed reduction is caused by a new feature of the program that produces a truer representation of images on the screen. With Version 1.0, if you used the ruler to draw a 5-by-5 box on-screen, the printed image appeared as 6-by-6. With Version 2.0, a 5-by-5 box prints as a 5-by-5 box.

Depending on your printer and the type of publications you produce, the slowdown may not be a problem for you. However, if you have noticed a substantial increase in the amount of time it takes to print a publication or if you have noticed a decrease in the quality of the printout, Version 2.01 offers the feature you need to enhance the printing capabilities of the program. As mentioned earlier in this chapter, Version 2.01 adds a scaled/unscaled feature that allows users to select whether they want to print the publication exactly as it appears on-screen (scaled) or whether the exact measurements are unnecessary (unscaled). There is not a drastic change in the appearance of the two options, so if you choose **Unscaled**, don't worry: the publications will not appear distorted. Unscaled mode offers you the flexibility of printing high-quality documents more quickly and, in some cases, with better character formation. Choose **Scaled** when you have a publication that requires printing exactly as the image appears on the screen (in accordance with First Publisher's rulers).

According to the developers of First Publisher, on certain printers, some small characters in certain fonts look better printed in standard mode rather

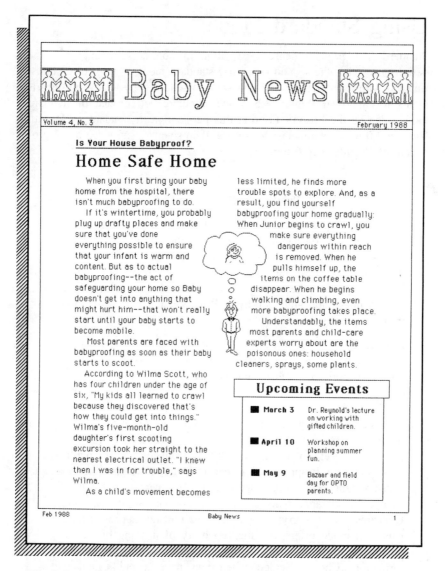

Fig. 8.5. A publication printed in standard mode.

than in smoothed mode. The left side of figure 8.6 shows a paragraph printed in 10-point Seattle text in standard mode. The right side of the figure shows the same paragraph printed in smoothed mode.

```
According to the developers          According to the developers
of First Publisher, some             of First Publisher, some
small characters in certain          small characters in certain
fonts may look better printed        fonts may look better printed
in standard mode than they           in standard mode than they
do in smoothed mode.                 do in smoothed mode.
```

Fig. 8.6. *A comparison of standard and smooth modes.*

Using Smoothed Mode

Smoothed mode is the highest quality you can get. Most users print a smoothed version of their publication only when they are finished with the project because of the longer print time.

Figure 8.7 shows a document printed in smoothed mode. This document took 46 minutes to print in Version 2.0. Printing this publication in unscaled mode with Version 2.01 took nine minutes. As you can see, choosing unscaled mode wherever possible can save you a substantial amount of time.

Installing Your Printer

In Chapter 2, you were introduced to the various installation procedures for different hardware configurations. In this section, the procedures for installing a dot-matrix and different laser printers are explained. If you have already installed your printer, you can skip to the "Printing with First Publisher" section.

The phrase *installing a printer* means to run a printer setup program to tell First Publisher what type of printer you are going to use to print your publications. That way, First Publisher will know what codes to send to the printer to communicate things like font changes, graphics layout, and other information about the publication. Check your printer manual to make sure that your printer is connected correctly (and also whether it's in the correct

Fig. 8.7. *A publication printed in smoothed mode.*

emulation mode, as appropriate). The printer setup program packaged with First Publisher is an independent feature; before you can set up your printer, you must exit First Publisher.

You should run the printer program *before* you begin creating or working with your publication. The basic steps are included in Chapter 2, but they are repeated in the next section for your reference. If you haven't run the Printer program, do so now, using the steps in the next section. If you are using a dot-matrix printer and you have already run the Printer program, you can skip to the section "Printing on a Dot-Matrix Printer."

If you are using a laser printer, you first need to set up First Publisher to work with your printer's available fonts by replacing the MASTER.FNT file packaged with the program. (These procedures are explained in the section "Installing a Laser Printer.")

Installing a Dot-Matrix Printer (Running the Printer Program)

To install a dot-matrix printer on a hard disk system, follow these steps:

1. Get to the DOS level by exiting your current program. (If you are using First Publisher, select **Exit** from the File menu or press Alt-E.)

2. Make sure that you are in the First Publisher directory by typing *cd\pub* and pressing Enter.

3. Type *printer* and press Enter. You see a numbered list of different printers. If you don't see the printer you need, you can press Enter to display another screen of printer choices.

4. Enter the number next to your printer and press Enter.

5. Select the port you are going to use by typing the number that corresponds to your printer port and pressing Enter. (If you are unsure how to determine which port you will be using, check your printer manual or contact the dealer or service outlet from which you purchased the system.)

Unless you change printers or install First Publisher on another machine, you will not need to modify these settings. Figure 8.8 shows the printer selection screen.

Users of the DeskMate version also must run the Printer program (by selecting Run... from the File menu) for the program to print properly.

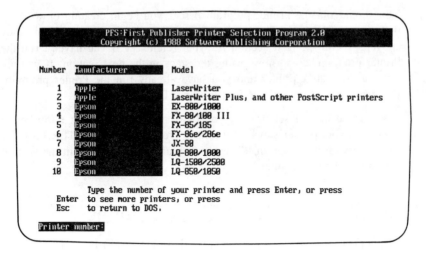

Fig. 8.8. The printer selection screen.

If you have a two disk drive system, follow these steps to install your dot-matrix printer:

1. Get to the DOS level by exiting your current program. (If you are using First Publisher, select **Exit** from the File menu or press Alt-E.)

2. Insert Program Disk 1 into drive A. (If you're using 3 1/2-inch disks, insert the Program and Fonts disk.)

3. When you see the A prompt, type *printer* and press Enter.

4. Enter the number that appears next to your printer.

5. Select the printer port by entering the correct number at the Printer port prompt and press Enter.

Installing a Laser Printer

The installation procedure for laser printers is a little more complicated because it requires manipulating some of First Publisher's font files and setting up First Publisher's laser support. First Publisher works with the following laser printers:

❏ Apple LaserWriter and LaserWriter Plus

❏ Hewlett-Packard LaserJet and LaserJet Series II

❏ Hewlett-Packard DeskJet (which is not really a laser printer but is recognized as such by First Publisher)

When you select a font, First Publisher searches in the MASTER.FNT file for the font you specified. If that font, style, or size is not found, First Publisher displays an error message. Whether you use a dot-matrix printer or a laser printer, all fonts accessed by the program are found in the MASTER.FNT file. If you want to add additional fonts to the program (as you do when you add laser support), you need to copy the fonts to the program's MASTER.FNT file.

To install laser printer support, you replace the MASTER.FNT file that came with your version of First Publisher with a laser version of the MASTER.FNT file. LaserWriter fonts are stored on the Laser Support Disk, and LaserJet and DeskJet fonts are stored on Program Disk 2. You rename your printer's font file as MASTER.FNT and copy the file to the hard disk. Then, if you want to add dot-matrix fonts, you can use FONTMOVE to add those fonts to your laser version of MASTER.FNT.

FONTMOVE is a program that allows you to transfer fonts in and out of First Publisher while staying within the program's memory restrictions. (Because FONTMOVE is a separate utility program that is packaged with First Publisher, it is discussed it fully in Chapter 10.)

The fonts, styles, and sizes initially displayed in the Font and Style menus are the dot-matrix fonts packaged with First Publisher. Many other fonts are available on the Fonts disk in the package; but when you initially install First Publisher, only the fonts shown in figure 8.9 are available. These fonts are the ones in the MASTER.FNT file.

Although the fonts initially available on the Fonts menu are dot-matrix fonts, they can be used by a laser printer, as well. You may want to consider using FONTMOVE to add those dot-matrix fonts to your laser version of MASTER.FNT. (Procedures for using FONTMOVE are discussed in Chapter 10.)

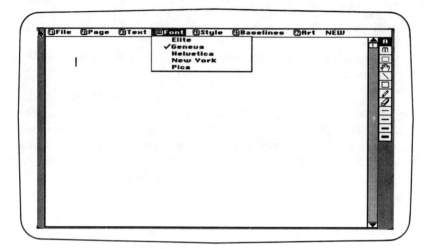

Fig. 8.9. *The fonts first available with First Publisher.*

Including both dot-matrix and laser fonts in your MASTER.FNT file gives you more flexibility in the design and production of your projects. You can print in a larger size some of the fonts that have limited size ranges, and you can save the time and trouble of changing the fonts in the publication if you upgrade from a dot-matrix to a laser printer.

In addition, First Publisher offers many different dot-matrix fonts, styles, and sizes, but only four First Publisher fonts can be used with compatible laser printers:

❏ Times Roman

❏ Helvetica

❏ Courier

❏ Lineprinter (offered by the Hewlett-Packard LaserJet only)

The Apple LaserWriter, a PostScript® printer, is capable of producing the largest variety of sizes and styles. Although the LaserWriter does not support the Lineprinter font, it does have two Courier sizes (10 and 12 points) and a range of Helvetica and Times Roman sizes from 7 to 48 points.

The Hewlett-Packard DeskJet is not really a laser printer but is recognized as such by First Publisher because of its high-quality output. This printer supports one size of Courier (12 points) and four sizes each of Helvetica and Times Roman, plus most of the rest of the cartridge fonts.

The LaserJet has the fewest fonts to offer because most LaserJet owners already own soft fonts. The LaserJet offers one size each of Courier, Helvetica, and Lineprinter (10, 14, and 8, respectively) and two sizes of Times Roman (8 and 10 points). Other cartridges and soft fonts available for the LaserJet can be added to the MASTER.FNT file. The soft fonts are available in virtually limitless styles, sizes, and so on. (See your dealer for more information on Hewlett-Packard soft fonts.)

Hard Disk System Installation

The procedure for installing laser support on a hard disk system is similar to the procedure for floppy disk systems. The only difference is the location of the font file you want to rename as MASTER.FNT. To install laser support, whether you use a LaserWriter, LaserJet, or DeskJet printer, follow these steps:

1. Exit to DOS. (If you have been using First Publisher, exit the program by selecting **Exit** from the File menu or by pressing Alt-E).

2. If you have been working in another directory, type *cd \pub* to change to the directory that stores your First Publisher program files.

3. Rename the existing dot-matrix MASTER.FNT file so that it will not be overwritten. To rename the file, type

   ren master.fnt dotmx.fnt

   This command line renames the file DOTMX.FNT. (Be sure to choose a name that reminds you that the file contains dot-matrix fonts.)

4. Copy the file to the hard disk, giving it the name MASTER.FNT. To do this, you could enter

   copy a:aplaser.fnt master.fnt

   This command line copies the Apple LaserWriter font file in drive A to a file named MASTER.FNT on the hard disk. If you use a LaserJet, you would enter *hplaser.fnt* instead of *aplaser.fnt*. The name of the font file for a DeskJet printer is *deskjet.fnt*.

When you copy the contents of your laser printer's font file to MASTER.FNT, you are not adding the contents of the two files; you are replacing the first file with the contents of the second one. For this reason, remember to save a renamed copy of the original MASTER.FNT so that later you can incorporate the dot-matrix files in the laser version of MASTER.FNT.

This completes the procedure for installing laser support on a hard disk system. As you may know, before a font can be used in First Publisher, its name must appear on the Font menu. This enables you to select that font and gives First Publisher the information it needs to find the specifications for the font. If you want to add the original dot-matrix fonts to your now-functional MASTER.FNT file, you can use the FONTMOVE utility (explained in Chapter 10). Figure 8.10 shows the fonts available in the Font menu after a Hewlett-Packard LaserJet has been installed.

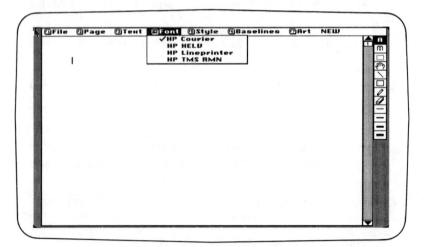

Fig. 8.10. *The fonts available for a LaserJet.*

Two-Drive System Installation for a LaserJet or DeskJet Printer

If you are using a two-drive system with a laser printer, the steps involved in installing the printer are slightly different.

The procedure for installing a LaserJet or DeskJet printer is as follows:

1. Insert the Fonts Disk in drive A and a blank, formatted disk in drive B.

2. Copy the MASTER.FNT file from drive A to drive B with a command such as:

   copy a:master.fnt b:dotmx.fnt

   Make sure you rename the file as you copy it.

3. Remove the data disk from drive B and insert Program Disk 2 (on which the laser font file is stored).

4. Copy the laser font file from drive B to drive A, renaming it as MASTER.FNT in the process:

   copy b:hplaser.fnt a:master.fnt

   This procedure copies the LaserJet font file over the original MASTER.FNT file, overwriting its contents. If you are using a DeskJet printer, substitute the file name *deskjet.fnt* for *hplaser.fnt*. You can use FONTMOVE to add the original dot-matrix fonts to the laser MASTER.FNT, if you want.

5. If you are using a DeskJet printer, one more step remains. Copy the DeskJet's additional font files to the Fonts disk so that First Publisher will have access to the fonts during printing. To do that, type the following commands, pressing Enter at the end of each line:

   copy b:fontsdj.dic a:
   copy b:fontsdj.wid a:

When you are working with a two-drive system, be aware of the amount of space you have on disk. First Publisher must have 40K available on the Fonts disk to store a backup copy of the current publication. Use the DOS DIR command to determine how much space is available on the disk, in the format *dir b:*.*.* This command tells you which files are stored on the disk in drive b and how much room is available.

Two-Drive System Installation for a LaserWriter Printer

To install a LaserWriter printer, use the following procedure:

1. Insert the Fonts Disk in drive A and a blank, formatted disk in drive B.

2. Copy the MASTER.FNT file from drive A to drive B with a command such as:

   copy a:master.fnt b:dotmx.fnt

   Make sure you rename the file as you copy it.

3. Erase the original MASTER.FNT file on the Fonts Disk by typing

   del master.fnt

4. Remove the data disk from drive B and insert Program Disk 1 (on which the laser font file and the PostScript files are stored).

5. Copy the PostScript files (the files ending with the PS extension) from Program Disk 1 (drive B) to the Fonts Disk (drive A). These files are LASERDEF.PS, SMOOTH.PS, and UARTPAT2.PS. Use the following format:

   copy b:laserdef.ps a:

   If you are using 3 1/2-inch drives, this step is not necessary because the font files and the program files are on the same disk.

6. Use FONTMOVE to create an empty MASTER.FNT file, then use the utility to move laser fonts from the Laser Support Disk to the newly created MASTER.FNT file.

Completing Laser Installation

After you have replaced the original MASTER.FNT file with the correct font file for your laser printer, you need to run the Printer program. This program is a utility that is independent of First Publisher; you must exit the program in order to use it. When the DOS prompt is displayed, type *printer* and press Enter to run the Printer program. You need to choose the correct printer model, and for LaserJet printers, you need to specify the cartridge, as well. Figure 8.11 shows the third page of the printer selection screen.

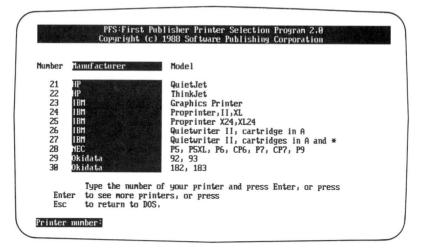

Fig. 8.11. *The third page of the printer selection screen.*

Printing with First Publisher

The process for printing with First Publisher is easy. The procedure is basically the same no matter what type of printer you are sending the output to. When you are ready to print, follow these steps:

1. Open the publication to be printed so that it is displayed on the screen. (If you have been working on the publication, remember to save it by using **Save** from the File menu or by pressing Alt-S.)

2. Select **Print** from the File menu. The dialog box shown in figure 8.12 is displayed.

3. Specify the number of copies you want to print (the default value is 1).

4. Specify the starting page.

5. Specify the ending page.

6. Check that the Destination is correct (the port to which your printer is connected).

7. Select the mode in which you want the publication to be printed (Draft, Standard, or Smoothed). If you have printed previously in this session, whatever mode you selected during that print job is still selected.

8. If you are using Version 2.01, you need to select whether you want to print the publication in scaled or unscaled mode.

9. Click the OK button.

Fig. 8.12. *The Print dialog box.*

A message box is displayed showing you what percentage of the document has been sent to the printer (see fig. 8.13). You can interrupt printing at any time by pressing Esc.

Fig. 8.13. *The message box displaying during printing.*

Printing with a Dot-Matrix Printer

Although the computer industry touts the motto "onward and upward," rest assured that no law says all desktop publishers must own laser printers. In fact, First Publisher produces surprisingly good output on dot-matrix printers.

There are a few things you can do to ensure that the output of your dot-matrix printer is the best you can get:

❏ Make sure that you are working with a new (or reasonably new) ribbon.

❏ Print final copies on high-quality paper.

❏ Select a font for the body text that looks crisp in dot-matrix output. (You may want to spend some time printing out sample of various fonts in different styles and sizes.)

❏ Stretch graphics only when necessary (the stretch may distort some angles).

❏ Use **Magnify** to smooth the rough edges of graphics before you print.

> The makers of First Publisher recommend that dot-matrix printer owners use **Pica** or **Elite** type for the body text and for text that requires a *monospaced* font. Monospaced means that each character uses the same amount of space, allowing characters to be aligned vertically in columns. These "built-in" fonts yield the highest quality (and readability) your printer is capable of producing, which is especially important for smaller point sizes.

Printing with a Laser Printer

If you are printing your First Publisher documents on a laser printer, you probably plan to take the copy to a printer for reproduction (unless you have enough toner and paper to print a few hundred copies yourself or you have a great photocopier). You want the quality of your design, production, and printing to shine through, so make sure that you have done all the following things before you start the printing process:

❑ Copy your laser printer's font file to the MASTER.FNT file as discussed earlier in this chapter.

❑ Use FONTMOVE to add dot-matrix fonts or soft fonts to MASTER.FNT (if you used dot-matrix fonts in your publication).

❑ Run the Printer program.

❑ Check the toner cartridge.

❑ Use high-quality paper.

❑ Modify graphics images to smooth out any rough edges.

❑ Make sure that the cable connection from the system to the printer is secure.

If you use graphics text instead of regular text, or if you save the publication as a MAC file and you are using a laser printer, the text will appear grainy, and you will not get the high-quality fonts available on the laser printer. To use the laser fonts, you must use the regular text tool to enter text. The text tool is found at the top of the tools row on the right side of the screen.

Using Soft Fonts

First Publisher supports all Hewlett-Packard and 100 percent compatible soft fonts. To make these soft fonts available to First Publisher at print time, you must first move the soft fonts into First Publisher's MASTER.FNT file by using FONTMOVE. Figure 8.14 shows the FONTMOVE opening menu.

When First Publisher prints a document that includes soft fonts, the program must have access to those font files. If you are using a hard disk system, you must be sure to copy the necessary soft fonts to your PUB directory before you print. If you are using a two-drive system, place the disk containing the soft fonts in drive A.

```
        PFS:First Publisher Fontmove Program 2.0

                     Main Menu

              F1  Move fonts

              F2  Add HP LaserJet soft fonts

              F3  Exit to DOS




          Copyright (c) 1988 Software Publishing Corporation
```

Fig. 8.14. The FONTMOVE opening menu.

When you select **Print** from the File menu, a dialog box is displayed. The box asks whether any soft fonts should be sent to the printer. You are also asked to specify where the program can find those soft fonts.

Once a soft font is sent to the printer, it stays in the printer's memory until you turn the printer off or copy other soft fonts over the ones in the printer's memory. Therefore, you need to send a soft font to the printer only once for each work session, no matter how many different documents you print using the same soft font.

Like your computer, the printer has a limited amount of memory. Before you use soft fonts, you should be aware of the memory capacity of your printer (check your printer's manual). If you download a soft font to the printer and the printer's memory is full, a soft font you sent to the printer earlier is overwritten. (To find out how much memory is used by a soft font, consult the soft font manual.)

Because of the amount of memory used by the DeskMate version of First Publisher, you may want to customize your MASTER.FNT file to store only the one or two fonts you use often.

There are two steps involved in using soft fonts with First Publisher:

1. Use FONTMOVE to add the soft fonts to the MASTER.FNT file. The fonts are displayed in the Fonts menu.

2. Make sure that the soft font files are accessible to First Publisher before you print (have the correct disk in drive A or copy the files to your PUB directory on your hard disk). First Publisher must have access to the files when the program prints with the soft fonts.

Printing Faster

When it comes to printing, First Publisher Version 2.0 is more like a tortoise than a hare. This lack of speed is understandable, particularly in smoothed mode. The program is sending much information to the printer, which the printer deciphers and applies to its task. When you need to print something in a hurry, however, First Publisher's print routine can seem slow.

Version 1.0 of First Publisher printed more quickly, but was less adept at proportioning graphics; more images came out stretched or squat, in sizes different than you expected. Version 2.0 resolved this problem and added more laser support, but there is a trade-off in print speed.

With Version 2.01, Software Publishing Corporation has introduced a feature that allows you to control further the print time and quality of the publications you produce. You can select **Unscaled** to print more quickly without worrying about whether the exact proportions of the images match the images on-screen. When you select **Scaled**, the publication is printed as it appears on-screen. Depending on the printer you use and the publications you produce, this may not be a problem for you.

Modifying Printer Margins

You probably will not need to modify the print margins set up in the **Define page** dialog box. When you use the Printer program to tell First Publisher which printer you will be using, the program assigns default margin settings according to the printer you specify. The makers of First Publisher configured the margins for all the printers available in the Printer program. Remember, however, that if you do change the settings in the **Define page** dialog box, any baseline modifications you have made previously on that document will be removed—even if you are only changing margins.

Evalute Your Printout

Once you have printed the publication, you need to stand back and take an objective look at it. The flexibility of First Publisher allows you to make modifications at any point during the creation and production of a process.

You don't like the way the printed banner looks? It's not set in stone; you can go back and change the look of the banner with a minimum of trouble. Here are some other questions you can ask yourself as you survey your work:

Do you like the font, style, and size you have chosen for the body text? In print, the type may look too big, too small, too light, or too heavy. You can change the font type, size, or style by capturing the text you want to change (refer to Chapter 5 for specific examples) and selecting new settings from the Font and Style menus.

Did the graphics print the way you intended them to? Your graphics may not print at exactly the same size you envisioned. For example, if you cut and pasted penguins from the clip art files and then resized them to fit in a certain space, the penguins may look ''stumpy'' when they are printed. This screen-to-printer proportion problem was more pervasive with Version 1.0; Version 2.0 prints a truer representation of what you see on the screen.

If you are unhappy with the way the graphics printed, you can modify them easily by selecting the image and using the **Resize** option on the Art menu.

Are the rules straight? You may have put a ''crimp'' in the line when you were outlining the document with the line tool. To fix the line, unfortunately, you must use the eraser tool to erase the part of the line that isn't straight. To help you redraw the line, use **Use grid** to lock the line into place.

Are the boxes effective? Have you used boxes to help organize the page? Boxes should give an article an inclusive look. For example, if you have a newsletter in three-column format on the top and two-column format on the bottom, unless you do something to set off the bottom article—such as enclosing the article in a box or separating it from the first article by running a rule across the page—the reader may get to the bottom of the first column and wonder "What am I supposed to read next?" A well-placed box helps contain the reader's gaze and shows the correct sequence of information.

Is the banner overwhelming? Are you pleased with the way the banner balances the printed page? If you don't like the way the banner turned out, you can get rid of it and start again, or make subtle changes until it conveys the message you want. Think of the banner's effect in terms of the audience, reading level, and goals of the publication.

Should the publication be printed in smoothed or standard mode? If you like the way the publication was printed—whether you used standard or smoothed mode—stay with your current print choice. If you are disappointed in the formation or clarity of some of the characters in smaller type sizes, however, you may want to consider changing the mode choice.

Printing to a File

When you think "printing" you probably think of the output a printer produces. There is another output device you can choose, however.

By printing to a disk file, you can save a First Publisher publication and print it later on a system that doesn't have the program.

Suppose, for example, that you have created a newsletter on your computer at home, but your laser printer is at work. You can use the Printer program to configure First Publisher for the laser printer you are going to use, print the file to disk, take it in to work, and print it. Simply print the file to disk by following these steps:

1. Make sure that the publication you want to print is displayed on the screen.

2. Select **Print** from the File menu or press Alt-P.

3. When the Print dialog box is displayed, change the Destination setting to indicate the drive to which you want to save the file. For example, if your data disk is in drive B, you type *b:* as the Destination.

4. Click the OK button or press F1.

The file is printed to the disk in the specified drive. After you take the disk to work, you can print the file by using the DOS COPY or PRINT commands. For example, the following command prints the file (named TRN2-23.PUB) to the LPT1 port, which connects to the printer:

```
copy trn2-23.pub lpt1:
print trn2-23.pub
```

If you decide to use the DOS PRINT command, press Enter after you type the preceding command line. A prompt is displayed, asking what output device you are printing to. Type *lpt1* and press Enter. Your publication is printed.

Chapter Summary

In this chapter, you learned about the various hardware and software setup requirements for printing with First Publisher. You also learned the technique for printing with soft fonts and for printing to a file. This chapter offered many printing tips gleaned from SPC's technical support line, answering questions often asked by new First Publisher users. In the next chapter, you will learn to create templates of your own for various publications, such as newsletters, fliers, and business cards.

Part III

Advanced Techniques

Includes

Creating Your Own
Templates

Using First Publisher's
Special Features

Creating Your Own Templates

Once you have created and assembled a publication—whether that publication is a flier, a business report, a newsletter, or any other type of project, you basically know the ropes. The next time you create something, the process will probably go much faster.

However, if you could skip the design stage and go right to plugging in new text and graphics on an existing publication, wouldn't you rather do so and save the time and trouble? For example, if you have finished with the first issue of *DT Publisher* (the January 1989 issue), you don't want to begin the February issue by starting back at square one, opening a blank publication.

To save yourself the work of re-creating a publication, you can make a template of an existing publication and work from that. A *template* is a file that already has some elements placed for you; elements that don't change between issues or versions of the publication. For example, in the *DT Publisher* example, the banner and the two column format stay the same from issue to issue. Additionally, the placement of the graphic item in the center of the page remains as is, meaning that the baselines of the publication are not modified for different issues. Figure 9.1 shows the publication as you last left it; figure 9.2 shows the *DT Publisher* template.

In this chapter, you will learn to create your own templates for newsletters, fliers, and business stationery, such as invoices and reports. First, however, before you learn to create templates, you need to review the templates that are packaged with First Publisher.

Publisher

January 1989
Volume 2, No.1

From the editors:
Happy New Year!

Welcome to 1989!

The staff of DT Publisher hopes this one will be a profitable and enjoyable year for you as you explore further into the world of desktop publishing.

We promised you the year would start off with a bang: so start the drumroll... .announcing DT Publisher's 1989 MakeOver Contest!

On page 3 of this issue, you will find the cover page of a newsletter badly in need of some TLC and some creativity. This newsletter is targeted at an audience of small business owners (that is, owners of small businesses, not small owners of regular-sized businesses). The entries will be judged and the winners will be contacted no later than May 5, 1989.

Prizes include publication of the makeover in the August issue of DT Publisher (and you have to tell how you did it), $500 cash, and a Hewlett-Packard ScanJet. Two second prizes of $200 will be awarded, and three third prizes of $100 will be given away.

Deadline Instructions

Entry deadline is February 28, so get busy on your makeovers right away. And here's a hint to get you started: You may want to consult our November 1988 issue to refresh your mind about important design tips.

DT Publisher MakeOver '89	
Place	**Prize**
1st	$ 500
2nd	$ 200
3rd	$ 100

Judges will include Ira Markowitz, owner and publisher of DT Publisher, Elizabeth Combs, commercial artist and president of The Last Word, Inc., a desktop publishing company operating out of Des Moines, Iowa; and Peter Sandbar, a professor at Duke University.

Scanners: Beam Me Up, Scotty

Technology is definitely evolving, and at a surprisingly affordable rate. If someone had told me two years ago that by 1989 I'd have a desktop publishing system elaborate enough to produce a high-quality newsletter, complete with scanned images, laser-quality print, and knock-out graphics, I'd have rolled my eyes and looked skeptical.

But today, here it is. The most recent addition to my dtp collection is a scanner. Scanners are peripheral devices that turn your printed material, photos, or drawings into digitized images that you can play around with on your computer screen. Im most programs, scanned images can be modified, resized, and treated as any other graphic element.

(*One aside here:* As I was considering how far we've come with the evolution and affordability of this type of peripheral, my seven-year-old son Scott walked up, eyes wide, looking at the scanner. As I picked it up to show him, he put his hands in front of his face. "Don't!" he said, "If you point that thing at me, won't I wind up on the Enterprise?" We've still got a long way to

Fig. 9.1. *The* DT Publisher *newsletter.*

Fig. 9.2. *The template file from* DT Publisher.

Reviewing First Publisher's Templates

Chapter 3 gave you an introduction to the templates that are packaged with First Publisher. For new users, these templates serve as a gentle introduction to design, creation, and layout—you simply plug in your own text and graphics in the predefined format. You don't need to modify baselines—although you may do so if you wish—and some of the rules have already been drawn for you. In some templates, graphics already have been added, as well. In this section, you will explore in a little more detail each of the templates included in First Publisher. This study will give you a "pattern" to follow as you begin to create your own First Publisher templates.

The NEWS.PUB Template

As its name suggests, NEWS.PUB is a template for a newsletter publication (see fig. 9.3). As you may recall, we used this template as the basis for the QuickStart exercise in Chapter 3.

The NEWS.PUB template uses two different formats: the top half of the page is formatted in three columns, and the bottom half is formatted in two columns. The template includes the rules that separate the identifier line (which lists the volume number and the date of the publication), as well as the box that delimits the second article space and the outline box. As you can see, headlines are indicated, as are kicker lines and photo space.

Although the baselines of the publication are not displayed, each column in the publication has been assigned a sequence number. This number tells you in which order the text will fill the columns. Figure 9.4 shows how the template looks on-screen when the baselines are displayed. (Remember, baselines appear only when one of the options in the Baselines menu is active.)

Everything on the NEWS.PUB template was produced using graphics text, graphics tools, or both. This means that before you begin to use the template, you must erase the items already there. Of course, you may want to leave the rules and boxes, and you may opt to leave the various elements in place and work on them one-by-one, as opposed to erasing them all and then creating your own elements. But when you want to insert your own

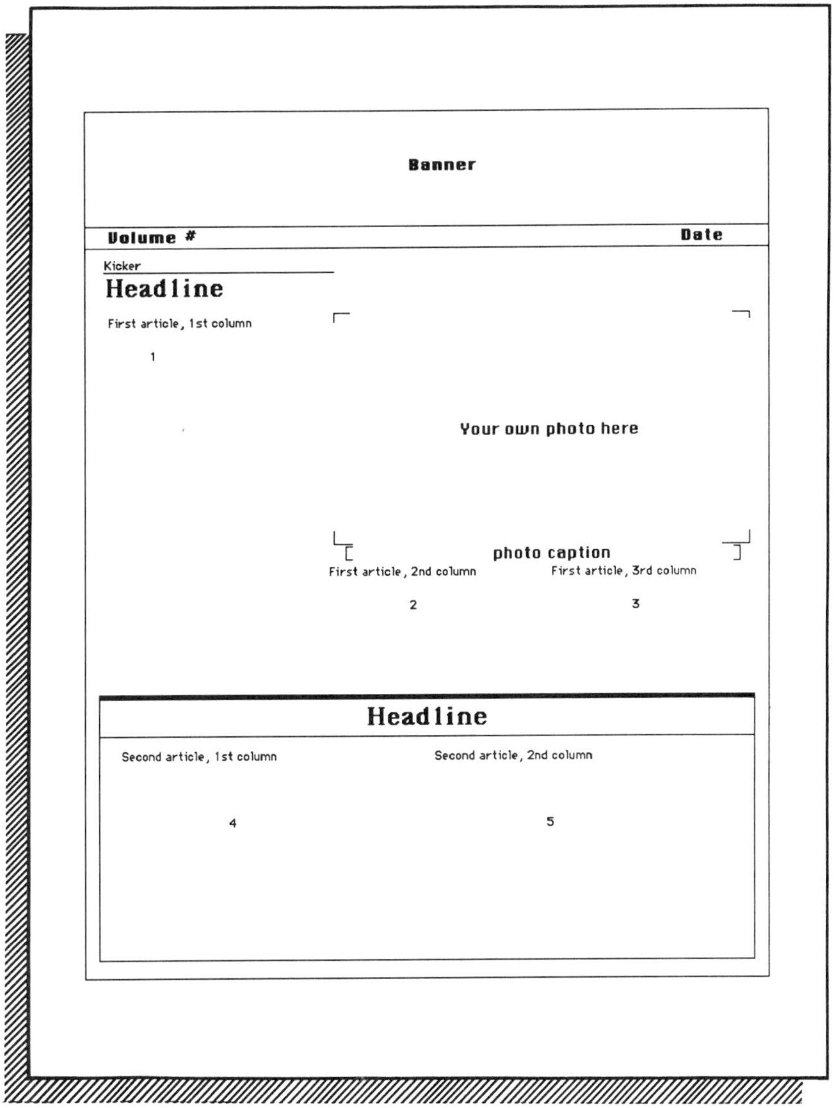

Fig. 9.3. The NEWS.PUB template.

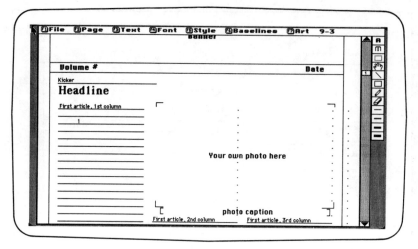

Fig. 9.4. *The baselines of NEWS.PUB.*

banner, for example, you first need to erase the word Banner that appears at the top of the template. (To erase the word, either use the eraser tool or use the selection tool to capture the word and then press Del.)

Although the NEWS.PUB template has a blocked-out space for a photo, you don't really have to paste a photo there. You can use that space for a graphics element, paste in a box that contains graphics text, or move the baselines so that text flows through that area.

> Remember to work with the backup copies of your template files. If you accidentally save a modified file without first changing the name of the file, the changed file will overwrite the original template file. To be safe, keep the original disks in a safe place and work only from copies.

The makers of First Publisher seemed to recognize that working with baselines to control text flow can be one of the most confusing things about the program. With Version 2.0, they included seven additional newsletter templates in various column formats and styles. These templates, which are found on Program Disk 2, can save you an enormous amount of time and effort. The seven templates are shown in figure 9.5.

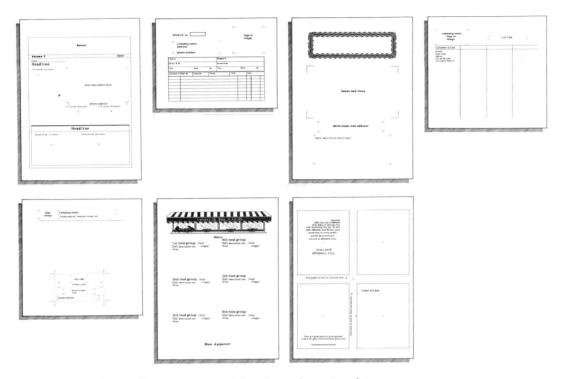

Fig. 9.5. *The seven additional newsletter templates.*

The FLYER.PUB Template

You can use the FLYER.PUB template to create advertising fliers for your business, party invitations, or a number of other attention-getting projects. Figure 9.6 shows the FLYER.PUB template.

Notice that on this template signifcantly more room is blocked out for graphics than for text. That's because a flier is meant to be a ''hit-'em-fast'' type of publication; you should rely on pictures and as few words as possible to convey your message.

The BUSINESS.PUB Template

The BUSINESS.PUB template is an extremely simple one: the most beneficial feature this template has to offer is the predrawn business card in the

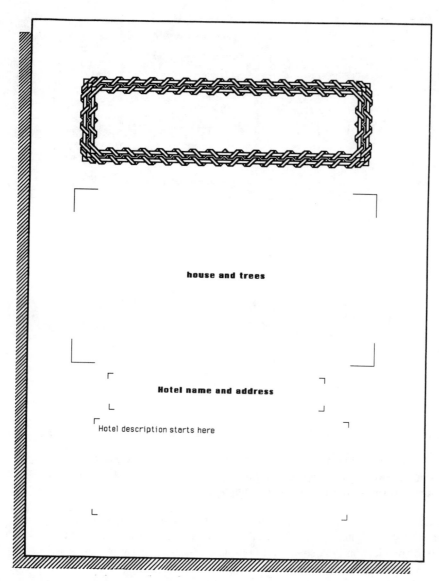

Fig. 9.6. *The FLYER.PUB template.*

center of the page. This "card" is drawn to the actual size of a business card and has crop marks so your printer will be able to reproduce the card and cut it to size with no additional work. (*Note:* Crop marks are the lines used to indicate where the cards will be cut.) Figure 9.7 shows the BUSINESS.PUB template.

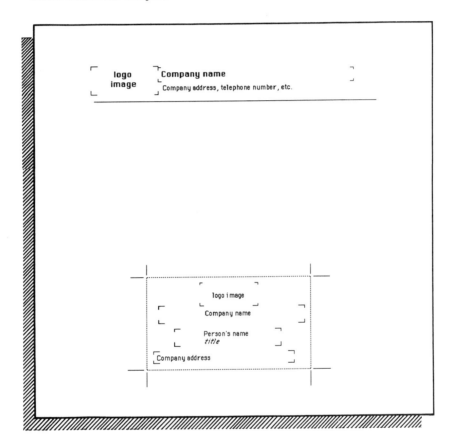

Fig. 9.7. *The BUSINESS.PUB template.*

Of course, this template offers you only one way to create your stationery and business cards. In the section "Creating Your Business Stationery," you will see some alternative ideas for sprucing up your business materials.

The INVOICE.PUB Template

The INVOICE.PUB template is one that is almost ready-to-use: just add your company name and your logo, and you have a usable invoice.

To extend the invoice entry lines farther down the page, use the selection tool to capture five or six lines and then select **Copy** from the Art menu or press Alt-C. Then select **Paste** or press Alt-V. First Publisher changes the shape of the cursor to a hand, and you can position the cursor and click the mouse button, and the program pastes the copied lines on the invoice. You then need to align the new lines so that the edges match (see fig. 9.8). If you have trouble matching the edges or leaving the same amount of space between lines, use **Magnify** to get a close-up look at the trouble spot.

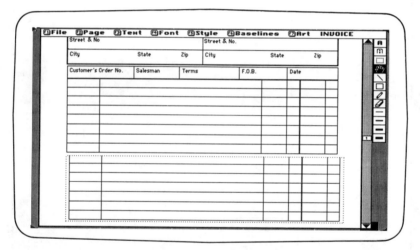

Fig. 9.8. *Aligning entry lines on INVOICE.PUB.*

The LIST.PUB Template

The LIST.PUB template offers you a four-column format for recording client names, supplier lists, phone lists, reunion information, and so on. This template could also be used to show items in a catalog form. Figure 9.9 shows the LIST.PUB template.

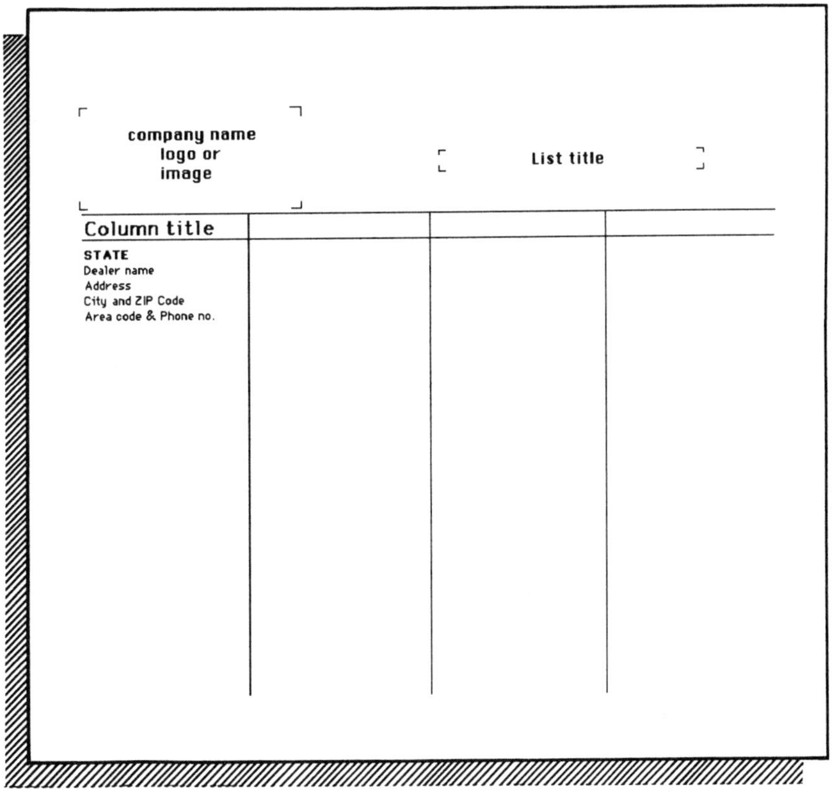

Fig. 9.9. *The LIST.PUB template.*

The MENU.PUB Template

The MENU.PUB template provides you with an almost-ready-to-use menu. The graphic is already there, as figure 9.10 shows. You probably will want to remove the words in the canopy and add your own restaurant's name. (The documentation provides steps for doing this.) You could use this template for menus, for dinner party invitations, or in the form of an avant-garde flier for a catering business. The developers of the template suggest you break the food down into food groups (that is, appetizers, sandwiches, and so forth—not meats, vegetables, dairy, and breads).

The CARD.PUB Template

This template is a little off the beaten path, but gives you an afternoon's diversion if you're feeling a little extra creative. With the CARD.PUB template, you can create your own cards—birthday, holiday, invitation, get well—any type of card you might want. Figure 9.11 shows the CARD.PUB template.

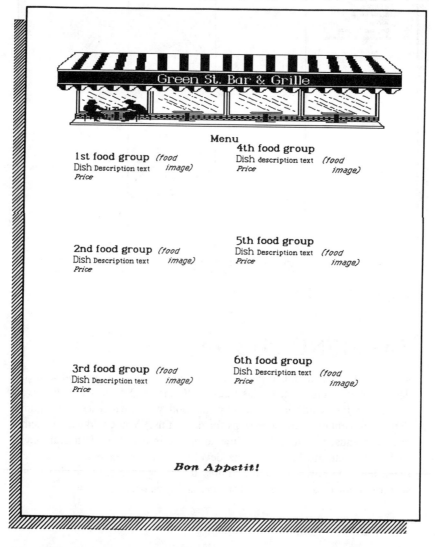

Fig. 9.10. The MENU.PUB template.

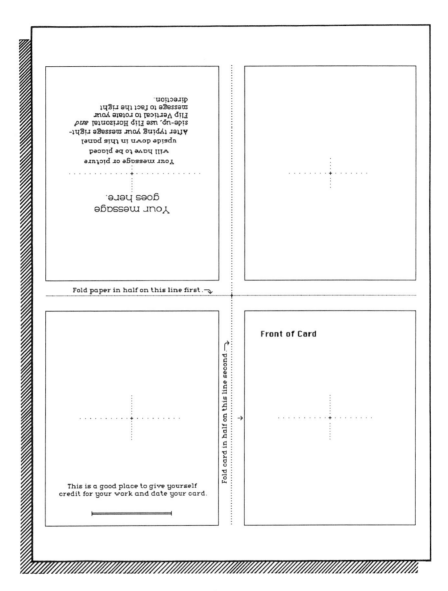

Fig. 9.11. *The CARD.PUB template.*

This template leaves more to your imagination than some of the other templates do. Instead of including borders, and blocked out areas for text, CARD.PUB explains where to position different text items, and illustrates where the inside text will be positioned when the card is folded.

When you are using the CARD.PUB template, you must use graphics text to enter the text that will be positioned inside the card. You need to be able to select and flip the text vertically so that the text will be placed correctly when the card is folded.

Now that you have explored each of the templates available with First Publisher, you need to find out how to make templates of your own.

Making Templates

Basically, a template is a "shell" of a publication that you can use again and again. A template should store only the information that *isn't* variable; things like a newsletter's banner, the company name on an invoice; the logo on business stationery. A template wouldn't be very functional if you must go through and delete text and graphics every time you want to use it. Therefore, your template should be the basic item on which you paste the variable text and graphics.

You have two options for creating a template:

❏ You can make a copy of an existing publication and delete all variable information

❏ You can create a template "from scratch," by copying and pasting items like a banner, logo, or name

Creating a Template from an Existing Publication

If you are like many people, by the time you are satisfied with the way a publication looks, you have modified it, tweaked it, and analyzed it until you want to stick it in a drawer and forget it. And, if you have gone to all that trouble, the idea of starting over next month and creating another issue may be overwhelming. Instead of starting over, you can make a template of this month's finished product, and then next month you can simply add text and graphics and save the file under another name. This process involves three steps:

1. Opening the publication you want to turn into a template

2. Deleting all variable information (text, changeable graphics, and so on)

3. Saving the publication under a new name

The paragraphs in this section explain these three steps by showing how a template is created from *DT Publisher*. Figure 9.12 shows how the finished publication looks.

Fig. 9.12. *The* DT Publisher *newsletter.*

To open the publication, select **Get publication** from the File menu. Specify the publication you want (in this case, the *DTP* file), and click OK or press F1. The file then is displayed on the screen.

Next, you need to decide what elements you will keep and what elements you will delete. Remove all items that are variable; that is, the items that will change from month to month. For example, in the identifier line, the date shows *January 1989*. For the template, you may want to delete only *January* and leave *1989*; or, if you would rather not have to change *89* at the end of the year, you could drop those characters, too. If you are making a template out of a newsletter publication, you probably need to delete the following items:

❏ The volume number and the date in the identifier line

❏ All text in articles

❏ Headlines that will change from month to month. (If you run a monthly column, such as "Letters to the Editor," you would leave that heading in place.)

❏ Graphics that are tied to a specific article

The items that you should consider keeping include the following:

❏ The banner

❏ Any portion of the identifier that is not variable

❏ The baseline settings

❏ Headers and footers

❏ Graphics items that are part of the design

❏ Any publishing information that is printed on every issue

Figure 9.13 shows *DT Publisher* after all the extraneous information has been deleted.

Fig. 9.13. *The publication after the variable information is deleted.*

After you delete the information, you are left with the publication that will serve as your template. You're now ready for the most critical step: saving the publication.

To save the publication, select **Save** from the File menu or press Alt-S. When the Save dialog box is displayed, enter a file name that indicates that the file is a template file (see fig. 9.14). For this example, the template file name used is DTPTMP. *Be sure to specify a new file name.* If you accidentally click OK, you may wind up overwriting the publication you took such pains to create.

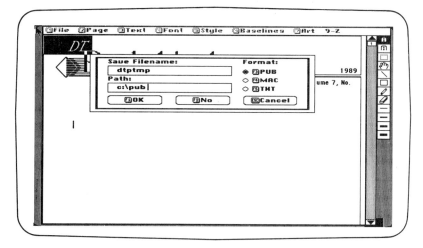

Fig. 9.14. *Saving the template file.*

Creating a Template from a New Publication

Although this process is easier to describe than the preceding process, it takes longer to carry out. The reason? When you sit down to plan out a publication, a lot of thinking time is involved. If you sit down with the objective of not only producing one publication, but of creating an effect so enlightening that you will want to commit yourself making a template out of that design, your burden may seem pretty heavy.

Most people start with a basic idea of what they like, what their audience likes, and what type of material should be included. From that point, they fine-tune features of the publication until they come up with something they can live with, or, if they're lucky, something they like. But this process generally involves going through several printings, showing the project around, getting feedback, and weeding through comments.

If you are planning on creating a newsletter template "from scratch," take a few minutes and look through the templates offered by First Publisher; you may find something you like. If not, charge ahead: but be aware that developing a good publication usually requires more than one sitting and more than one opinion.

Creating new templates for publications less complicated than a newsletter is significantly easier. A flier, for example, would be fairly easy to create as a new template. To create a flier template from scratch, you would need to assemble the following things:

❑ Your company's logo

❑ Any graphic element that should appear on every version of the flier. (Generally, this type of graphic is part of the company name.)

❑ Your company's address

❑ Your company's motto (if you have one)

❑ A border (if you plan to use the same border on subsequent fliers)

Figure 9.15 shows a sample of a flier template. The section for text (blocked out in the middle) is reserved to include variable information about sales and seasonal discounts.

When you want to save the publication, you just select **Save** from the File menu or press Alt-S. When the Save dialog box is displayed, enter a file name that in some way reflects the fact that this is a template file for fliers. After making sure that the path designation is correct, click OK or press F1. First Publisher then saves the file under the name you specified.

How Do You Use a Template?

Now that you have a template, what do you do with it? To use a template, you simply open the file and begin building the project, just like any other publication. Add text and graphics, fine-tune the layout, follow whatever process is most comfortable for you. In fact, the only real difference between a template file and a regular publication file is that in the template, some of the work has already been done for you. And also, because you want to preserve the template so that you can use it again, you need to be sure to save the modified file under a new name so that the publication file is not overwritten.

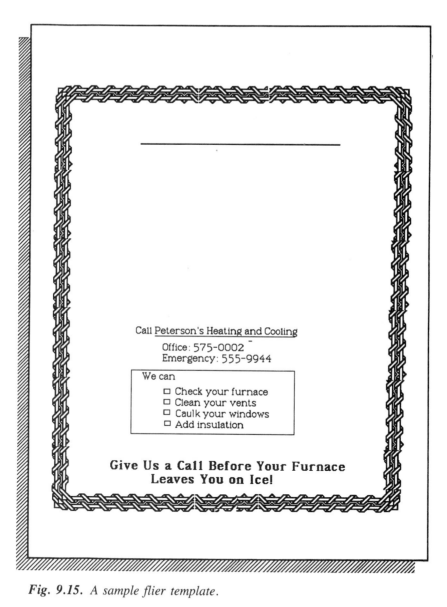

Fig. 9.15. *A sample flier template.*

> In the procedures of creating and using templates, there are two crucial points to remember:
>
> ❏ When you save the created template, be sure to enter a unique file name.
>
> ❏ When you save a publication you have created by using a template, specify a new name for the finished publication. If you save the modified file under the template file name, the template will be overwritten.

For example, suppose that you have created a publication from your template file and you are ready to save the publication. If, in the Save dialog box, you click the OK button when the default name (the name of the current file) is displayed, the template file will be overwritten. When you are using template files to build your publications, then, make sure that you specify another file name in the Save dialog box.

To save a publication that was created from a template file, follow these steps:

1. Select **Save** from the File menu or press Alt-S.

2. Enter a new file name that in some way describes the content of the file (such as DTPFEB). First Publisher automatically assigns the extension for you, according to the radio button that is checked.

3. Make sure that the path designation is correct.

4. Click the OK button or press F1.

For the remainder of this chapter, you will see how three different templates are created and used.

Template Applications

In this section, you will see how three different First Publisher users produce publications from templates. Whether you are the editor of your community newsletter, the person responsible for producing advertising materials in a small business, or a desktop publishing entrepreneur, you will find that using templates cuts the repetitiveness out of your desktop publishing tasks, and, consequently, saves you time and trouble.

Example 1: The HighFlyer Newsletter

Bob Howard is the editor-in-chief of *The HighFlyer*, a monthly newsletter for radio-controlled airplane enthusiasts. He inherited this job because he's the only one in the group with a personal computer. Although the club boasts almost 200 active members, the president almost swallowed his pen when Bob sheepishly asked about dipping into the funds to buy a $795 desktop publishing program.

When Bob found First Publisher, *The HighFlyer* was never again to be produced on a typewriter. He had already envisioned the banner he wanted and felt that even though First Publisher's clip art didn't include a picture of an airplane, a helicopter was close enough. The template for the *The HighFlyer*, shown in figure 9.16, was created and assembled in this way:

1. The banner was created first. Bob selected the graphics text tool, New York font, 36-point size, and typed the name. He then used the selection tool to select the name and used the **Rotate** option in the Art menu to move the name to align vertically with the left edge of the page. He then used the **Show page** option to see how the banner looked in that position, and, deciding that it still looked too small, he returned to the publication, selected **Resize** from the Art menu, and stretched the name until it touched the left edge of the screen.

2. Details were then added to the banner. Bob typed the word *The* in New York, 24-point type. He then selected the area around the word by using the selection tool and chose **Invert** from the Art menu. He then moved the inverted word to a position where it would complement the main section of the banner.

3. Next, rules were added to enclose the banner. One rule was added to the top, and two were placed close together below the banner. Another line was added horizontally across the top of the page, leaving enough room for text. Lastly, the straight line tool was used to produce an arrow, which was placed at the end of the left-most rule.

3. An identifier line was added across the top in Geneva, 14-point bold type.

4. The publishing information box was added as graphics text, using Geneva, 9-point normal type. The box tool was used to produce the box.

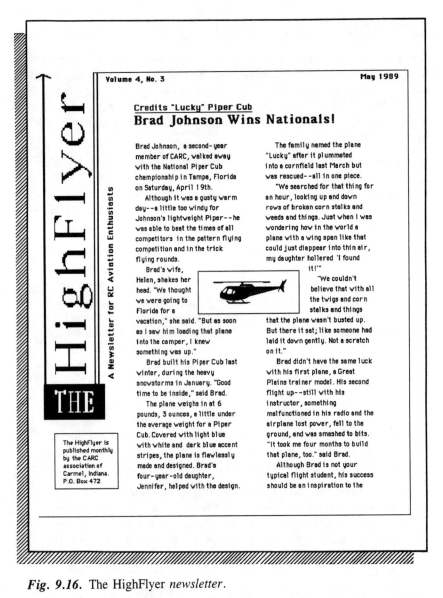

Fig. 9.16. The HighFlyer *newsletter.*

5. Bob then modified the baselines, which was a multistep process. When he first defined the page (using the **Define Page** option in the Page menu), he set the publication for two columns. Figure 9.17 shows how the baselines look before they are modified.

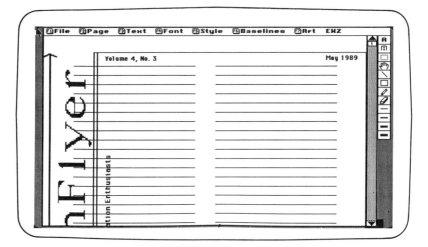

Fig. 9.17. The baselines before modification.

First, he selected the **Adjust column** setting from the Baselines menu, and moved each column down far enough to leave room for headings. Next, he clicked on the top baseline in the left column, and dragged the left handle to the right, thereby shortening that baseline and all baselines in that column. Then he shortened the far-right column; and finally, he adjusted both columns so that the right and left columns were of equal length. The panels in figure 9.18 show these steps.

Next, he used **Adjust single** to adjust the baselines around the graphics box in the center of the page (see fig. 9.19). Figure 9.20 shows the baselines after the modifications have been made.

Example 2: Peterson's Advertising Flier

Karla is the office manager for Peterson's Heating and Cooling. When she was initially introduced to First Publisher several months ago, Karla was still relatively new to computers in general. She had used one file program to keep track of stock inventory; someone else in the office did the book-keeping with an accounting package. Until recently, she had produced fliers by using press type and cutting and pasting pictures out of clip art books. She delivered the "finished" version to the printer, with a variety of items pasted or taped onto one page.

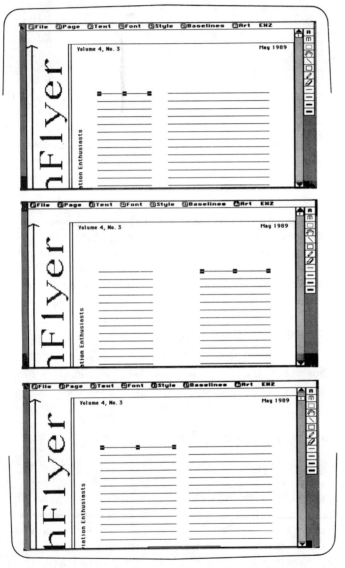

Fig. 9.18. *Modifying the baselines for the* HighFlyer.

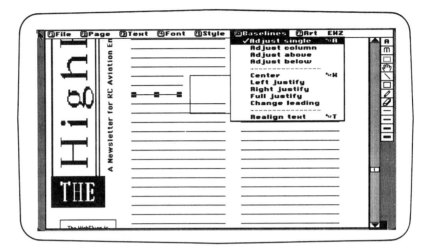

Fig. 9.19. *Adjusting single baselines.*

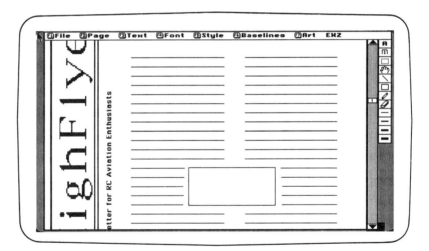

Fig. 9.20. *The finished baselines.*

First Publisher allows you to put the tape and the paste in a drawer—and leave them there. With First Publisher, Karla was able to pick the border she wanted to use, and cut and paste it (electronically) to fit the measurement she wanted. She chose from a variety of clip art so that she could include something that would catch the reader's eye and still tie in to the message she wanted to convey. The variety of fonts gave her the freedom to make parts of the document stand out, while still giving the rest of the document a professional look. The advertising flier for Peterson's Heating and Cooling shown in figure 9.21 was produced—entirely on the graphics layer—in the following steps:

Fig. 9.21. The advertising flier.

1. Karla first looked through the clip art files and found the border she wanted to use. She used the selection tool to select the border (see fig. 9.22). Because the selection tool always selects items within a rectangular area, part of the MasterCard and Visa symbols were selected as well. (But that's all right, for now—once the image is placed on the page, the extra images can be erased.) She then selected **Save art** from the Art menu and entered the name *BORDER* when it was requested.

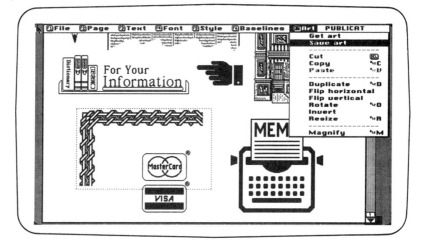

Fig. 9.22. Selecting and saving the border.

2. She then selected **Start over** from the File menu so that a blank page would be displayed.

3. She selected **Get art** and selected BORDER from the displayed names. (The path she used when she saved the art is offered as the default.) After she clicked the OK button, First Publisher changed the cursor to the shape of a hand. When she clicked the mouse button, the border was pasted onto the page. She then selected the unwanted image of the MasterCard emblem and pressed Del to delete it.

4. Next, she needed to copy and move the border sections so that they enclosed the page. She selected **Duplicate** from the Art menu; the cursor changed to the hand icon. She clicked the mouse button, and a copy of the border was pasted onto the page at the position she had placed the hand icon (see fig. 9.23).

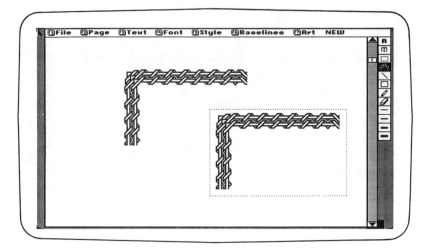

Fig. 9.23. Copying the border section.

5. Next, she flipped the border section so that it would fit in the upper-right corner by selecting **Flip horizontal** from the Art menu. Then, she selected and moved each border section to its corner.

6. To create the corner pieces for the bottom of the page, she selected the two top corner pieces, chose **Duplicate** from the Art menu, positioned the hand icon, and clicked the mouse button. A copy of the selected items was positioned on the page. She then selected the new images and chose **Flip vertical** from the Art menu, which caused the bottom corners to be flipped so that they would align with the bottom of the page (see fig. 9.24).

Sometimes the process of moving graphics down a page can seem slow—if you use the method of selecting the image with the selection tool and using the hand tool to drag the image down the page. To speed things up, use the cut-and-paste method instead. First select the image with the selection tool; then press Del; then press PgDn to get to the part of the page you want, and press Alt-C. The deleted image then is restored at the cursor position.

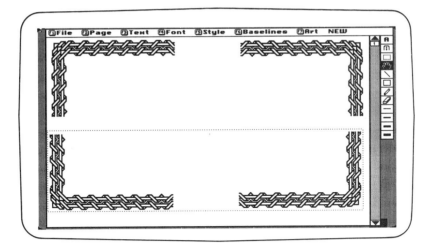

Fig. 9.24. *Flipping the bottom corners of the border.*

7. To fill in the border along the edges, Karla selected a piece of the longest side of the border (see fig. 9.25). She then copied it several times, rotating each piece to fit the area in the border.

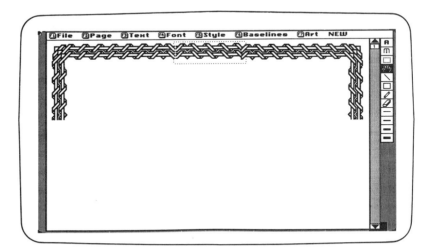

Fig. 9.25. *Filling in the border.*

8. She then selected the font she wanted to use and, using the graphics text tool, typed in the name, address, and phone number of the business.

These items—the border and the company information—are the only things on this flier that are not variable; the picture of the penguins and the "catch lines" at the top of the flier will vary depending on the season and the promotion being offered. For this reason, Karla saves the publication as her template at this point, under the name FLITMP, and then returns to the publication to finish the winter flier.

Example 3: Business Cards and Stationery

Desktop publishing overtook John quite by accident. A political reporter for his local paper and an occasional free-lancer, John had always considered himself a dyed-in-the-wool writer; he did the creating and left the corrections and the other production activities to the editors and publishers.

In doing some research for an article, however, John ran across a review of First Publisher, and his interest was sparked. He got the program and, within hours, had created his own business card and stationery. As he circulated his card, others began coming to him to produce their business materials. Several months later, John was owner of a desktop publishing business that created custom business materials for clients. In order to keep the development time to a minimum, John decided to keep four different template styles for stationery and cards, and he encourages his clients to pick from those styles. He then assembles the publication by building on the basic template style he created previously.

Because this audience is so specialized, John can set up a template only as far as fundamental graphic items are concerned; until he talks with the individual client, he cannot add clip art items or the name or motto of the business. For the business packet shown in figure 9.26, John built on a template that consisted only of the rules and the boxes; he added the logo, business name, and other variable information.

To create the business packet shown in figure 9.26 (which consists of business cards, stationery, and invoices) for a client, John followed the procedures in the following sections.

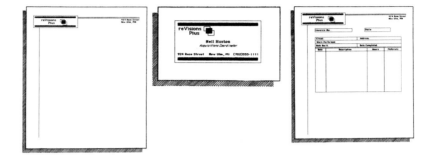

Fig. 9.26. *Business stationery, a business card, and an invoice.*

For stationery, he follows these steps:

1. John selects a new publication by choosing **Start over** from the File menu.

2. He then enables the grid by selecting **Use grid** from the Page menu. (This displays guide dots on the screen.)

3. Because he plans to draw two rules side by side, he needs to change the size of the grid. To do this, he selects **Set grid size** from the Page menu, and enters the smallest allowable setting (.12) for both the horizontal and vertical settings. The dots are then displayed much closer together (see fig. 9.27).

4. He turns on the ruler feature by selecting **Ruler** from the Page menu. (Rulers appear across the top and down the left edge of the screen.)

5. Using the line tool, he draws a rule of regular width from a location 2 1/2-inches below the top edge of the page.

6. Next, he selects the second width setting to draw the companion rule. However, he finds that even though the grid setting is small, it still does not allow him to draw the rule as close to the first rule as he would like.

7. To solve this problem, he disables the grid by selecting **Use grid** again from the Page menu. The dots disappear.

8. He then captures the second rule by using the selection tool; then clicks on the hand tool and moves the rule up underneath the first rule (see fig. 9.28).

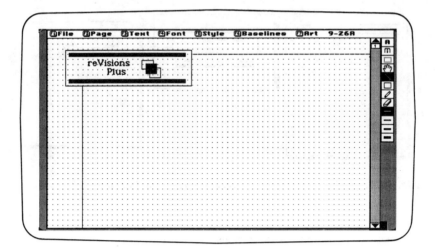

Fig. 9.27. The grid with the smallest settings specified.

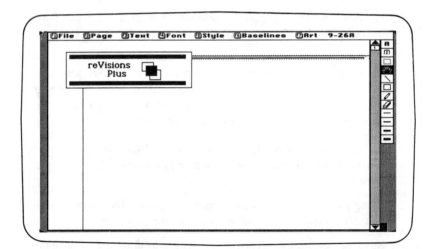

Fig. 9.28. Moving the second rule.

At this point, John saved one version of this publication for the client; then deleted the client information and saved the publication as a template file.

Producing Business Cards

To produce the business cards, John worked on a smaller scale model of the graphics used on the stationery. He wanted everything to tie together visually. He first used **Show rulers** to measure off the area for the card—3 1/2-inches by 2 inches—and then he added a smaller version of the rules. Next, he selected **Get art** and specified the ART file that stores the design element. When he pasted the image onto the publication, he selected **Resize** and reduced the size of the camera so that it wouldn't look overwhelming on the small card.

> You may notice when you use the **Show rulers** option that the rulers don't seem to be of equal measurements. The top ruler looks okay, but the ruler down the left edge of the screen looks exaggerated. Go ahead and create the card—or any graphic— according to the rulers; when you print the publication, it will be printed in the right proportions. On-screen, however, your business card may look more like a square than a rectangle.

Producing the Invoice

To be consistent with the design used on other publications, John modified the stationery design to create the invoice. By consolidating the logo and using rules and boxes to create the data entry area, he created the finished invoice after just a few minutes' work.

Chapter Summary

In this chapter, you learned how to create and use your own templates with First Publisher. Additionally, you took a closer look at the templates packaged with the First Publisher program. The last half of this chapter used three desktop publishing examples to show you how templates—and First Publisher in general—can be used for different applications. The next chapter concludes the book by introducing you to some specialized uses of First Publisher: importing and using scanned images, and using FONTMOVE and SNAPSHOT.

10

Using First Publisher's Special Features

In this chapter, you will learn about the special features of First Publisher that don't fit neatly into one of the chapters up to this point. This chapter focuses on more specialized applications, including the following:

❏ How to import and use scanned images in First Publisher publications

❏ How to use the FONTMOVE utility to move fonts in and out of your MASTER.FNT file

❏ How to use First Publisher's screen-capture utility, SNAPSHOT, to "take a picture" of your screen, and SNAP2ART to develop the picture

Using Scanned Images

Before starting to explore the possibilities of importing scanned graphics in First Publisher publications, you need to know the answers to a few basic questions.

What is a scanned image? A scanned image is a graphic that is converted from a photograph or line drawing—on paper—to an on-screen, electronic representation of the image.

How can you use scanned images? Scanned images can be used in the same way a photograph or other art is used. But, instead of pasting photos at layout stage or having the printer inlay art, scanned images give you the freedom of importing the graphic to First Publisher, modifying the image as necessary, and saving it on disk to use again.

How do you scan art? The photos and art for scanning are digitized through the use of a scanner—a device that uses accompanying software to "read" the image and translate the data to dot patterns. The dots—or pixels—can then be modified, copied, or manipulated as any other First Publisher graphic.

What scanners are compatible with First Publisher? First Publisher can accept digitized images from any scanner capable of scanning at 72 dpi. Many scanners on the market today scan at 300 dpi—a dot ratio too high for First Publisher to use. Most of these same scanners, however, are capable of scanning at a lower rate as well as the higher one. Be sure to check your scanner's manual before attempting the scan. You may be able to get around this dpi limitation, however, if you have a paint program that is capable of using a higher resolution graphic. For example, you might be able to import the scanned image into your paint program and then transfer the file into First Publisher.

What type of scanners are available? There are three types of scanners available: sheetfed scanners, flatbed scanners, and hand-held scanners. With a sheetfed scanner, the image is scanned as it moves across the glass area inside, not unlike the traditional photocopier. Flatbed scanners also are similar to copiers without the autofeed mechanism: you lay the photo or art face down on the glass, close the cover, and the image is scanned. To use the hand-held scanner, you hold the scanner and move it across the image. The hand-held scanner is not much larger than your average mouse and is used primarily for scanning small images, such as company logos, banners, and other small graphic items. Prices range from $1,995 for the top-of-the-line flatbed and sheetfed scanners to $199 for the lower resolution hand-held scanners.

What type of images produce the best results? When you are considering whether you want to invest in a scanner or have an image scanned by a service, carefully consider the material you want to scan. Look for contrast, sharp lines, clean images. A good, crisp black-and-white photo is probably the ideal image for scanning, but you can use color photos as well. Choose a picture in which the central image has a sharp contrast against the background. If the background is too light, the detail and definition of the scan may be lost—especially when the image is scanned at 72 dpi.

If you don't have a scanner of your own but would still like to incorporate scanned images in your First Publisher publications, you have the option of finding a scanning service to scan the image for you. Many printing houses have this service now. Just make sure that you find a company with a scanner that is capable of scanning at 72 dpi and converting the file to a format readable by First Publisher or by a compatible paint program.

Figure 10.1 shows a photograph that was scanned at 72 dpi and imported into First Publisher. In this photo, the central figure was caught in the flash of the bulb (it was not a great photograph because of that), but this caused the image to stand out clearly, making it easy for the scanner to pick up.

Fig. 10.1. *A photograph scanned and imported into First Publisher.*

Compare figure 10.1 with figure 10.2. The photograph in figure 10.2 was professionally taken, and the balance of background and foreground was less startling. However, because of this and the lightness of the background, the photo did not scan as well at 72 dpi and the result is a darker image.

Once you import a scanned image into First Publisher, you can treat the image as you would any other graphic. You simply retrieve the file by choosing **Get graphics** from the File menu. Then select the image by using

Fig. 10.2. *A professionally done photograph imported into First Publisher.*

the selection tool and save it as an art image by choosing **Save art** from the Art menu and assigning it a name.

Figure 10.3 shows a line art image in **Magnify** mode. That same image is later used on the front of a publication advertising a church function (see fig. 10.4). For more information on modifying graphics, see Chapter 6.

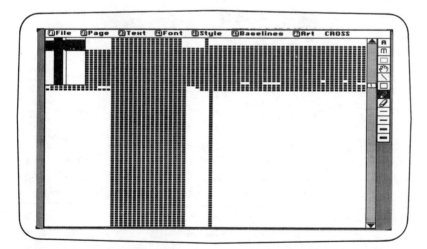

Fig. 10.3. *You can modify a scanned image like any other graphic.*

Fig. 10.4. *The scanned image used on a publication.*

In the next section, you will learn how to use First Publisher's utility FONTMOVE to add fonts to the program's MASTER.FNT file.

Using FONTMOVE

At several points throughout this book, you have seen references to the First Publisher utility FONTMOVE. Don't be intimidated by the phrase ''utility'' or by the fact that it is a miniprogram that runs independently of First Publisher.

FONTMOVE is simply a small program that moves fonts in and out of First Publisher. Because systems always have a limited amount of memory available, First Publisher is packaged with only a few of the available fonts installed on the Fonts menu. The default fonts available in the Fonts menu are the following:

Elite
Geneva
Helvetica
New York
Pica

These fonts give you a sampling of the various types of fonts available. New York is a serif type, meaning that the characters have small lines that cross at each end of the letter, and Helvetica is a sans serif type, meaning the characters do not have those lines.

Other fonts are available, however. On the Sampler Disk, in a file named EXTRA.FNT, First Publisher has the following additional dot-matrix fonts:

Athens
Chicago
London
Los Angeles
Monaco
Seattle
Toronto
Venice

These fonts give you a wide variety of styles from which to choose, from ornate fonts like London to a simple, sans serif Monaco font.

If you want to use any of these additional fonts, you must use FONTMOVE to place the fonts on the Fonts menu. Additionally, if you are using a laser printer, you need to use FONTMOVE to add the fonts from your printer's font file to the Fonts menu. Whether you are using an Apple LaserWriter or a Hewlett-Packard LaserJet or DeskJet, First Publisher already has the font file for your printer. You simply need to rename the program-supplied MASTER.FNT file (which contains dot-matrix fonts) and copy and rename your printer's font file to MASTER.FNT. (This procedure is explained in detail in Chapter 8.)

> For any operations requiring the use of a First Publisher program disk, remember to use backup copies instead. If you haven't already made backup copies, refer to Chapter 2 for copying procedures.

Starting FONTMOVE

In order to use FONTMOVE, you need to exit to the DOS prompt. If you are working on a First Publisher document, remember to save the publication by selecting **Save** from the File menu or by pressing Alt-S. Then exit First Publisher by selecting **Exit** from the File menu or by pressing Alt-E.

If you are using a system that is equipped with a hard disk, then you can start FONTMOVE from the PUB directory by typing *fontmove* and pressing Enter. If you are using a two disk drive system, place Program Disk 1 in drive A and the Fonts Disk in drive B; then type *fontmove* and press Enter.

After you press Enter, the FONTMOVE Main menu is displayed (see fig. 10.5). Table 10.1 gives you an overview of each of the commands used with FONTMOVE.

With the DeskMate version, you can run FONTMOVE by selecting Run... from the File menu.

```
            PFS:First Publisher Fontmove Program 2.0

                         Main Menu

                F1  Move fonts
                F2  Add HP LaserJet soft fonts
                F3  Exit to DOS




            Copyright (c) 1988 Software Publishing Corporation
```

Fig. 10.5. The FONTMOVE Main menu.

The FONTMOVE Menu System

The FONTMOVE Main menu only has three options:

Move fonts
Add HP LaserJet soft fonts
Exit to DOS

If you are moving the fonts from First Publisher's EXTRA.FNT file into the program, or if you are adding First Publisher fonts you purchased separately, you use F1 to access the next menu. If you are adding Hewlett-Packard soft fonts to the Fonts menu, you press F2 to access the correct menu. Each of these options is discussed more fully in the sections related to their functions.

Table 10.1
Commands Available in FONTMOVE

Key	Command	Function
F1	Help	Displays the functions of the FONTMOVE commands
F2	Dir	Lists all font files (FNT) in the specified directory
F3	Show	Displays all fonts in the selected font file
F4	Destination	Chooses file to which selected font will be copied
F5	Create	Creates a font file
F6	Copy	Copies font to the destination
F7	Erase	Erases font
Esc	Quit	Displays the FONTMOVE Main menu

> Although First Publisher does support Hewlett-Packard LaserJet soft fonts (for LaserJet and LaserJet Series II only), the program *does not* support DeskJet soft fonts.

Creating Another MASTER.FNT File

As you read in Chapter 8, MASTER.FNT is the file that First Publisher searches to find the font you specify. Before you can use a font with First Publisher, you must use FONTMOVE to move the font to the MASTER.FNT file.

When you set up the fonts for your laser printer, you replace the MASTER.FNT file—which originally stores dot-matrix fonts—with the laser fonts for your printer. You may want to have a mixture of dot-matrix and laser fonts, however, so that you have more flexbility in the fonts and sizes you use.

If you want to combine a few dot-matrix fonts with your laser printer fonts, you can create a new MASTER.FNT file and move those fonts to the file.

You also can choose to have several font files—perhaps one for each category of publication you produce— but there can only be one font file named MASTER.FNT at one time.

To create a new MASTER.FNT file, first choose **Create** from the FONTMOVE menu by pressing F5. Then enter the file name of the new font file. (Remember that if a version of MASTER.FNT already exists, you must save the font file under a different name.)

Adding Fonts

After you have started FONTMOVE, you are ready to move fonts into the program. If you are using a two disk drive system, Program Disk 1 should be in drive A, and the Fonts Disk should be in drive B. (If you're using 3 1/2-inch disks, place the Program and Fonts Disk in drive A.)

To select and add the fonts to the font file, follow these steps:

1. Press F1 to select **Move fonts**.

2. Press F2 to choose **Dir**. Specify the drive and directory where the program can find the font file (see fig. 10.6). If the fonts are on a disk, insert the disk in drive A and type *a:* as the path. After you specify the path, press Enter. (If you are using 5 1/4-inch disks, before pressing Enter, remove the Program Disk from drive A and insert the disk with the font file.)

3. Press F3 to select **Show**, and enter the name of the file you want to show. The program then displays the contents of the font file selected (see fig. 10.7). Use ↑ and ↓ to scroll through the list.

4. Press F4 to select the **Destination**. This file is the one to which you will copy the fonts. First Publisher looks in MASTER.FNT to get the fonts displayed in the Font and Style menus. If you have created a second font file, specify that file name. If you haven't yet created the file, select F5 (**Create**), and FONTMOVE creates the file and assigns it as the destination.

5. Use the arrow keys to move the highlight to the font you want to copy (refer to fig. 10.7). Then press F6 to select **Copy**. The file is copied to the destination file. Repeat this step until you have copied all necessary fonts.

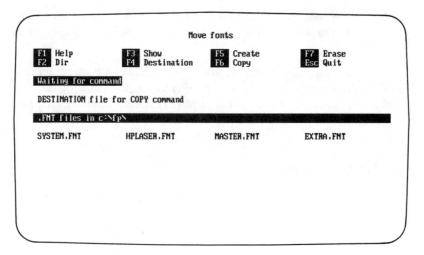

Fig. 10.6. Choosing **Dir** *in* FONTMOVE.

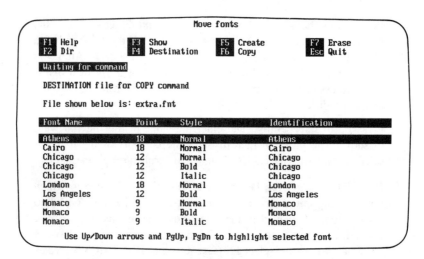

Fig. 10.7. Showing the contents of the font file.

Soft Fonts and FONTMOVE

Soft fonts are fonts stored on disk that can be loaded into your program and then downloaded—or copied—to the printer when you print a document that uses that particular font. First Publisher supports soft fonts for the Hewlett-Packard LaserJet printers, but does not, at this time, support soft fonts for the DeskJet printer.

Like other fonts in First Publisher, before you can use a soft font, it must be made available on the Font menu. You need to add the soft font to the MASTER.FNT file by using the FONTMOVE program.

Before you begin, be sure that you know the file name of the soft font you want to add because you are asked to enter the file name later in the procedure. If you are using a two disk drive system, make sure that Program Disk 1 is in drive A (or the Program and Fonts disk, for 3 1/2-inch disks), and the soft font disk is in drive B.

Then, to add the soft font to your font file, follow these steps:

1. At the FONTMOVE Main menu, press F2 to select **Add HP LaserJet soft fonts**.

2. Type the path to the soft font file. Then press Tab.

3. Type the destination path and font file where you want the soft font to be copied. (If you type the name of a FNT file that has not yet been created, First Publisher will automatically create the file.)

4. Enter the name of the font as it should appear in the Font menu.

5. Enter the path to First Publisher (such as *c:\pub* for a hard disk system), and press Enter. (If you're using a two disk system, and the Fonts Disk is in drive A, you can simply press Enter.)

If you have additional soft fonts to add, repeat the last few steps as many times as necessary. If you are using a two disk drive system, remember to leave at least 40K on the Fonts Disk so that First Publisher will be able to store the working backup copy of your current publication.

Remember that the procedure for using soft fonts with First Publisher is twofold:

1. You must use FONTMOVE to add the soft font to your MASTER.FNT file.

2. At print time, you must have the disk containing the soft fonts in drive A or copy them to the hard disk. Even though the soft font file names appear in the Font menu, First Publisher must have access to these files at print time.

Erasing Fonts

After you load a few fonts into MASTER.FNT, you will find that the available memory goes quickly. To remove fonts in order to make room for additional fonts—or just to free up some extra space—you can erase a font by using FONTMOVE. If you are using 5 1/4-inch disks, place the Fonts Disk in drive A. Then, follow these steps:

1. Press F2 to select **Dir**. FONTMOVE lists the available files.

2. Press F3 to choose **Show** and enter the name of the file you want to work with. MASTER.FNT is the file that stores the fonts listed on the Fonts menu. First Publisher displays the contents of the selected file.

3. Use ↑ or ↓ to highlight the font you want to remove.

4. Press F7 to choose **Erase**.

Remember that once you have erased a file, it's gone. Don't forget to keep a backup copy of all your font files before using **Erase**.

That wraps up our discussion of FONTMOVE. In the next section, you will learn about First Publisher's screen-capture utility, SNAPSHOT.

Using SNAPSHOT

As you have been reading through this book, you have seen illustrations that show actual screen images—called screen shots—that depict an action taking place on the screen. The figures are not "representations" or "artist's renderings" of the screen; they are electronic photographs taken of the screen while the operation was in progress. These photographs are taken by a program called a *screen-capture utility*, which works "behind" your program and takes a picture of the screen when you press a specified key or key combination.

What Is SNAPSHOT?

SNAPSHOT is First Publisher's screen-capture utility. But, unlike some utilities of this sort, SNAPSHOT does not have the capacity to "develop" the pictures it takes. To develop the picture by turning it into an ART file usable by First Publisher, the utility SNAP2ART is used.

When Would You Use SNAPSHOT?

Granted, the number of applications that would require the use of a screen-capture utility may be limited. Such a program would be useful, however, if you are creating any of the following projects:

❏ A software manual

❏ Training materials

❏ An advertising flier for your desktop publishing business

❏ A newsletter related to computer hardware and software

❏ Any document that would incorporate on-screen spreadsheets

Activating SNAPSHOT

You can use SNAPSHOT whether you have a hard disk system or a two disk drive system. As you know, SNAPSHOT is an independent screen-capture utility that works outside of First Publisher. If you are using a two disk drive system, first put Program Disk 1 in drive A; if you have 3 1/2-inch drives, put the Program and Fonts Disk in drive A; and if you are using a hard disk system, make sure that c:\pub is the current directory.

Then, to activate SNAPSHOT, you simply type *snapshot* and press Enter. The following lines then are displayed:

```
Snapshot program version 1.1
Copyright 1987, 1988 Software Publishing Corporation
Press [Shift-PrtSc] to take a snapshot.
Use SNAP2ART program to create .Art file from snapshot.
```

Selecting a Hot Key

In the message displayed when SNAPSHOT is activated, the third line lists the key combination you use to take a picture, with SNAPSHOT. By pressing the Shift and the PrtSc keys at the same time, you tell SNAPSHOT to capture whatever is displayed on the screen at that moment.

You have the alternative of selecting a different key combination—or *hot key*—used to tell SNAPSHOT to take a picture. If you want to customize SNAPSHOT in this way, you simply start the program by typing *snapshot k* instead of the regular *snapshot*. After you press Enter, you need to type the key that you want to use as the activator.

> If you specify a hot key for SNAPSHOT rather than use the default activator key combination Shift-PrtSc, be careful to select a key that is not used in the program you will be photographing. For example, if you select F1 as the hot key for SNAPSHOT and then you use First Publisher, you will be unable to use the F1 key for normal First Publisher operations. Choose instead a key you use rarely, such as the right bracket (]) key.

Capturing a Screen Shot

Whether the screen you are taking a picture of is a First Publisher screen or a screen from another program, SNAPSHOT stays dormant "behind" the program until you need it. When the screen you want is displayed, simply press Shift-PrtSc or the hot key you specified.

Immediately after you press the key to activate SNAPSHOT, you will hear a beep, which indicates that SNAPSHOT has taken the picture of the screen. If you hear a buzzing noise, SNAPSHOT was unable to take the picture.

> SNAPSHOT captures only graphics screens if you are using a Hercules card.

One major limitation of SNAPSHOT arises from the fact that you can only take one picture at a time. In order to do this, you must exit the program, use SNAP2ART (discussed in the next section) to turn the picture into an ART file, and then return to the program. If you have several screen shots to capture, this can be a frustrating process.

"Developing" the Screen Shot

As mentioned previously, you must use SNAPSHOT's companion utility, SNAP2ART, to convert the picture to an ART file usable by First Publisher. Like SNAPSHOT, SNAP2ART is an independent utility that runs outside of First Publisher. If Program Disk 1 is in drive A (on a two disk drive system) or PUB is the current directory (on a hard drive system), you can use SNAP2ART by following these steps:

1. Type *snap2art* at the DOS prompt.

2. Name the picture and press Enter. SNAP2ART shows the picture on the screen. A Help screen is available, allowing you to make modifications to the picture or save it as captured (see fig. 10.8).

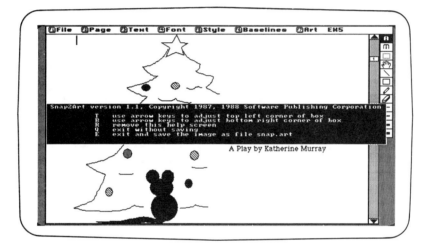

Fig. 10.8. *The SNAP2ART Help screen.*

3. Remove the Help screen by typing *r*.

4. Press E to save the picture and exit the program.

If you want to quit SNAP2ART without saving the picture, type *q*.

After the file is saved in ART format, you can retrieve the file and use it in your publications by selecting **Get art** from the Art menu. You can then modify it as you would any graphic image in First Publisher.

Cropping the Screen Shot

You have the option of selecting only a portion of the SNAP2ART image by cropping the picture. A flashing box encloses the selected area; this is the area saved (see fig. 10.9). You use the options in the Help screen, at the top of the screen, to move the sides of the flashing box. (If you have removed the Help screen and want to restore it, press ?.)

Fig. 10.9. The flashing rectangle encloses the area to be saved.

Chapter Summary

This chapter introduced you to three very different but important features of First Publisher. The first section explored the possibilities of using scanned images with First Publisher; the second section explained FONTMOVE and showed you how to add and erase fonts from the program's MASTER.FNT file; and the last section illustrated SNAPSHOT, First Publisher's screen-capture utility, and explained SNAP2ART, the utility used to turn the snapshot into an ART file usable by First Publisher. This chapter concludes the chapters in this book, but two appendixes and a glossary follow.

Turning Your Publication into a Finished Product

N ow you have worked all the way through the book, probably producing award-winning publications, and you're ready to take the publication to the printer.

Many new desktop publishers feel "out of their element" once they walk into a print shop. They think they don't know what questions to ask, what the "normal" choices are (paper weight and size, ink, and so on), or what price range to expect.

This appendix attempts to help you with those questions. The best advice for working with printers, however, is the following:

> Find a printer who is willing to advise you, who shows creative judgment you can trust, and who gives you a reasonable price. If you are satisfied with the quality, turnaround time, and cost, stay with that printer. Developing a business relationship with one printer is good business sense for a budding desktop publisher, and it will work to your company's best interest in the future.

359

How Should the Publication Look When You Take It to the Printer?

Many times, when you finish a publication, you will not want to look at it anymore. Part of the reason may be that you're tired of reworking and revising it; the other part may be that you're afraid you will see something else you want to change.

Generally, when you consider yourself "finished" with a publication, you should take one last careful look. Make sure that the rules are where you want them to be; read over the publication for grammatical and punctuation errors; check your graphics to make sure that they printed correctly.

If you have had to manually paste down anything, make sure that it is secure and neatly done (big wads of rubber cement don't indicate professionalism). Lastly, have all your pages together in the right order.

Typical Newsletter Orders

More and more, businesses are going to a more polished, sophisticated newsletter style. Gone are the days of the typed-and-photocopied company newsletter. Now house organs use eye-catching color, custom art, and laser or typeset quality type to create a dramatic effect for their publications.

These publications typically are four-page newsletters, which is actually one sheet of a fairly heavy-stock paper, printed front and back and folded in the middle. One half of the last page is reserved for the mailing panel, to which mailing labels are affixed. The bulk mailing rate also may be printed in the top-right corner of the panel. A print run of a publication of this type may be anywhere from 2,000 to 4,000.

Although that type of high-investment "typical" order may be the norm for the corporate world, there are plenty of people who are still producing informational newsletters for nonprofit organizations, parent-teacher organizations, and businesses. This type of business relies on First Publisher most, making good the use of the program's clip art, flexibility, and wealth of features.

Paper

What paper weight do you want? This question is one of the first your printer will ask you. For newsletters, a 60-lb offset paper is best. The coarseness of the paper can stand up to printing on both sides. If you're on a low budget, you can use a 50-lb offset paper, but you run the risk of the ink bleeding through when you print on both sides of the page.

If you are producing a brochure for mailing, you should use a different type of paper. You can select from a flat finish, enamel (high gloss—which also strengthens the paper), text stock, or card stock. (Text stock is a relatively lightweight paper that folds easily; card stock is heavier paper, often used for producing materials that include business-reply cards, and so on.) Unless you are including a business reply card that will be detached and mailed separately by the recipient, an enamel text stock is a good choice for a mailer. It folds neatly, doesn't need to be scored like card stock does, and costs less in postage. (The term *scored* refers to the process of cutting lines at the folds of the publication so the heavy stock can be folded neatly.)

What size should the paper be? For a typical four page newsletter, printers most often use one 11-by-17-inch sheet. The sheet is folded vertically in the center, giving you the "book" effect of having four pages. If you have stayed within the First Publisher margins set in the program, your printer will be able to print the pages on 11-by-17-inch paper. If you have modified the margins and extended the graphics to the edge of the page, or if you want a graphic image—like a rule or border—to bleed off the page, the printer must print the publication on a larger size paper and then cut the pages back to 11-by-17-inch size. For publications other than the standard 8 1/2-by-11-inch size, keep in mind that the process may require cutting and/or printing on a larger or smaller size paper. (Naturally, the larger the paper size or the more work involved, the more you pay.)

If you are producing business cards, be sure to create the publication card at actual size: 2 inches by 3 1/2 inches. If the card is larger than standard business card size, the printer must photograph it, electronically reduce it, and print from the reduced copy. This process can detract from the readability of the card. It's best to create it at the size you need; then you can simply print the card, take it in, and let the printer do the rest.

What color paper should I use? You have a choice in the color of paper you use for your publication. From real "colors" like blue, pink, and yellow, to more business-like colors of gray, off-white, and white, you can choose the paper color that best suits your publication. Remember that you want a paper color to complement the ink color you use on the publication, so if you're using red ink as part of a company logo, a publication on pink paper might make your readers cringe. Before you decide, ask the printer to see the color selection available.

How much will the paper cost? Several factors figure into the price of the paper you use: the weight, the size, the finish, and the quantity. Heavier paper costs more, but often is a necessity; and larger stock costs more than regular sizes. Keep in mind that most printers offer a substantial price break for buying in quantity. If you have taken on the responsibility of printing your organization's newsletter for 12 months, for example, and you expect to print at least 500 copies a month, you may want to buy all your paper for the year at one time. Most printers will store the paper for you, and this gives you a significant price break on the paper, as well.

Inks

What color ink should I use? As you might expect, black is the least expensive ink you can use. Most printers also have standard inks in several different colors. If you are trying to match a specific color, or simply don't like the selection you have seen, you do have the option of requesting custom colors, at a possible additional cost. For custom ink color, you select the color from a chart (much like the paint scales at your local hardware store), and the printer mixes it for you. Usually, there's an additional fee of $25 per ink used for standard ink (the price may be more or less, depending on your area), and an additional $10 to $15 charge for custom colors.

You can cut costs on printing in special ink and printing in quantities with one blow, if you prefer. Suppose that in addition to the mass amount of paper you purchased in the last example, you also wanted to print the company's masthead—in a custom royal blue ink—on the top of every page. The rest of the publication will be done in black ink. In this instance, you can buy the paper in bulk, and have the color printed for the whole amount at one time. This keeps you from having to buy the paper and pay the specialized ink fee every month when you print the publication. Then, when you take the monthly publication in to be printed, the cost will be minimal.

Copying

Is it cheaper to photocopy? Depending on your project, the type of audience you're reaching, and the quantity you want, photocopying is probably not your best bet. Although most people think "I'll just take this flier down and run off 50 copies," the quality they get for the price they pay may be pretty poor. Here again, think in terms of quantity. Is the flier you're producing a one-time, seasonal promotion that will have a limited shelf life? Or is it a flier you will be able to use several times throughout the year, by circulating it to different client groups? If you can justify printing 100 or 150, have the printer reproduce it for you. The quality will be much better, and the cost is still minimal: about $12 for 100 copies.

Additional Printing Tips

Let the printer make suggestions. The printer has worked with many clients, some of whom must have produced publications similar to yours. Rely on the printer's experience to tell you what paper, ink, envelope weight, and so on, works best for your particular project. Most printers keep samples of recent works, so you can feel the various paper weights, see the inks, and examine the layout.

Keep a folder of publications you like. This tip was included in the design section also. It's important to identify the styles that catch your eye; those styles will catch other readers' eyes, as well. If you like the paper, the ink, or the size, keep it with your publication's file; then take it to the printer with you. The printer will be able to make suggestions based on your likes and dislikes.

Ask questions. If you don't understand something about the printing process or about your responsibilities in preparing the material, don't be afraid to ask. An informed customer is much easier for the printer to deal with than a customer who doesn't understand the process.

Remember to get a guaranteed print date. Most printers will give you a target date or time by which they will have finished the publication. And reputable printers stick to that deadline. However, bear in mind that sometimes even in the best of situations, deadlines get bumped; so if your printer misses by a little bit, don't write him off—unless that becomes a pattern.

B

First Publisher
Design Tips

This appendix gives you a quick look at the various design tips scattered throughout the book. Tips are broken down into the following categories:

- ❑ Overall design tips
- ❑ Newsletter tips
- ❑ Business stationery tips
- ❑ Flier tips
- ❑ Tips for training materials

Overall Design Tips

Consider what you want to accomplish with your publication. Are you trying to enlighten, amuse, inspire, or inform people? Do you simply want to get your business's name out in front of the largest number of people possible?

Think about the tone of your publication. Plan everything—from the design to the content—to correspond with the tone your audience will expect.

365

Picture your audience. Are they businesspeople or members of the PTO? Do they sell stocks and bonds or roses and daffodils? Think about the type of publication your audience would expect to see. Sketch a rough draft of the publication before you begin. Decide where you will position different elements, and, if you will be using more than one page, sketch out additional pages, too.

After you have created some of the basic elements on the page, print a copy, using draft mode. This printout will give you a paper guide —something you can continue to sketch ideas on or use to decide what to do and *not* to do as you continue the design stage.

Think about the way a reader's eye scans text. Choose columns and place graphics in such as way that it encourages the reading flow rather than interrupts it.

Use rules and boxes judiciously to help enhance the organization of the publication and lead the reader's eye.

Keep a folder of styles you like so that you can try to emulate those publications using First Publisher.

Newsletter Tips

What does your banner say about the publication? Make sure that the banner is appropriate for your audience. Should it be dramatic? Try inverting the banner so that it is white text on black. Is it lighthearted? Use a clip art item as a side graphic and work that into the banner.

Use one of First Publisher's newsletter templates if you want to vary the column layout.

After text is placed in the multicolumn layout, check to make sure that there are no "bad breaks;" that is, words or letters that wrap to the top of the next column or the next line, leaving a confusing, unbalanced look.

Don't overdo it with graphic elements. Remember that graphics are meant to support the text; not the other way around. Use one or two graphic elements on each page. More than two elements of art on one page detracts from the readability of the newsletter.

Use only one or two fonts within a document. Don't run the risk of cluttering your publication and detracting from its effect by trying out various fonts in one publication. Select one or two typefaces you like, and then stick with them throughout the document.

Never use graphics instead of text in a newsletter. In other words, don't try to convey a message in a graphic that isn't conveyed in text. Readers may go searching for the text that supports the art.

Make sure that the baselines in columns align so that even though the text wraps to the next column, the text in the two columns is aligned.

Use a box to enclose a secondary article. This helps highlight the article and, at the same time, confine the reader's eye.

Use shadow boxes in a newsletter as callout boxes. Callout boxes summarize an important concept in the text and display the message in larger type. This allows the reader to scan the article quickly and pick out the major points.

Enlarge the banner by stretching it with **Resize** and by using the **Magnify** option to smooth out rough edges.

Be sure to include on page one a table of contents box (use graphics text to create this text).

Use the **Change leading** option in the Baselines menu to change the amount of white space around headlines.

Create and use a template if you will be doing the same publication month after month.

Business Stationery Tips

Keep a collection of stationery and logos that you like. This will help you in deciding what is appropriate for your business stationery.

Create a logo that is in some way connected with your business. First Publisher has several logos available in the program-supplied clip art file, and other clip art files for businesses can be purchased separately from Software Publishing Corporation

Make sure that the letterhead you choose does not overwhelm the page. There is a fine balance there—selecting an image that sticks in the reader's mind but doesn't dominate the page. Again, looking through a file of stationery you like will help you identify what might work for you.

Use rules across the top of the page and down the left edge, if you like. Remember that in most cases, also running rules down the right and bottom edges—in effect, boxing in the page—gives the page a ''confining'' feel.

Use the logo on all your business items: stationery, business cards, envelopes, invoices, and any other business forms. Use the logo as an identifier for your business.

Keep the design of your letterhead simple and memorable. Don't overload your readers with your creative talent. Do something subtle that will linger in the reader's mind.

Remember that the white space is just as important as the printed space on a publication.

Position the elements on the page so that attention is called to your company's name.

Flier Tips

In most publications, white space is as important as printed space. In a flier, white space may be *more* important than the printed space. Use white space to highlight the message you are trying to convey.

Remember that if a reader cannot scan the flier quickly, it doesn't work. If a reader has to sit down with a cup of coffee in order to read the volume of text on a flier, that flier isn't effective, and probably won't be read.

Place the business name and address so that the reader's eye will be drawn to it.

The fewer the words, the better.

Use graphics to catch the reader's eye. (Make sure that the graphics in some way are tied to your business or your message.)

Use a border to give the page an organized look or to call attention to a specific promotion.

Make sure that you include your company logo somewhere on the flier.

Tips for Training Materials

Keep the handout brief, with only enough information to refresh the reader's memory later.

If you have room on the publication, add space for notes.

Include an agenda box that lets readers know what to expect from the course. (Use graphics text to create this box.)

Use graphic elements to highlight important points.

Use rules to help organize the flow of text.

Be sure to include captions on any figures or graphs.

C

First Publisher for DeskMate Users

In February, 1989, Software Publishing Corporation introduced another version of PFS: First Publisher. The new version, PFS: First Publisher 2.01—DeskMate®, was created to run with the DeskMate program available for Tandy and other IBM-compatible computers.

What Is DeskMate?

DeskMate, an interface program produced by Tandy Corporation, is a shell from which you can run application programs on a Tandy or IBM-compatible computer. DeskMate includes many applications to help you manage data. These applications include a calendar, a file program, a word processor, a spreadsheet, a draw program, a communications application, and a music program.

All application programs run from within DeskMate look and work similarly. After you learn how to use the menu system in one application, you can apply that knowledge to the other applications as well.

If you currently are using the DeskMate program, adding First Publisher to your collection of applications programs gives you the flexibility to turn your system into a complete desktop publishing package. Armed with a word processing program and First Publisher, you have everything you need to produce effective newsletters and brochures, as well as business reports, press releases, and many other publications.

371

What Do You Need To Run First Publisher's DeskMate Version?

You can use First Publisher with DeskMate Runtime, included with the packet of First Publisher disks, or you can purchase DeskMate 3.0 from Tandy Corporation.

What Is DeskMate Runtime?

If you purchased PFS: First Publisher 2.01—DeskMate, you actually have a version of First Publisher created to run with the Desk-Mate program. The DeskMate program is not packaged with First Publisher; only the necessary commands for running the program are included. If you need to get the entire DeskMate program (with First Publisher included), you can purchase DeskMate 3.0 from Tandy Corporation.

To run PFS: First Publisher 2.01—DeskMate, you need the following hardware and software:

❏ A Tandy, IBM, or 100-percent compatible computer

❏ 640K of memory

❏ Two floppy disk drives or one floppy disk drive and one hard disk

❏ DOS Version 3.2 or higher

❏ One of the following graphics cards: Hercules, CGA, EGA, or VGA (Tandy or IBM)

❏ A mouse from one of the following manufacturers: Tandy, LOG-ITECH, Microsoft, or Mouse Systems. (*Note:* The use of a mouse is optional but highly recommended.)

❏ A dot-matrix or laser printer supported by First Publisher. For a list of compatible printers, see Chapter 8.

The amount of memory your system has is crucial to the operation of First Publisher. Before you start the program, be sure that you do not have any other active memory-resident programs. If you do, reboot your computer and restart First Publisher to free the memory needed for First Publisher to make use of all program features and fonts. For tips on increasing the amount of memory space you can use for First Publisher, see "Tips for Using PFS: First Publisher —DeskMate," later in this appendix.

Because of the memory required by the DeskMate version of First Publisher, users who currently use the stand-alone IBM version of the software should not consider this version a sufficient upgrade for the program they are now using. Although the DeskMate version does enhance some of the features introduced in Version 2.0, the product was designed specifically to run under the DeskMate interface program. If you are currently using the stand-alone version of First Publisher and do not plan to use the program with DeskMate, don't despair. You can expect to see the extra features of this version in subsequent releases of First Publisher.

What's New about First Publisher for DeskMate?

Whether you use the First Publisher 2.0 or 2.01—DeskMate, the program's basic operation is the same. In this section, you learn about a few of the differences encountered when using the DeskMate version.

The User Interface

The user interface of the DeskMate version of First Publisher resembles the interface of other DeskMate applications. Figure C.1 shows the screen displayed after you start First Publisher.

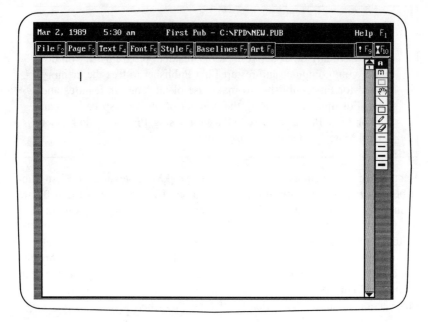

Fig. C.1. *The opening document screen.*

Understanding the Information Line

First Publisher displays the date and time in the information line at the top of the screen. The name of the program also is displayed (First Pub) in this line, and the current directory is listed to the right of the program name. On the right side of the information line is a reminder that you can access help at any time during the program by pressing F1.

Using the Menu Bar

The menu bar, directly below the information line, lists the First Publisher menus. (Note the absence of F1, the key used only to display help screens.) Next to the menu names are the function keys you can press to open the windows. Table C.1 lists the various menus and their function key alternatives and provides a basic description of the purpose of each menu.

Table C.1
First Publisher Menu Options

Menu	Key	Description
File	F2	Use the File menu to open, close, save, delete, and print files; to run other programs; to check the status of the current file; and to exit First Publisher. (For more about the File menu, see Chapter 4.)
Page	F3	Use the Page menu to define the page by setting columns, margins, and leading; to toggle the **Picturewrap** feature on and off; to enable and disable the grid and change grid size; to move to other pages; to add new pages; and to display the entire current page. (For more about the Page menu, see Chapters 4 and 7.)
Text	F4	Use the Text menu to retrieve and save text, and to cut, copy, and paste selected text items. (For more about the Text menu, consult Chapter 5.)
Font	F5	Use the Font menu to change the current typeface on the text and graphics layers of the document. (For more about the Font menu, see Chapters 5 and 10.)
Style	F6	Use the Style menu to change the style and/or size of the typeface you choose from the Font menu. (For more information on the Style menu, see Chapter 5.)
Baselines	F7	Use the Baselines menu to control the flow of text in your publication. (Chapter 7 explains more about the Baselines menu.)
Art	F8	Use the Art menu to retrieve and save art images, and to cut, copy, and paste selected art items. (In Chapter 6, you find additional material about the options available on the Art menu.)

You can open a menu in two ways:

1. By clicking the mouse button on the menu name

2. By pressing the function key next to the menu name

Similarly, you can close the menu in two ways:

1. By clicking the mouse button outside of the open menu

2. By pressing Enter or Esc

Selecting Menu Options

Now that you know how to open the menu and display the available options, you need to select the options. For example, suppose that you want to select the **Open...** option on the File menu (see fig. C.2). You have three methods of making this selection:

1. You can use the ↓ key to position the highlight bar on the item and press Enter.

2. You can move the mouse pointer so that the highlight rests on the item and then click the mouse button.

3. You can press Ctrl-O.

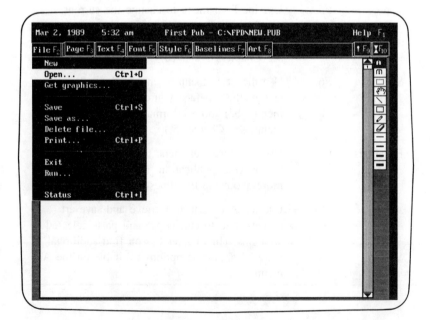

Fig. C.2. *Selecting the **Open...** option from the File menu.*

This last method involves a speed key combination. *Speed keys* are key combinations that enable you to bypass the keystrokes for opening menus and selecting options (or if you are using the mouse, you can bypass the necessary mouse operations). The DeskMate version of the program uses the Ctrl key with an alphanumeric key for each combination; First Publisher 2.0 uses the Alt key and an alphanumeric key for speed key combinations.

In the next section, you learn more about the menus unique to First Publisher's DeskMate version.

Using the F9 and F10 Menus

The first seven menus available in the menu bar (File, Page, Text, Font, Style, Baselines, and Art) are almost identical to the menus used in First Publisher 2.0. The two main exceptions are the several options added to the File menu—such as an option for running programs like FONTMOVE and Printer from within the program, and separate options for opening new and existing publications—and the function key alternatives are changed so that Help is available when you press F1. (Chapter 3 explains more about each of the menus.)

In the DeskMate version, however, two new menus are available: F9 and F10. The F9 menu has no name other than F9, and, if you are using First Publisher's DeskMate Runtime version, the options on this menu are unavailable to you. If you select the menu by clicking the name or pressing F9, the menu shows the message ‹ Empty ›.

You use the F10 menu, called the DeskMate Accessories menu, to tell DeskMate and First Publisher what type of mouse you are using and how fast you want the double-click speed to be. (Double-click speed is the measurement of the time between clicks in a double-click.) You also can set the communications settings (for DeskMate only), the date and time, the printer settings (for DeskMate only), and the colors you use on-screen.

> Although the DeskMate Accessories menu provides you with the means to change the printer settings, you *must* run First Publisher's Printer program for the program to print your documents correctly. For more information on running First Publisher's Printer program, see the section ''Specifying Printer Settings,'' later in this appendix.

When you select the DeskMate Accessories menu by pressing F10 or clicking the menu name, one option is displayed: **Setup**. When you select the **Setup** option, the screen shown in figure C.3 is displayed.

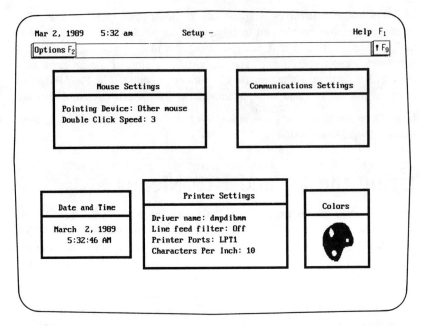

Fig. C.3. *The screen produced by selecting the* **Setup** *option.*

As you can see, five boxes appear on-screen, displaying the current settings for each of the following elements:

> Mouse Settings
> Communications Settings
> Date and Time
> Printer Settings
> Colors

To change any of the settings displayed, select the Options menu by clicking the menu name or pressing F2. The menu shown in figure C.4 is displayed.

Specifying Mouse Settings

After you select **Mouse...** from the Options menu, the screen shown in figure C.5 is displayed.

Select the item that best describes the type of mouse you have by positioning the mouse pointer on the item's setting button and clicking the mouse button or by pressing Tab to move to the appropriate setting and pressing the space bar.

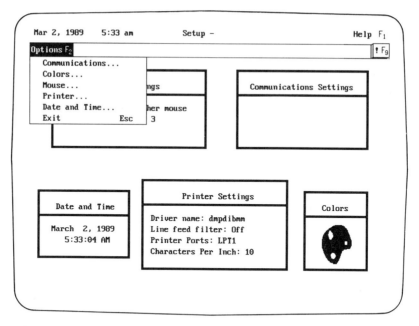

Fig. C.4. *The Options menu.*

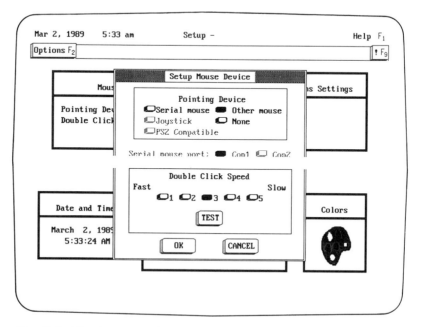

Fig. C.5. *The Setup Mouse Device screen.*

If you are unsure about which type of mouse you are using, refer to the section "The Mouse," in Chapter 2. If you are still uncertain, consult the manual packaged with the mouse or contact your local dealer.

Depending on the type of mouse you select, some of the options on this screen may be disabled, meaning that these options cannot be selected. You can tell which options are disabled by their appearance: the unavailable options are lighter than available options.

In the bottom half of the Setup Mouse Device box, you can set the amount of time allowable between clicks in a double-click. For example, if the user does not click the second time quickly enough, First Publisher doesn't recognize the action as a double-click. The program sees the two clicks independently. Try different settings to see which is most comfortable for you. Use the Test button to try the speed you have selected. When the Test button flashes, you have double-clicked the mouse button within the allowable time limit.

Specifying Printer Settings

Although the DeskMate Accessories menu has a Printer Settings box, you must run First Publisher's Printer program to ensure that your documents are printed correctly. Use the Printer Settings box on the DeskMate Accessories menu to specify printer settings used with other DeskMate applications.

To run the Printer program from within First Publisher's DeskMate version, follow these steps:

1. Select the File menu by pressing F2 or clicking the menu name.

2. Select **Run...** from the File menu. The screen shown in figure C.6 is displayed, asking you to enter the name of the program you want to run.

3. Type *printer* and press Enter (this action automatically "presses" the OK button). The screen shown in figure C.7 is displayed.

4. Type the number that corresponds to the printer you are using.

5. Specify the printer port and whether you are using scaled or unscaled printing. (For more information about scaled versus unscaled printing, see Chapter 8.)

When you press Esc to return to First Publisher, a blank publication screen is displayed, and the program can be configured for your printer type.

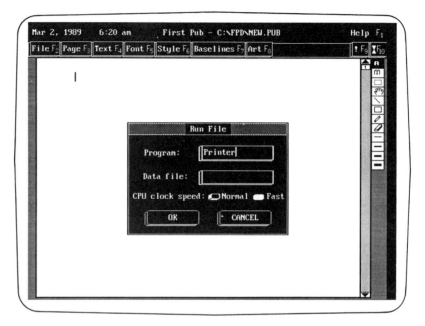

Fig. C.6. *The Run File window in which you specify the program you want to run.*

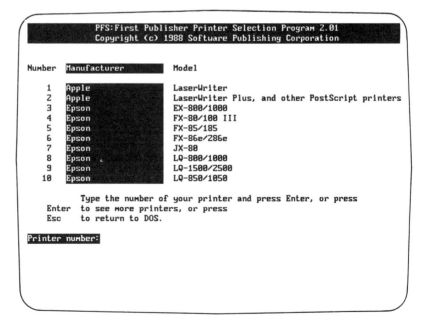

Fig. C.7. *The first screen of the Printer program.*

Running the FONTMOVE Program

FONTMOVE is a utility program that First Publisher uses to move fonts in and out of the program. In First Publisher 2.0, users often find that adding fonts from the EXTRA.FNT file is necessary to merge fonts for dot-matrix and laser printers or to create a custom MASTER.FNT file. (*Note:* MASTER.FNT is the name of the file in which First Publisher looks to find the fonts listed in the Font menu.)

With the DeskMate version of First Publisher, FONTMOVE becomes even more important because the memory limitation is a greater consideration. You may want to select only two or three fonts to use in the creation of your First Publisher document and include only those fonts in your MASTER.FNT file. This process reduces the amount of data First Publisher must store in RAM, and therefore increases the amount of RAM you have available for First Publisher documents.

To run the FONTMOVE program from within First Publisher, follow these steps:

1. Select the File menu by pressing F2 or clicking the menu name.

2. Select **Run...** from the File menu.

3. When the screen asking you to enter the name of the program you want to run is displayed, type *fontmove* and press Enter. The screen shown in figure C.8 is displayed.

When you finish moving fonts with First Publisher, press F3 to get back to the First Publisher document screen. (For more information on using FONTMOVE, see Chapter 10.)

Changing Colors

Discussing the DeskMate Accessories menu leads to another new feature of the DeskMate version that most people notice right away: Color. First Publisher 2.01—DeskMate enables you to choose foreground and background colors, designing your screen in whatever color scheme works best for you.

To display the current color settings, follow these steps:

1. Press F10 to open the DeskMate Accessories menu or position the mouse pointer on the menu name and click the mouse button.

2. Open the Options menu.

3. Select the **Colors...** option. The window shown in figure C.9 is displayed.

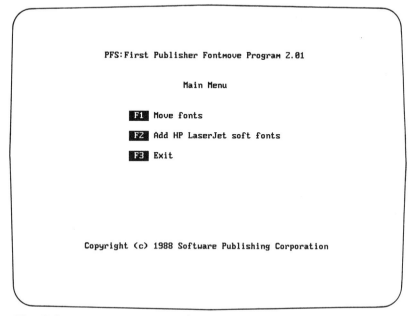

PFS:First Publisher Fontmove Program 2.01

Main Menu

F1 Move fonts

F2 Add HP LaserJet soft fonts

F3 Exit

Copyright (c) 1988 Software Publishing Corporation

Fig. C.8. *The FONTMOVE Main menu.*

In this pop-up window, you can examine the various active color settings and modify those settings if you want. In the top left corner of the window is the Palettes box. If you look to the right of the items in that box, you see (in the Colors column) the color selected for that item.

To change the color of an item, follow these steps:

1. Select the name of the element you want to change (for example, **Text background**).

2. Click the arrows at the end of the red color control panel to add a smaller or larger amount of red to the item color. If you are not using the mouse, you can use Tab to move to the color control panel you want and use the → and ← keys to indicate more or less color.

3. When you are happy with that item's color, repeat steps 1 and 2 for any other elements you want to change.

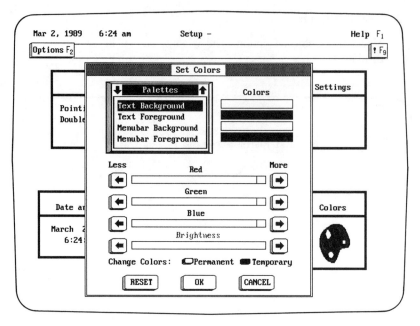

Fig. C.9. *The Set Colors screen.*

Background and Foreground: Which Is Which?

First Publisher for the DeskMate throws you a slight curve when referring to *background* and *foreground*. If you have ever seen First Publisher operate on a black-and-white monitor, you know that the document appears white and the text and graphics placed on the document appear black.

With DeskMate's color scheme, the definition of background and foreground is reversed. If you want the DeskMate version of First Publisher to display as black text on a white background, therefore, you need to set the *background* to black and the *foreground* to white. Similarly, to get yellow text on a blue background, set the background to yellow and the foreground to blue. Although this process seems backwards, when you get back into First Publisher, you see the correct settings.

4. When you have set all the colors the way you want them, tell First Publisher whether you want these changes to be in affect for only the current session (temporary) or to be made the default colors for every session (permanent).

5. You now have three choices: You can select RESET to do away with the changes you made and return the display to the color scheme selected previously; you can choose OK to accept the color scheme you have chosen; or you can select Cancel to abandon changes.

The color scheme you choose depends on your personal preferences. The following are a few general suggestions for selecting a good color scheme:

❏ Pick colors that are not too bright; remember that extremely bright characters are difficult to read and a background that is too bright overwhelms the text.

❏ Make sure that the overall color combination scheme is not too dark. Picking three different shades of blue, or choosing two dark blues and a dark green for the text, menu background, and foreground results in a screen that requires a lot of effort from the reader.

❏ Choose a combination of colors you like. You can even get a little exotic.

❏ Remember that one of the keys to choosing a good color combination is in the degree of contrast. If you can choose your colors for foreground and background so that they go well together, show enough contrast to make the necessary items stand out easily, and don't overwhelm you with brightness, you have a good screen.

Tips for Using PFS: First Publisher—DeskMate

This section summarizes the DeskMate suggestions appearing throughout this book:

❏ Remember that the DeskMate version uses a considerable amount of memory. You must disable all memory-resident programs before running First Publisher. (Otherwise, your use of available fonts and possibly the program may be inhibited.)

❏ To free up RAM that can be used by First Publisher, create a MASTER.FNT file including only one or two fonts you use often. (Chapter 10 explains more about customizing the MASTER.FNT file and using FONTMOVE.)

❏ Use FONTMOVE from within First Publisher by selecting **Run...** from the File menu and typing *fontmove* in response to the program name prompt.

❏ Remember that you must run First Publisher's Printer program to correctly configure the printer for the program. Using DeskMate's Printer Settings screen is not sufficient for printing First Publisher documents. You run the Printer program by selecting **Run...** from the File menu and typing *printer* in response to the program name prompt.

❏ Remember that you cannot use DeskMate's built-in clipboard while First Publisher is active. When you use First Publisher's text and graphics clipboards, anything previously placed on DeskMate's clipboard is erased.

Glossary

Alignment. A phrase used to describe the positioning of text within a column or on a page. In First Publisher, you can choose the alignment of text from the **Define Page** option in the File menu or by choosing individual baseline adjustment features in the Baselines menu.

Art clipboard. The unseen clipboard to which items from the graphics layer of the publication are copied, cut, or pasted.

ART file. A First Publisher file that can be used—or pasted—directly onto a publication.

ASCII. An acronym for American Standard Code for Information Interchange. This is the "common denominator" form of saving data: most word processing programs have the capacity to save data in ASCII format, which is without formatting or font specifications of any kind. First Publisher can then import the ASCII files.

Autoleading. A short form of the phrase *automatic leading*. First Publisher changes the amount of space between lines (leading) automatically, according to the largest font you have used on that line.

Bad break. A term used to indicate the situation when a word fragment or section of a sentence is wrapped to the next line or column, giving the publication an unbalanced look.

Bar cursor. The bar cursor marks the position on the page where text will be inserted if you begin typing.

Baselines. The baselines are the lines on the text layer on which text is positioned.

Bleed. The phrase *bleed off the page* indicates a graphic element, such as a rule or box, that continues off the edge of the page.

Body text. The text of the publication that is entered on the text layer.

Box tool. The tool in the tools row used to draw boxes on the graphics layer.

Brochure. A small, folded pamphlet.

Callout. Text that is used to highlight an element in a figure or in a shadow box to summarize concepts introduced in the text.

Clipboard. First Publisher has two clipboards: a text clipboard and an art clipboard. The text clipboard stores the text block most recently cut, copied, or pasted; the art clipboard stores the art element that was most recently retrieved, cut, copy, or pasted.

Columns. With First Publisher, you can format the document in up to four columns of text.

Crop marks. Lines on the publication used to indicate to the printer where the publication should be cropped (or cut).

Cursor. First Publisher actually has two cursors. The cursor for the text layer is the bar cursor. The cursor for the graphics layer takes on the shape of the tool you're using.

Desktop publishing. A computerized method of publishing printed materials.

Directory. An area on the hard disk in which a specific group of files are stored.

Dot-matrix printer. A printer that creates characters and images in patterns of dots.

dpi. Dots per inch. First Publisher's screen display is 72 dpi.

Drag. A word indicating that you press the mouse button, hold the button down, move the mouse cursor to the point you want it, and release the button.

Elevator. The small white box in the elevator bar that indicates your position on-screen.

Elevator bar. The vertical bar on the right side of the screen area that has one arrow at each end and the elevator in the center. You use this bar to scroll through First Publisher files by clicking on either the gray sections of the bar or the arrows.

Eraser tool. The tool in the graphics tools row that is used to erase elements on the graphics layer.

Font. One complete set of characters in a specific typeface, size, and style. For example, Geneva, 12-point bold is one font.

FONTMOVE. The miniprogram used to move fonts in and out of First Publisher's Font and Style menus.

Footer. Lines of text that appear on the bottom of every page in the publication.

Graphics overlay. The layer of a First Publisher document that stores all graphic elements.

Graphics text tool. The tool in the graphics tools row that is used to enter text on the graphics layer.

Grid. A mesh of nonprinting dots that helps you align rules, boxes, and graphic elements as you place them on the page.

Gutter. The amount of white space between columns.

Handles. Three small black rectangles that appear on a selected baseline. You use handles to move, zero-out, shorten, or lengthen baselines.

Hand tool. The tool in the graphics tools row that is used to move or place selected images.

Header. A line of text that appears at the top of every page of a publication.

Highlight. Turns black text on a white background to white text on a black background. Before performing operations on text on the text layer, you must first highlight the text.

I-beam cursor. Also called the *mouse cursor*, this cursor marks the position of the mouse pointer. When you choose one of the graphics tools, this cursor takes on a different shape, according to the tool you choose.

Insert mode. This mode (activated by pressing Ins) wipes away all text past the insertion point on the screen. This allows First Publisher to accept without delay the text you type. To deactivate insert mode, press Ins again.

Justified text. Justified is a text alignment setting that adds space between words so that the beginning and end of each baseline are aligned.

Laser printer. A high-resolution printer that uses laser technology to produce print that rivals electronic typesetting equipment.

Layout. The phase of putting all elements together to form a publication.

Leading. The amount of white space between lines in a paragraph or block of text.

Left-justified text. Left-justified is a text alignment setting in which the left ends of all baselines are aligned.

Logo. A company's symbol or graphic image that is used on stationery, cards, invoices, and so forth.

MAC file. A First Publisher clip art file. You can create MAC files of your own, but you can only use the art saved in those files after you save the individual art pieces to ART files.

Magnify. An option on the Art menu that allows you to display a large image of a selected area of a graphic so that you can edit the image pixel-by-pixel. Then, when you return the graphic to normal display size (by pressing Alt-M), the graphic shows the modifications.

Margin. The amount of white space reserved on a publication, and in which text and graphics are not printed.

MASTER.FNT. The font file First Publisher uses to find the fonts displayed in the Font and Style menus.

Masthead. Another word for banner, which refers to the name and publishing information usually located at the top of a newsletter.

Menu bar. The bar across the top of the First Publisher screen in which all the menu names are displayed.

Mouse. A small peripheral device used in First Publisher to point to and select menus, commands, options, tools, and graphic elements. A mouse is not mandatory for use with First Publisher, but one is recommended.

Mouse cursor. The small, I-beam shaped cursor that moves in accordance with the movement of the mouse. This cursor changes shape according to the selected tool.

Offset printing. High-quality, professional printing done on a printing press.

Path. The drive and directory where First Publisher can find or save files you specify.

Pencil tool. The tool in the graphics tools row that is used to draw "freehand" on the graphics layer.

Picturewrap. A feature available on the Page menu that allows you to flow text around an image automatically.

Pixel. The smallest element in the publication—a dot. Every character and image is composed of a pattern of pixels.

Point. A measurement of the height of a character, as in 12-point type.

PUB file. The extension of a First Publisher publication file.

Pull-down menu. A menu you can display by using the mouse to ''pull it down'' or by pressing specified function keys.

Rule. Line used as a graphic element to enhance the page.

Ruler. An option, available on the Page menu, that displays rulers across the top and down the left edge of the screen, allowing you to produce correctly proportioned graphics.

Sans serif. Type without the small cross-lines that appear on the ends of characters in a serif font.

Scanner. A peripheral device similar to a photocopier that digitizes images into an electronically usable form.

Scroll. The term used to describe the action of moving the screen display.

Selection tool. The tool in the graphics tools row used to select elements on the graphics layer.

Serif. Type with small cross-lines across the ends of the characters.

SNAP2ART. The companion program for SNAPSHOT, which develops the ''picture'' taken by SNAPSHOT.

SNAPSHOT. An independent screen-capture utility that allows you to take a picture of a current application on-screen.

Soft font. A font packaged on disk that is copied to the printer at print time. To install soft fonts for use by First Publisher, you must use the FONTMOVE utility.

Speed keys. Keys displayed in the menus of First Publisher, showing you alternative methods of selecting the options without using the pull-down menus.

Template. A publication skeleton upon which you build the actual publication. Use templates, for example, to save time when you create similar publications or subsequent issues of a newsletter.

Text overlay. The text layer of First Publisher upon which text entry and editing takes place.

Text tool. The tool at the top of the graphics tools row. This tool is the only one *not* used on the graphics layer. Used only for text, this tool is active whenever you are working on the text layer.

Tools. First Publisher offers you a set of tools that you use in the creation and maintenance of all your First Publisher documents. The top tool is the text tool, used to manipulate text on the text layer. The other tools are used on the graphics layer of the publication.

Wordwrap. First Publisher automatically bumps words to the next line when the words you type pass the right end of the baseline. This action is known as *wordwrap*.

Index

393

G

Q

More Computer Knowledge from Que

SELECT QUE BOOKS TO INCREASE
YOUR PERSONAL COMPUTER PRODUCTIVITY

MS-DOS User's Guide, 3rd Edition

by Chris DeVoney

This classic guide to MS-DOS is now better than ever! Updated for MS-DOS, Version 3.3, this new edition features several new extended tutorials and a unique new command reference section. The distinctive approach of this text lets you easily reference basic command syntax, while comprehensive tutorial sections present in-depth DOS data. Appendixes provide information specific to users of DOS on COMPAQ, Epson, Zenith, and Leading Edge personal computers. Master your computer's operating system with *MS-DOS User's Guide*, 3rd Edition—the comprehensive tutorial/reference!

Managing Your Hard Disk, 2nd Edition

by Don Berliner

Proper hard disk management is the key to efficient personal computer use, and Que's *Managing Your Hard Disk* provides you with effective methods to best manage your computer's hard disk. This valuable text shows you how to organize programs and data on your hard disk according to their special applications, and helps you extend your understanding of DOS. This new edition features detailed information on DOS 3.3, IBM's PS/2 hardware, and new application and utility software. If you own a personal computer with a hard disk, you need Que's *Managing Your Hard Disk*, 2nd Edition!

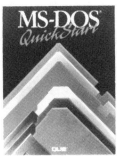

MS-DOS QuickStart

Developed by Que Corporation

The visually oriented approach to learning MS-DOS! More than 100 two-page illustrations provide a detailed view of the MS-DOS environment and help readers rapidly become familiar with their operating system. This fast-paced book demonstrates MS-DOS basics and shows how to implement commonly used commands, such as COPY and FORMAT. The perfect learning aid, for all beginning users of DOS—through Version 4.0!

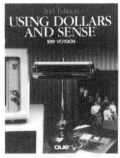

Using Dollars and Sense on the IBM

by Steve Adams

Using Dollars and Sense on the IBM is a practical guide to this popular financial management program. After helping you customize Dollars and Sense for your personal needs, this book shows you how to manage your checkbook and budget, analyze your portfolio, determine your net worth, and estimate your tax liability. Managers of small businesses will appreciate the sections on tracking income and expenses, as well as the information on maintaining accounts receivables and payables. If you use Dollars and Sense on an IBM or compatible personal computer, this is the book for you!

ORDER FROM QUE TODAY

Item	Title	Price	Quantity	Extension
838	MS-DOS User's Guide, 3rd Edition	$22.95		
872	MS-DOS QuickStart	21.95		
837	Managing Your Hard Disk	22.95		
877	Using Dollars and Sense: IBM Version, 2nd Edition	19.95		

Book Subtotal _____

Shipping & Handling ($2.50 per item) _____

Indiana Residents Add 5% Sales Tax _____

GRAND TOTAL _____

Method of Payment

☐ Check   ☐ VISA   ☐ MasterCard   ☐ American Express

Card Number _____ Exp. Date _____

Cardholder's Name _____

Ship to _____

Address _____

City _____ State _____ ZIP _____

If you can't wait, call **1-800-428-5331** and order TODAY.

All prices subject to change without notice.

FOLD HERE

_____

_____

_____

_____

Que Corporation
P.O. Box 90
Carmel, IN 46032

REGISTRATION CARD

Register your copy of *Using PFS: First Publisher* and receive information about Que's newest products. Complete this registration card and return it to Que Corporation, P.O. Box 90, Carmel, IN 46032.

Name _____ Phone _____

Company _____ Title _____

Address _____

City _____ State _____ ZIP _____

Please check the appropriate answers:

Where did you buy *Using PFS: First Publisher*?
☐ Bookstore (name: _____)
☐ Computer store (name: _____)
☐ Catalog (name: _____)
☐ Direct from Que _____
☐ Other: _____

How many computer books do you buy a year?
☐ 1 or less   ☐ 6–10
☐ 2–5   ☐ More than 10

How many Que books do you own?
☐ 1   ☐ 6–10
☐ 2–5   ☐ More than 10

How long have you been using PFS: First Publisher?
☐ Less than 6 months
☐ 6 months to 1 year
☐ 1–3 years
☐ More than 3 years

What influenced your purchase of *Using PFS: First Publisher*?
☐ Personal recommendation
☐ Advertisement   ☐ Que catalog
☐ In-store display   ☐ Que mailing
☐ Price   ☐ Que's reputation
☐ Other: _____

How would you rate the overall content of *Using PFS: First Publisher*?
☐ Very good   ☐ Satisfactory
☐ Good   ☐ Poor

How would you rate the *First Publisher Quick Start*?
☐ Very good   ☐ Satisfactory
☐ Good   ☐ Poor

How would you rate *Appendix A: Turning Your Publication into a Finished Product*?
☐ Very good   ☐ Satisfactory
☐ Good   ☐ Poor

How would you rate *Appendix B: First Publisher Design Tips*?
☐ Very good   ☐ Satisfactory
☐ Good   ☐ Poor

What do you like *best* about *Using PFS: First Publisher*?

What do you like *least* about *Using PFS: First Publisher*?

How do you use *Using PFS: First Publisher*?

What other Que products do you own?

For what other programs would a Que book be helpful?

Please feel free to list any other comments you may have about *Using PFS: First Publisher*.

_____

_____

_____

_____

_____

FOLD HERE

Que Corporation
P.O. Box 90
Carmel, IN 46032

Place
Stamp
Here